BEYOND
SURVIVAL

Theresa Saldana

BEYOND
SURVIVAL

BANTAM BOOKS
TORONTO · NEW YORK · LONDON · SYDNEY · AUCKLAND

BEYOND SURVIVAL
A Bantam Book / October 1986

Library of Congress Cataloging-in-Publication Data

Saldana, Theresa.
  Beyond survival.

  1. Saldana, Theresa. 2. Victims of crimes—California
—Los Angeles—Biography. I. Title.
HV6250.3.U53L 1986 362.8'8'0924 [B] 86-47621
        ISBN 0-553-05133-4

Published simultaneously in the United States and Canada

Bantam Books are published by Bantam Books, Inc. Its trademark, consisting
of the words "Bantam Books" and the portrayal of a rooster, is Registered in
U.S. Patent and Trademark Office and in other countries. Marca Registrada.
Bantam Books, Inc., 666 Fifth Avenue, New York, New York 10103.

PRINTED IN THE UNITED STATES OF AMERICA

MV   0 9 8 7 6 5 4 3 2 1

To my loving family—
Anthony, Divina, and Maria Saldana.

And to Jeffrey Allan Fenn,
who saved my life.

ACKNOWLEDGMENTS

I would like to thank my friends and relatives, who gave me their love, their support, and their compassion throughout the ordeal: Betty and Olive Abbott, Jill and Larry Aiossa, Robert Arcaro, Gusti and Ruth Bogok, Catlina Crespo, Robert DeNiro, Shelly D'San Juan, Sam Elia, Jenny and Peter Elia, Fred Feliciano, Lorena and Nino Feliciano, Laurie Gross, Don Gurler, Gwendolyn Green, Bob Gale, Bob Higgins, Joseph and Patricia Hindy, Sally Kirkland, Joan Kobin, Caroline Kosloff and family, Mayra Langdon, Rene Leask, Kay Michaels, Alan Marshall, Ally Mills, the Miranda family, Julian and Patsy Myers, Gabrielle Patalano, Elizabeth Randall, Loyda Ramos, the Rendeiro family, Michael Riesman, Selma and Ben Rubin, Maria Smith, Steve Solberg, Wendie Jo Sperber, Susan Walsh, Brenda Wingfield, Iggy Wolfington—and to all who sent their prayers, their kind thoughts, and their good wishes my way.

Special thanks to the nurses, doctors, staff and administration of Cedars-Sinai Hospital and the Motion Picture and Television Fund Hospital—and to the Actors Fund of America—for the care and services they so generously provided.

And—for helping to make this book a reality—I am deeply grateful to my agent, Ed Victor; my advisor, Wally Wolfe; my typist, Carolyn Parqueth; and my editor, Jeanne Bernkopf.

—*Theresa Saldana*

This book could not have been written without the guidance and support of John Driver.

PROLOGUE

In March of 1982, I was leading a happy and fulfilling life. My career as an actress was on the rise, I enjoyed attending college part-time, and my handsome husband and I lived in a lovely apartment in trendy West Hollywood. Fred and I were close to our families, had plenty of good friends, and were active socially.

But on March 15, 1982, just a few yards away from the home I loved, I became the victim of a grisly, premeditated, brutally violent crime.

During the course of one morning, I was changed from a healthy, optimistic, high-spirited young actress into a terrified, barely breathing, pain-racked invalid, clinging weakly to life itself.

The assault upon my body lasted only a few minutes, just long enough to bring me to the brink of death. But the assault upon my mind, my heart, my soul was to last far, far longer.

That sunny, lovely spring day, I was hurled into an entirely new reality devoid of the comfort and normalcy of the past. I now shared with other victims of violent crime the bond that sets us apart from the rest of the world: the personal, shattering knowledge of the depth of pain and trauma one human being is capable of inflicting upon another. Suddenly I had been reborn into a world where peace, safety, and trust no longer seemed to exist. Suddenly, I had become a victim—not of a flood, an accident, or a disease, but of another human being. The thought sickened me.

As I fought desperately to survive, hooked up to tubes, machines, and monitors, and racked by dizzying pain, I felt cut off, apart, like a lone survivor trapped on an ice floe, a swift-moving current carrying me farther and farther away from civilization.

I felt increasingly isolated by my experience as the days and weeks passed. It seemed so hard for others to grasp or fully understand my utter horror at being harmed—almost killed—by a *person*.

And so I decided to write, to let others know what it was like: to explain, from an insider's point of view, how a victim *feels*. To share my journey back from the depths of physical and emotional torment.

The purpose of my book is not to make others suffer vicariously through my agony but, rather, to show how essential it is to create something positive out of an ugly, wrenchingly painful experience.

I started writing when I was still in the hospital, but it was not until further along my road back to complete recovery, when I founded Victims for Victims and became very active in working with other victims of crime, that my concept of this book changed. Yes, I wanted to tell my own deeply personal story about the climb back from bitter despair, but I also wanted to share many other victims' experiences of tragedy and triumph— stories that have amazed, enriched, and inspired me.

The victims and their loved ones portrayed in this book are real—as are their strength, stamina, and determination— although their names, residences, and other identifying characteristics have been changed.

My book is designed to give concrete, tangible advice about what people can do to help themselves—or someone else—survive and flourish after a victimization. I hope that people will take from it what they need and will freely adapt its suggestions and contents to work for them.

I am neither a psychiatrist nor a psychologist, but I do have an in-depth, firsthand knowledge of the world of pain and isolation so familiar to victims of crime and their loved ones.

For readers who are themselves victims of crime, I hope this book offers the comfort of knowing that *you are not alone*— that many, many others have been through devastating ordeals like your own and have managed in a variety of ways to wade through their horror and misery, to get on with their lives.

But I want also to bridge the gap between those who have been victimized and those who haven't. In truth, we all have much in common; with so many crimes occurring every day, few of us go about our lives without taking security precautions: locking doors, worrying about our children's safety, being careful when out at night, and so on. Although many people (thank God) are not themselves actual victims of crime, they are in fact victims of the *fear* of crime. And as such, they have much in common with those who have directly suffered an attack.

The collective experiences shared in this book will, I hope, shed some light on the human condition not only in the *worst* of times but also in the most triumphant of times.

—*Theresa Saldana*

CHAPTER 1

THE ATTACK

Since my early teens I have been decidedly career-oriented. I started out as a stage actress in New York City and then moved to Los Angeles in order to work in films and television.

Before the attack I had starred or played featured roles in such films as *Defiance* opposite Jan-Michael Vincent, *I Wanna Hold Your Hand* and *Nunzio* for Universal Studios, and Brian DePalma's *Home Movies*. I appeared as a frequent guest star on numerous television series, played a recurring role on *Gangster Chronicles*, and co-starred as Sophia Loren's sister in the NBC film *Sophia Loren: Her Own Story*. But by March of 1982, I was probably best known for my role as Robert De Niro's sister-in-law in Martin Scorsese's *Raging Bull*.

Between my career and home life I was always extremely busy. My husband, Fred Feliciano, was a counselor for alcoholics and drug abusers, and we lived in a lovely West Hollywood neighborhood. Fred was as active as I, working all day and attending classes at UCLA at night. He was proud of my hard work and supportive of my career.

But on March 8, 1982, everything began to change. It was about six o'clock and Fred and I were having dinner when my mother called from New York. Excitedly, she explained that she had just received a telephone call from Martin Scorsese's assistant. Apparently Mr. Scorsese was in London and needed to reach me immediately. My mother had given the assistant my telephone number, but he'd insisted on having my address as well. He'd explained that the telephone lines were down in England and that Mr. Scorsese might need to send me a telegram. Since the caller was insistent and so concerned about being able to reach me immediately, my mother thought it best to give the information directly, rather than have him call my manager. She had never before given out my address to any business contact, but she was convinced that the caller was Scorsese's assistant; after all, Scorsese's office had my parents' unlisted telephone number, and she thought the caller must have gotten it from someone there. (We would later learn that he had hired a detective to track me.)

I was as excited and curious as my mother about why Scorsese needed to reach me so urgently.

I have a vivid memory of the half-hour following my mother's call. I told Fred the news; he was just as curious and happy as my mother and I had been. I was hopping around the apartment singing and dancing, sure that Scorsese had another film role for me. Considering my excitement, I am surprised I didn't pack my bags and get out my passport. Fred was tickled by my behavior, but he had to leave for UCLA, so he packed up his books and gave me a kiss for luck as he left.

Moments later, my manager, Selma Rubin, called from New York. Sounding distraught she said, "Theresa—there's a *nut* looking for you. I'm very worried." Selma went on to tell me that a man had called her four times, assuming different names each time, claiming to be a producer, a photographer, an agent, a publicity man. With each call he insisted she give him my home address and telephone number. Selma refused to give out the information, and during the second attempt she realized it was indeed the same person. What worried her most was that, during the fourth call, the man had begun to giggle and had sounded deranged. At that point Selma had warned him never to phone her again or she would call the police.

When Selma told me one of the names the caller had

used, my body became rigid with fear. It was that of the "director's assistant" who had phoned my mother.

Hurriedly I told her about the telephone call to my parents' home and that the caller had persuaded my mother to give him my home address. There was a moment of silence; then Selma said, "Get out of the house."

Shaking, I hung up the phone and ran to the door, peering out of the peephole. Our apartment was in a typical West Hollywood courtyard-style building, with a swimming pool in the middle. I could see no one through the peephole, but my view was limited.

My heart pounding, I ran to the door of my neighbor Mrs. Hahn, just a few feet across the hall. I hammered on it with my fists and the elderly lady quickly brought me inside.

Trembling, I told her what had happened and asked if I could use her telephone. First, I tried to contact my husband at UCLA. I dialed one number after another—security, administration, general information. . . . Twenty minutes later, I was told by a security person at the university that unless I knew the exact classroom Fred was in, they would not be able to reach him before his class was dismissed. Mrs. Hahn told me not to worry: I could stay with her until Fred came home.

I was now afraid that the caller might harm Fred, so we decided to slide a note under my door for him. Mrs. Hahn insisted on going with me. We literally ran to my apartment door and back, leaving the message for Fred.

Next, I called the West Hollywood Sheriff's Department, explaining the situation to the officer on duty and asking him to send a patrol car. I was informed that unless I was actually being harassed, they did not have the manpower to dispatch an officer. Stunned, I replied, "What if he *kills* me?"

The officer reassured me that such calls were common for people in the media; usually the callers were simply trying to get an address where they could send fan mail. He explained that the odds of this caller's being dangerous were slim. By the time I hung up I felt so relieved that I was almost embarrassed about the whole thing. Nevertheless, I remained in Mrs. Hahn's apartment.

At eleven, Fred came home and picked me up at Mrs. Hahn's. When we were safely inside our apartment we discussed what to do. Neither of us wanted to jump to negative conclusions, but there was clearly an element of danger involved.

Fred is a third-degree black belt in karate, and so we felt confident of his ability to protect us both from harm. But he could not be at my side night and day. We needed to consider our alternatives.

We talked about moving, but Fred and I loved the apartment and felt that leaving it would be both rash and premature. We thought of asking friends if I could stay with them temporarily, but both of us resented the idea of allowing this unknown caller to force us to separate.

Exhausted, Fred and I agreed to get some rest and make a decision in the morning. Six hours later when we awoke, the events of the night before seemed more like an unpleasant dream than a threatening reality. We actually teased each other about it, yet beneath our laughter, anxiety lurked. We decided that Fred should walk me to and from my car and that whenever he wasn't home, I would stay at Mrs. Hahn's or with other friends.

That morning at the end of my singing class I told the professor what had happened. He suggested that I go to the music office to have my records pulled from the files so that no one could trace me that way. After all, it was possible that the caller was someone who worked at or attended the college. I went directly to the office. The music department head was very understanding and had my records pulled immediately.

In each class, I told one or two key people to watch out for me. By the end of the afternoon, I felt that I was safe at least at the college.

By the end of the week nothing unusual had happened, and both Fred and I began to feel we had perhaps been overreacting. After all, we told ourselves, the caller had known my telephone number and address for five days and had made no attempt to reach me. Mrs. Hahn, who spent most days at home, had diligently kept watch on the entrance to the building. Fred and I had checked the courtyard, the garage, and the alleys whenever we went out. None of us had seen anyone suspicious.

*   *   *

A week to the day after my mother's phone call, I prepared to go to a music class at L.A. City College. Fred told me I looked lovely. I had dressed to suit my cheerful mood in a nautical suit and red-and-white-striped sailor blouse—and I felt terrific. I was certain I was going to get a guest-starring role on a *Hill Street Blues* episode I'd auditioned for a few days earlier. And I'd been to church the day before and vowed to go about my life unafraid.

As I gathered my books, Fred asked me to wait till he got dressed so he could walk me to my car. I gave him a kiss and told him to stay in bed. My last words to him before I left were: "Don't worry. I'll be fine."

Shortly before ten A.M. I left the apartment. The day was bright and sunny; as I went through the entrance gate and down the front steps, I affirmed to myself: "I am unafraid and no harm shall come to me."

My car was parked on the street in front of the building next door. As I put my key into the door, a voice spoke the words that have echoed in my mind ever since: "Are you Theresa Saldana?" I looked around and saw a person immediately to my left.

Instinctively I knew this was the caller. Without answering, I tried to run, but he caught me in a viselike grip. At the same instant, he reached into the bag slung from his shoulder and raised his hand high above his head.

For one shocking split second, I stared in horror at the five-inch kitchen knife held tightly in his fist. Before I could move, he plunged the knife deep into my chest.

A scream erupted from me as I tried to fight him off, but he thrust the knife into my body again and again. The world began to spin; I felt myself being literally ripped apart.

"He's killing me. He's killing me!" I heard myself shrieking these words over and over again. I could sense that people were coming out into the street, but no one came forward to help me.

I kicked the attacker and tried to block his blows with my arms, but I could not stop his steady assault.

As physically painful and unbearable as this vicious attack was, the most vivid and horrific memory I have of the event is one not of physical suffering but of psychological anguish.

Never in my life will I forget the indescribable horror I felt when I stared into the assailant's eyes and realized that his intention was to murder me.

"He's killing me! He's killing me!" I continued to scream. And still no one came to help as again and again he plunged the knife into my body.

Finally I was able to reach out with my left hand and grasp the blade of the knife. But even with my hand clenched tightly over it, he continued to flail about with the knife, cutting tendons, nerves, and muscles.

Unable to bear the physical torture any longer, I released the blade, only to feel it thrust into me yet again.

Just as I felt the last of my strength slip away, I looked up and saw an angel. There behind the assailant was a tall, beautiful blond man. As if in slow motion, I saw him pull the attacker away from me.

I fell to the ground and lay motionless for about ten seconds. Then I was overcome with a desperate fear that the attacker would stab me still again. My sudden terror catapulted me to my feet. Somehow I found the strength to stumble toward my building.

Looking down, I saw that my clothing was entirely red. Blood seemed to be streaming from my very pores. As I stumbled along I heard a hideous sound. With every breath I took, blood was spewing out of a chest wound, causing a sucking noise. Instinctively, I pressed my right hand over the wound and lurched up the steps, slipping and sliding on my own blood.

As I passed through the gate and entered the empty courtyard, I was consumed with an overwhelming feeling of sadness and loneliness. I sensed that some of my neighbors could see me from their windows. But still they hid in fear, capable of watching me bleed to death in front of their very eyes rather than risk coming to my aid. I raised my blood-soaked arms and wailed at the hidden faces: "Help me. I'm dying."

Just as I began to fall, Fred ran out from our apartment and caught me in his arms. He screamed, "Who did this to you?"

"It's *him*," I whispered.

Fred carried me into the apartment and laid me down just inside the door. Frantically he called the hospital and the police.

My lung had collapsed completely, and I was fighting for air. Again and again I whispered, "I'm dying."

Fred kept saying, "No, you're not. You're going to be fine."

A neighbor, Joe, came in and knelt by my side. Fred, worried that the assailant might return, left me with Joe. He ran to the front of the building and discovered that the attacker was already inside the sheriff's car.

When Fred returned to the apartment he found me chanting quietly, "I love my family. I love God." But my pain was gripping; it was so severe that I prayed for death. I could not catch a full breath of air and I felt as though I were being asphyxiated. My body was in the process of shutting down; death loomed closer and closer. Yet I continued to fight desperately for air, and with each gasp, I heard the gurgling, sucking sound in my lung.

My eyes were drawn upward. I stared at the white ceiling high above me, yet my vision did not end there. I began to see a picture of the future—a time when all the pain would be over. Suddenly I felt myself beyond all that had happened, all that I was now enduring. This was not, however, an "out of body" experience. I was still very much present, there on the floor, bleeding profusely and in unspeakable agony. But I somehow saw beyond it all and realized that eventually the pain would end. I didn't know or care at that moment if the end of pain meant my death. For some reason, the physical torment became bearable because I knew that it wouldn't last forever.

As the seconds passed, I felt weaker and weaker. A group of neighbors were now gathered around, and from the way they looked at me, I could tell they believed I was about to die. A girl bent down and began to give me mouth-to-mouth resuscitation, but a neighbor with experience in CPR (cardiopulmonary resuscitation) told her to stop. As she withdrew her lips and raised her head, I saw that her mouth was now covered with my blood.

Fred had been holding a pillowcase over my chest wound. Its pastel pink was now stained bright red.

My eyes looked steadily upward; my lips kept forming the words "I love my family. I love God. I'm dying." At this point the breaths I was taking were so shallow and painful that I realized I couldn't last much longer.

Suddenly the paramedics burst through the door and ordered everyone except Fred to leave. The room reverberated with loud, tension-filled voices. The medical team knelt over me and placed an oxygen mask on my face—what an exquisite relief it was. Almost magically, the oxygen cleared my senses. Though the pain remained intense, for the first time since the attack I felt I could pull through.

As they cut much of the clothing from my body, the paramedics found one wound after another. With each new discovery, a medic would shout out a brief description to his partner, who relayed the information by walkie-talkie to Cedars-Sinai Hospital. There were ten separate wounds.

The paramedics put me into a "trauma suit"—a pair of rubberlike pants which, when inflated, forced the blood from my legs up to my vital organs. I had been sure I was stabbed in the heart. From their conversation, I realized that the paramedics also considered this a possibility.

After what seemed an eternity, the ambulance arrived and I was driven with a wail of sirens toward Cedars-Sinai. Because the medics needed every inch of working space in the vehicle, they did not allow Fred to ride with me.

My body was repeatedly jostled by the lurching movements of the ambulance. Every inch of my flesh cried out in agony; I was terrified that the pain itself would kill me. Yet I clung to the last vestiges of life, fighting to remain conscious, sensing that passing out would mean death. Once again I concentrated on a future time when I would be well again.

We screeched to a halt at Cedars-Sinai. Voices screamed, "CODE BLUE!" meaning Near Death, and I was raced down the corridors to the pre-operating room.

A team of doctors and nurses began working to save my life. The wounds were so widespread that they literally had to work on my body in individual sections. It was bizarre: One doctor worked on my leg, another on my chest, others on each arm.

Somehow, throughout these procedures I remained awake and alert. I talked incessantly to those around me, knowing these might be my last words and feeling an overwhelming need to let others know what had really happened.

"He tried to kill me . . . kill me . . . kill me," I whispered to them. I felt it was important for them to know that the assailant had tried to *murder* me, not merely harm me. The nurses patted my shoulder and said that I was safe now.

Again and again I asked the nurses and doctors if I would die, and they repeatedly assured me that I would make it through. But the looks on their faces and the sadness in their voices belied their words.

One doctor, who had been treating my right arm, told me I would undergo surgery. Everyone was amazed when I responded by asking them please to remove my contact lenses. (Later, they told me this had most likely saved me from corneal damage.)

Then the doctor who was attending to my chest wounds told me he had to do something very painful. To my mind, there was no way the pain could possibly get any worse. I was wrong.

The doctor inserted a thick, hollow metal pipe through my left side directly into my lung. Shocked, I reeled in agony—I had never known such pain existed. As weak as I was, I let out a piercing scream. Then, utterly spent, I told myself that the torment would all be over soon.

As they were about to take me to surgery, a nurse leaned close to me and asked tearfully, "What do you want, Theresa?" At that instant I realized that they all expected me to die. I whispered, "I want my parents."

Seconds later they brought me out of the pre-op room and into the corridor. Fred rushed to my side, kissed me, and said, "I love you. You're going to make it." Then they wheeled me into the operating room.

When I saw the surgeon, I stared into his eyes and said, "I'm an actress. Please be careful with the scars." He promised me he would do his best.

Then the anesthetist said, "You're going to sleep now," and suddenly the pain ended and I drifted away.

CHAPTER 2

THE AFTERMATH

My surgery lasted four and a half hours. When I woke up in the intensive care unit of Cedars-Sinai, I saw a kaleidoscope of light. Disoriented, I struggled to clear my mind, which was cloudy from anesthesia. When my vision focused, I saw a young blond nurse standing nearby, her back to me.

I took in the strangeness of my surroundings. Tubes seemed to protrude from every part of my anatomy. Most of my face was covered with a rubbery oxygen mask and I was connected to innumerable machines which hummed and whirred beside me.

An onrush of relief flooded over me. *I'm alive, I'm alive, I'm alive!* raced through my mind. I was deeply, undeniably, wondrously happy to be there in that stark white hospital room—*alive*.

But in seconds, pain gripped me with ghastly intensity. With every breath my chest felt as though it would split apart. When I tried to cry out, I could manage only a faint, dry moan. Still, the nurse heard me and rushed to my side with an injection of Demerol. The shot began to take effect almost immediately. Yet the pain continued under the dulling mask of the drug. It was to remain there for many months to come.

I wanted desperately to know my condition. With great difficulty I raised my head enough to look at my body. Gasping with horror at the sight, I dropped back upon my bed.

Both my arms were attached to long, wooden boards, and I was swathed in bloody bandages. Under the thin white sheet draped loosely over my torso, I was completely naked. My hands and fingers were splinted and bandaged, and IVs had been inserted into what seemed to be every available vein. My throbbing feet and legs were elevated and surrounded by pillows. I remember thinking that with my arms outstretched in this crosslike position and with bloody bandages covering my body, I looked like the living victim of a macabre crucifixion.

I turned my head to the nurse and whispered weakly, "What did the doctors do?" She explained the basics of the operation that Dr. Alexander Stein had performed and also told me how special he was. It seems that when he learned of my case, he had just finished performing a grueling seven-hour operation. The surgeon on call had not yet arrived, and I was lying there with massive internal bleeding, hovering on the brink of death. So Dr. Stein went right back into the operating room to try to save my life.

The doctor had been forced to perform thoracic surgery, opening my chest from just below my collarbone and sawing through the sternum. This, the nurse informed me, was necessary in order to repair my left lung, which had been punctured in four different places by the assailant's knife. I knew now why I felt the strange pulling sensation of being about to "rip apart."

I whispered, "He tried to kill me," over and over again. Now, intense emotional pain was added to my physical suffering, and for the first time since awakening, I cried. Sobbing would have hurt my aching, sutured chest, so I wept in stillness, tears trickling down my face. I then nodded off briefly, into a sleep induced by the combination of the drugs I'd been given and sheer exhaustion.

When I next awoke, my state of mind was completely altered. Renewed by pain-free sleep, I felt suddenly elated at how very lucky I was to have survived at all. I realized I owed my life to God, to the man who had stopped the assailant, and to the surgeon. Silently I thanked them.

Voices outside the door interrupted my thoughts, and Fred came into the tiny room. He kissed my cheek gently and gazed at me in silence for a moment. This husband of mine, so athletic and usually so full of life and energy, looked pale, shaky, and consumed with grief. Already it was apparent that I was not the only one who would suffer.

He explained that my parents had taken the first available flight out of New York and were due at the hospital in little more than an hour. I had feared that I would die without seeing my parents again. Now, filled with relief, I couldn't wait for them to arrive.

Fred told me that Detective Kalas of the Los Angeles Sheriff's Department was waiting out in the hall and needed to speak to me immediately. I was far from up to answering questions, but Fred said that the detective considered the meeting imperative. Seconds later, the nurse ushered the detective in.

"He tried to *kill* me," I croaked again and again. I desperately needed to let Detective Kalas know that it had been an attempted *murder*, not just a stabbing.

In a calm tone of voice Detective Kalas informed me that the assailant, whom he described as a Scottish drifter, had fixated upon me after seeing me in films. A journal had been found on his person which detailed minutely his deranged plan to kill me in order to "send me to heaven." He then wanted to be executed so that he could join me in "paradise."

According to the journal, the attacker felt I was a "beautiful angel"—too lovely and good to live in this terrible, evil world.

Detective Kalas showed me a sample of the writings contained in the journal. I could bring myself to read only a few words. The handwriting was abnormally tiny, and my gaze was so unsteady that the print seemed to dance before my eyes. Besides, I was horrified to see the written, tangible proof of this gruesome plot against me. I turned my head away, repulsed.

Feeling weaker by the minute, I struggled to give the detective the details he needed. I was able to answer most of the questions without pause. But as I recalled the attack, the images of it began to upset me.

Sensing my distress, Detective Kalas asked only what was absolutely necessary and left, assuring Fred and me that the case was airtight.

As soon as he was out the door, I again reverted to repeating, "He tried to *kill* me!" In the midst of my chanting, I experienced a vivid flashback of the attack—so highly graphic and detailed that I truly believed I was back there on that street in West Hollywood. I whimpered, moaned, and screamed for help. Nurses came in and injected me with a powerful sedative to keep me from harming myself in my hysteria. That was the first of the many flashbacks that would plague me during my lengthy recuperative period.

I came out of my drug-induced stupor when my parents arrived. Despite my grogginess, I could sense immediately their heart-wrenching shock at my condition. Later, they were to describe to me the sunken black eyes that stared up at them in agony and their own feelings of overwhelming despair.

As they approached my bedside, the first words I said to them were: "Don't worry. I look a lot worse than I feel." They kissed me and touched my cheek, my brow, and a tiny section of my upper arm—the few areas where I was not cut or seriously injured.

But their faces were ashen as they fought to hold back their tears. Instinctively I begged them not to cry; that was very important to me. I felt that I could somehow remain more controlled if those around me gave at least the illusion of optimism.

All I wanted was for my parents to take care of me. This marked the beginning of a lengthy period of reversion to a state of childlike dependency.

My mother, Divina, kept a constant vigil by my bedside. This tiny woman, scarcely five feet tall, was a tower of strength, never letting me sense for a moment that she felt I would die. She has always been a devoted wife and mother—a lady who enjoys caring for others and actually thrives on it.

During those post-attack months, my mother's faith in God and trust in people were put through a terrible test. She was torn apart by grief and agony. Her usually bright eyes were clouded over with sadness. It would be more than a year before my mother would smile or laugh again.

My father, Tony, also visited me almost every waking hour. Ever since I can remember, I have relied on my handsome, gentle father's support and the trust he has in me. When I first began to perform, he attended every show—ballet recitals in dance halls, school talent shows, local productions, and, finally, professional theater in New York City. He never said very much, but the pride and happiness on his face gave me the incentive to do well.

During the trying days after the attack, his quiet belief in me provided the strength I needed. His confidence in my recovery was contagious. His warm, crinkly hazel eyes beamed at me whenever I made even the tiniest step toward recovery.

But, despite the confidence he exuded during his visits, my father was inwardly consumed by pain and anger. Within two weeks his hair turned completely gray.

In the weeks following the attack, I was completely incapable of being left alone. I became agitated or even totally hysterical at the mere suggestion of being in a room by myself. Some of the nurses said my demand for constant company was a childish desire to be pampered or coddled in this time of crisis. The truth was that my desperate need to be surrounded by others stemmed from an all-consuming, uncontrollable terror. I believed with my soul that if I were left alone, I would be killed.

I spent the first few days after the attack fighting for my life in the intensive care unit. Pain enveloped me like a blanket and I was barely able to hold out from one shot of Demerol to the next.

By the final half-hour between shots, I began to moan— softly at first and then more and more loudly. As the minutes ticked by I would be reduced to tears, and my moans would alternate with small, animal-like yelps and whimpers. Finally I would resort to begging, pleading with the nurses to give me the next shot earlier than scheduled. Sometimes my abject misery persuaded them. Had I been able to *move* during those hours of screaming agony, I would probably have sprung from my bed, taken a syringe from a nearby tray, and injected myself.

My mother was always there at my side. Whenever I wept or worried about my scars, she would exclaim, "Your face is still so beautiful, Theresa. Thank God for that!" Mother applied compresses, held my hand, spoke to me quietly, and gave me the strength to endure it all. I believe she felt the pain even more intensely than I did.

By my second day in ICU, I began to have increased awareness of my surroundings. My room, scarcely more than a cubicle, was crammed with lifesaving equipment and medical devices, leaving barely enough floor space for more than one person to walk to my bedside. The only permissible visitors were my immediate family: Fred, my father, and my mother.

What fascinated me most in the room were the amazing machines I was hooked up to. With their dronelike hums and whirrs, they seemed to pulse with more life than I could muster.

Although I was immobilized, there were frequent medical procedures performed: Blood was taken, injections given, tests administered. All produced discomfort and many were extremely painful. The twice-daily chest X ray was one of the most unbearable procedures of all. A portable X-ray machine was rolled into my room, and two nurses lifted me to a sitting position. The pain in my chest wounds and in the surgical incision made me feel as though I would go mad. Whenever the robotic-looking, many-dialed X-ray machine was rolled in, I felt I was about to be the human sacrifice in some demented ceremony.

Worse still was the daily routine of being rolled over on my side so the nurses could make the bed. The jostling hurt my wounds so much that I wept, moaned, and even screamed. Every one of the more than a thousand stitches in my body felt as though it would burst open. Sometimes the movement really did jar the incisions enough so that they would ooze blood, which terrified me. Again and again I felt the sensation of being about to rip apart.

My husband was often present while the medical procedures were being performed. He would sit there silently, hating the pain he knew I was feeling, but unable to stop it. I could sense that Fred was deeply troubled, torn, and confused. He cared, he felt, and he hurt. But it was all locked up inside him. Everyone was so busy with my survival and recovery that his severe depression went unchecked.

Emotionally, I experienced dramatic ups and downs. These mood swings would fluctuate hour by hour, even minute by minute. At times I would feel elated at having lived through it all, and hopeful and positive about complete recovery. I would babble on and on about making my comeback as an actress and proving to the world that I was alive.

Then, only minutes later, I would sink into a quagmire of depression and despair, allowing my physical and emotional suffering to engulf me. Feeling helpless and angry, I would rock my head back and forth, back and forth—it was the only part of my anatomy I could move.

Dr. Stein, who had performed the lifesaving surgery, was often present during this period of turmoil. He examined me frequently, reporting to my family any changes in my condition. His wry British sense of humor helped to alleviate the tension. Dr. Stein loved to tease me. He discouraged any indication of self-pity and stressed a positive, active approach on my part. Even when I was at my lowest point emotionally, Dr. Stein could usually manage to coax a smile out of me.

One day he commented on how delicious a small box of Godiva chocolates looked. I invited him to help himself, and he promptly gobbled down all eight of the chocolates, said "Jolly good sweets, those!" winked at me, and left the room. I couldn't stop giggling for half an hour.

Another day, I told him I was worried that people might consider me weird because of what had happened to me. Without batting an eye he said, "Oh don't worry about that, silly! I've already taken a poll of all the resident doctors here and they all feel that stab victims are both sexy and mysterious!" I feel lucky to have had a doctor who not only possessed great surgical skills but who was also funny.

Then a new fear gradually began to obsess me. I became convinced that the assailant would somehow escape and kill me in my hospital room. Everyone assured me that very strict security measures had been taken for my protection. Nonetheless, my terror was overwhelming. Whenever a new male technician or orderly entered the room, I would tremble in terror and whimper like a baby until he explained who he was and convinced me that he really *was* part of the hospital staff.

On one occasion, a Catholic priest came to bless me. Feeling that I was certainly in good hands, my parents and Fred left the room. I looked up at the large, stocky priest, and listened to him intoning prayers in a thick foreign accent. He moved his hands in the air, making the sign of the cross. The slight movement triggered something in my mind. Gripped by panic, I thought, *He's not a priest! He's going to kill me!* I had to get away from him at all costs, and tried to wriggle myself over to the far side of the bed. Sensing my distress, he leaned over even closer and raised his hand to bless me. I shrieked for help, utterly convinced that he was about to punch me in the chest with his fist. My family and the nurses rushed into the room. Everyone, including the well-intentioned priest, was totally confused.

I could do nothing but whimper, "Please ask him to leave. He scares me. Please, please, ask him to leave." The priest, understanding my fear, left quietly.

Later, I felt sorry for that priest, for I'm sure my behavior was upsetting to him. But I simply could not control my reaction.

Usually, in the first hour after receiving a dose of pain medication, I was able to discuss my inner feelings with my parents, with Fred, and even with the nurses and doctors who cared for me. I've always loved to talk to people and am stimulated by good conversation. As it turned out, my penchant for talking became a useful therapeutic tool. I took my feelings of impending dread or anxiety and talked them out with others—and afterward I felt relief. But I became aware that the kinds of problems I faced required more than a loving listener. I needed professional help. And so I asked to see a psychiatrist.

From my third day at Cedars-Sinai, I was visited by Dr. Paul Joseph, a psychiatric resident. We met five times a week. These sessions were invaluable; I don't think I could have made my psychological recovery so swiftly and completely without them.

Questions plagued me. *Why me? How could this have happened? Wasn't God watching over me? Will I ever trust people again? Why should I bother to recover, only to return to the ugly world that contains people like this monstrous would-be killer? How can I ever walk in the streets again? Will I have a complete mental breakdown? Will I survive at all?* My body was unable to function, but my mind never seemed to stop questioning.

On my third day in ICU, Dr. Stein brought me a blue plastic instrument that looked like an air pump and was meant to strengthen my lung. Because my entire chest area was in so much pain, it was natural for me to take very shallow breaths. This made me a prime candidate for pneumonia. Dr. Stein told me to inhale deeply through the mouthpiece of the device; the air being sucked in would cause a little ball to rise to the top of the plastic cylinder. Every hour I was supposed to get the ball to reach the top at least ten times.

But whenever I inhaled or exhaled into the instrument, the pain in my lung and chest was piercing. Soon I would burst into tears at the mere mention or sight of the "toy," as we came to call it.

And the exercise itself made me weep in frustration. For although I tried to inhale as deeply as possible, the ball would hardly budge, let alone rise up.

Time and time again Dr. Stein warned us of pneumonia. Fred and my parents begged, pleaded, and cajoled me. Desperately I struggled to breathe more deeply. Finally I got the ball to move and then to rise a few inches. But try as I would, I could not get it to the top.

Since childhood I have been strong-willed and goal-oriented. My inability to move that ball made me feel like a loser and tore at my confidence. I hated the exercise, the pain, my helplessness, and—most of all—my *failure* to accomplish this seemingly minuscule achievement.

Within two days I contracted pneumonia. A block of phlegm was lodged in my lung and unless I could dislodge it by coughing very deeply, the doctors would be forced to perform an excruciatingly painful procedure. The blockage would have to be removed with an instrument inserted down my throat and into my lung. The prospect petrified me.

Feverish and frightened, I tried to cough again and again. Each time, my unhealed sternum, which was wired together with steel, felt as though it were being cracked open. I wept; my mother became unnerved; my father and Fred stood by, helpless and pale. Then my fever rose to 104 degrees. The doctors said there was no other choice. It was imperative that they perform the procedure.

At this news I burst into uncontrollable sobs. The weeping itself caused me still more pain, which sent me into a fit of deep, racking coughs. Thankfully, the coughs were so intense that they dislodged the substance in my lungs. As soon as the congestion was relieved, the pneumonia began to clear up. With a few hours my fever had broken and the crisis was over.

Despite the quality of care I received from doctors and nurses alike and the loving attention of my family, there were times when my pain and anxiety made me hysterical and demanding. In short, I was often a crotchety pain in the neck. Crime victims who are seriously injured often act out in ways that can be difficult for those around them to cope with. Speaking from personal experience, all I can say is that this behavior is a natural response. When your formerly healthy body suddenly becomes a source of unrelenting stress and pain, the helplessness and anguish you feel can cause a major—though usually temporary—personality change. I was a perfect example of this: I threw things, I yelled and screamed, I pounded the pillows, and I caused general disruption.

One day I tried on a nightgown someone had sent me as a gift. It was pink silk and beautifully hand-embroidered. When my mother tried to get it over my bulky chest bandages, the delicate pink lace flowers at the bodice burst apart. Angry and frustrated, I literally ripped the gown off and threw it to the ground, cursing and yelling all the while. The nightgown was ruined.

My tolerance level had become practically nonexistent. Even small problems and disappointments seemed huge to me. I'd had such a large dose of trouble and horror that I wanted everything now to go smoothly. But unfortunately, life doesn't usually work that way. So my rages surfaced often and I vented my anger with whatever strength I could muster. Afterward I'd feel embarrassed and would apologize to everyone.

I'm so grateful to those who stood by me and allowed me to express my emotions. As unpleasant as it may seem at times, it is actually healthy for a patient to discuss his inner feelings or even weep or scream about them. It is far better than submerging these feelings so that they fester and eventually explode.

Dr. Joseph encouraged me to express even my blackest thoughts. He also helped my family to cope with my extreme reactions. I looked forward to each session with him. Although he had no special training in the care of victims, he was so supportive, considerate, and caring that he was able to help me through those psychologically grueling first few weeks. Whenever I felt distraught I could "beep" Dr. Joseph. He would respond quickly, often helping me over the phone.

I was especially glad that my psychiatrist was *male*. In some cases, victims of a violent crime perpetrated by a man prefer to be counseled by a woman. But I felt that *because* I'd been harmed by a man, it was good for me to be *helped* by men now. I did not want to risk hating or even resenting men forever. I was glad that the two people responsible for my physical and psychological well-being, Dr. Joseph and Dr. Stein, were both men.

Three days after the attack, I was ready to be moved out of ICU into Cedars' thoracic wing. As they pushed me to my new room, I saw other patients walking slowly down the halls. For the first time I wondered how long it would be before I, too, would walk again.

I'll never forget the moment they wheeled me into my private room. I felt as though I'd entered a flower shop. Incredible arrangements of flowers and plants were everywhere, even in rows along the floor. The nurse told me that the first flowers to arrive had been sent by Robert De Niro, Joe Pesce, Martin Scorsese, and Steven Spielberg—people I'd done films with before. There were gifts and cards from countless other members of the film and television industry, co-workers from the New York theater scene, and dozens of friends and relatives. The sight of that flower-filled, love-filled room made me realize how lucky I was.

The attack had received a tremendous amount of publicity, particularly in Los Angeles. Oddly enough, my family and I actually learned many new facts about the case by watching television. It was strange for us to see the bizarre story unfolding on the news programs. We even joked about it at times, saying that some people in Hollywood probably believed that the whole thing was a publicity gimmick. But despite the humor, watching the news stories was often highly stressful and depressing.

Viewing the coverage one day, we were all upset when suddenly we saw a close-up of my blood on the pavement outside my apartment. Quickly, Fred turned off the TV set. But none of us has ever forgotten that gruesome image.

Yet in a certain way, listening to news reports helped us to keep the attack in true perspective. We existed only in the isolated world of the hospital, and at times everything apart from that existence seemed to be a dream. But hearing the reporters on the six o'clock news talking about the attack turned the dream into undeniable reality.

The horrifying events were taking their toll on the entire family. Everyone was tense and exhausted, and the problems never seemed to end. In addition to coping with the direct psychological and physical results of the attack, we also had to contend with the financial crisis caused by my ever-growing medical expenses. Detective Kalas informed us about the State of California's District Attorney Victim Witness Assistance Program, which exists to help crime victims, witnesses, and their families.

Lori Nelson, director of the program, visited me personally at Cedars-Sinai. She explained that I was eligible to apply to the State Board of Control for reimbursement against medical expenses, but that the amount the state would pay was limited to $10,000. She went on to explain that I would be personally liable for any expenses over $10,000, and that it usually took more than a year for the reimbursement to come through.

When the reality of Lori Nelson's words hit me, my reaction was loud and hostile. I was, and still am, outraged to be *paying* because I was stabbed, outraged to be *paying* for the painful treatments, the endless doses of medication, the exhausting examinations, the lengthy hospital stay.

There was no question that my bills would be astronomical. After insurance and the maximum reimbursement from the state, I would still end up paying many thousands of dollars because I happened, by pure chance, to be the victim of a crime.

Thankfully, I did have an insurance policy. But so many of the crucial treatments, like the psychiatry and physical therapy which I would need for over a year, were not covered. And many other medical costs were only partly covered. If I had not been insured, the attack would have left me no choice but to declare bankruptcy. Many less fortunate victims are forced to do so.

While we house, clothe, feed, and medically and psychologically care for alleged and convicted criminals, we do not accord the same treatment to the innocent victims who suffer at their hands. Can any one of us consider this to be justice?

Now that I was permitted visitors, many of my friends flocked to see me. I loved having people around; the activity and conversations cheered me and helped to bring me to life again. And the visitors allowed Fred and my parents to get some badly needed rest.

Of course, none of my friends had ever dealt with a stab victim before, and they were usually nervous at first, self-conscious and unsure of how to act around me. Once I understood that the IVs, the bandages, and my lacerated body frightened people, I would try to ease the initial awkward moments by joking with my visitors. I wanted them to see that neither my personality nor my sense of humor had been stripped away.

But unfortunately, having visitors led to an unexpected and depressing side effect. Once my friends had gone I was left feeling isolated and bereft. I would lie in bed and fantasize about doing things my friends did when they left the hospital: taking dance classes, seeing shows and films, going to auditions. I longed to be out there too. But my family and I were trapped in our corner of Cedars-Sinai.

The silence in my hospital room was most oppressive right after my visitors left. Fred and my parents experienced the same let-down feeling. For hours, we would stare mutely at one another, shaking our heads.

Fred had become withdrawn and exhausted. We missed the closeness we'd shared as husband and wife. Now, both of us were just two small cogs in the machinery of the hospital world. We had little time alone together; my dependence upon my parents was still as strong as that of a small child. Fred and I were both filled with pain and loneliness, but we didn't know how to deal with each other. There was a huge gap between us which neither of us knew how to bridge.

My overall physical condition improved with each passing day. The doctors were able to reduce my medication a bit, and all but one of the IVs were removed. I was thrilled when, only one week after the attack, Dr. Stein told me I could take my first walk or, as he called it, my "first hobble."

The nurses lifted me out of bed and I leaned on the arms of Fred and my father. The pain in my chest made me stoop over. Although I took only tiny scuffling steps, every one of my injuries hurt. The nurses pushed the IV pole along beside me, and the sorry-looking procession made its halting way down the corridor.

Still, I was on my feet again! Even if I was hunched over and taking only pathetic little steps, at least I was *moving*. I felt wonderful. I knew that I was, both literally and figuratively, making steps toward a complete recovery.

The injured finger on my right hand was healing nicely, but I was having trouble with my left ring finger and middle finger, which had been much more seriously wounded when I'd closed my hand over the assailant's knife. These two fingers remained immobile. Dr. Stein called in a hand surgeon, who felt that microsurgery was necessary to repair the damaged muscles, nerves, and tendons.

So, just ten days after the attack, I underwent a second operation, which lasted about two and a half hours. I awoke from the anesthesia and saw the large cast that extended from my fingertips to my elbow. The entire arm was in traction. And every nerve in my hand was screaming in pain.

Only now was I informed that hand surgery is among the most painful of operations, particularly when the nerves are involved. The doctors increased my dosage of Demerol and I was catapulted backward into a pain-racked state not unlike that of my first few days in ICU. I tried not to fight the pain, to let it wash over me. Since rebelling against it and upsetting myself only made me ache even more, I tried to stay as calm as possible and put my energies into meditating or resting. While doing so, I'd try to focus my mind on positive things and positive people.

One person was constantly in my thoughts: Jeff Fenn, the Sparkletts water deliveryman who'd rescued me from death at the hand of the assailant. I asked to see Jeff and when I heard that he was going to visit me at Cedars, I was ecstatic.

But the day before the meeting was to take place, the press found out about it and asked my family and me for permission to have reporters present. Although I have always had respect for the press, I wanted this special meeting to be a private one. So only Jeff, his wife Claire, Detective Kalas, and my family attended.

When the man who had so bravely saved my life walked into the room, I felt a bit disoriented and confused. It was hard to grasp that this was the blond "angel" who had literally pulled me from death's jaws.

Fred and my parents thanked him emotionally for what he had done. Then Jeff walked to my bedside. The moment he was next to me, we reached out and embraced. I felt an onrush of gratitude and love for this courageous man. The bond between us was unbreakable—I owed him my life. As we clung to each other, I felt as though I would burst with emotion. Everyone present was swept up in the feeling.

Then I presented Jeff with a trophy I'd had made for him. It was engraved with the words TO MY HERO, JEFF FENN. THANK YOU. THANK YOU. THANK YOU. WITH LOVE AND GRATITUDE FOREVER, THERESA SALDANA. As Jeff left the hospital, he showed it to the reporters outside and said that he would keep it always.

Only three days after my microsurgery, the pretrial hearing was held. With my arm still in traction, I went to court in a wheelchair, accompanied by my husband. Fred, too, had been subpoenaed as a witness. We were driven in a police vehicle from Cedars to the courtroom.

Trembling, I was helped out of the car and into my wheelchair. Reporters were everywhere, flashing pictures and asking questions. So many strangers. I was terrified on many different levels.

Would the attacker try to hurt me? Were there any other "crazies" in the courthouse? Would someone in the crowd bump me and hurt me accidentally? Would my mind go blank during my testimony?

The reporters questioned me, but I'd been instructed by Detective Kalas not to say anything that might jeopardize the case, so I said as little as possible.

In the waiting room I sat surrounded by Fred, Jeff Fenn, and other witnesses. The prospect of seeing and identifying the assailant turned my blood to ice water. I could hardly breathe.

They wheeled me into the hearing room. At my request, the lady judge allowed my wheelchair to be placed parallel to the assailant, rather than facing him. I answered the official questions in a robotlike monotone, but my pulse raced and my throat felt parched and constricted. The judge asked me to identify the attacker. I forced myself to look in the direction of the person who had, barely two weeks earlier, plunged a knife into me ten times.

My only thought when I glanced at him that day was that he personified the word *evil*. An aura of malice and derangement seemed to emanate from his being. The sight of him made me feel sickened and deeply, unutterably depressed.

Finally the hearing ended and I was wheeled out of the courtroom and driven swiftly to the hospital. Riding in the police car back to Cedars-Sinai, my mind reeled with the intensity and bizarreness of it all.

My entire life had been turned upside down. I remember thinking that I had become part of a freak show, an injured animal placed on display at the courthouse carnival. I could almost hear a crazed circus barker yelling, "Come and see the little stab victim, folks. Just step right up!"

Moments after my arrival at Cedars, my nurse announced that court-ordered photographers were waiting outside. At their request, she removed my nightgown and discreetly covered me with three small towels. The photographers came in and systematically took pictures of each of my injuries. I felt like a corpse in a morgue. That ghoulish photo session was one of the most deeply humiliating experiences of my life.

In the hospital that night, I tried to rethink the day's

courthouse experience rationally and unemotionally. Why were the press and onlookers there in full force? Were they really out seeking to get a thrill from this macabre little sideshow? Well, I reasoned, perhaps a few really were voyeurs. But it had seemed that most of the press and public were genuinely concerned and interested in seeing how I was after the ordeal. I realized that many of the courtroom spectators were, in fact, well-wishers. And I'd certainly been treated kindly and courteously by everyone.

From that day on, I began to perceive people's interest in me as positive. Without the care and support I received from them, I could never have thought of working publicly in the field of victim advocacy. The next crucial step had to come from me. I needed to start thinking of myself not as a "freak show animal," but as a role model for others who had been victimized.

Three weeks after the attack I entered a new phase of recovery. My condition was now listed as serious but no longer critical. Yet my entire life still felt completely out of balance. The pain, medical procedures, and drugs were part of a dull pattern, a dreary, day-to-day hospital-bound routine.

About eighteen days after the attack, Dr. Stein came to my room to inspect my wounds. He had to remove both the bandages and the Steri-Strips (butterfly-stitchlike pieces of special tape which held together and partially concealed the wounds). My stitches, thank God, were not the kind that had to be cut and pulled out one by one. They would remain in place and eventually dissolve.

When Dr. Stein was through, I asked for a mirror. He suggested that I wait to look at myself until the swelling went down. But my combined curiosity and anxiety were insurmountable. Again I requested a mirror, and the nurse reluctantly complied.

First, I stared at my face, grateful that it had remained untouched by the attacker's knife. Then, I brought the mirror lower, holding it in front of my chest and upper torso. What I saw made me gasp in shock. All my worst fears were confirmed: I was ugly, disfigured, horrible to look at. Too upset even to cry, I looked stonily ahead, my face a frozen mask of revulsion.

Dr. Stein explained that the swelling would go down soon, the redness would fade, and I would see marked improvement in the weeks and months ahead. I stared, still in a daze, at the mirror, and let his words sink into my consciousness. The most encouraging thing Dr. Stein told me was that plastic surgeons could do wonders in cases like mine. I looked up at him dubiously. But at least I felt some hope.

The cruel truth of that mirror image made me question further: How could I come to terms with the fact that neither my mind nor my body would ever be the same again?

One of my best physical features had always been my skin, which people often told me was "absolutely flawless." Now, it was not only flawed but terribly disfigured.

I realized that if I was going to cope with the negatives in my life, I had to concentrate on the positives. Every day I thanked my lucky stars that my face had not been disfigured. Each morning, I took the time to do a complete makeup job: lipstick, rouge, base, mascara, eyeshadow—the works! Then my mother brushed my hair and either braided it or put it in pigtails, adding ribbons to match whatever I was wearing. In a way, I resembled a painted, beribboned china doll.

For hours I would stare into a mirror, gaining confidence and hope from the fact that I could still look pretty. It was so very important to find ways to make myself attractive in spite of my terribly injured body.

When people asked what I'd like them to bring me, I usually answered, "Oh, a nightgown, please." These gowns made up my entire wardrobe for quite a while, and I relied on their prettiness and softness to cheer me and to help me be presentable to visitors. I often changed nightgowns two or three times a day, selecting each garment with care. It might have seemed silly or even vain, but I felt that all the primping I did was a necessary step toward accepting myself again.

In order to start getting into the frame of mind that would help me recover as swiftly as possible, I asked myself: "What is it that makes me happiest?" And the answer was: *working*. When I am on stage or in front of a camera I feel vibrantly, exquisitely alive—and *happy*.

And yet it was through my work as an actress that the attacker had fixated on me. Naturally, this made me consider getting out of show business—but only for a moment or two!

Abandoning my profession would destroy everything I'd worked for all my life. I told myself: *This complete stranger has already disrupted and nearly ruined my life. I'm not going to let him take my career away from me too!*

And so I made a vow: to put every ounce of my strength into achieving a recovery that would allow me to resume my career as soon as humanly possible.

For hours I talked on the phone with my manager, Selma, and with my agents and friends, discussing plans for my return to work. It may have sounded strange to them, coming from a woman who was lying in traction in a hospital bed. But even the act of *talking* about a return to my career made it seem like a real possibility.

Obviously I couldn't perform from my hospital bed— although my friends and relatives were entertained when I'd get carried away in conversation and start waving my good arm around expressively. I guess I looked pretty demented. But the creative side of me desperately needed an outlet. The one other method of expression I'd always loved was writing. In fact, it had always been a secret dream of mine to write a book. But with my demanding career, I'd never found the time to work on one. Now, perhaps writing was the answer to my need for artistic fulfillment.

My mind started spinning with ideas. It struck me that the most helpful thing I could do was to share my experience and relate the effects that this hideous crime had upon me and upon my family. Suddenly my feeling of uselessness evaporated. I couldn't wait to get started.

Yet, despite my eagerness and excitement, even the relatively effortless task of putting pen to paper was physically impossible. One of my hands was splinted and bandaged, the other was suspended in traction.

I told my good friend, Bob Gale, about my predicament. Despite his hectic schedule as a producer/screenwriter, Bob somehow managed to visit me almost every day. When Bob heard my dilemma, he used his writer's instincts to come up with the perfect solution. The next morning, Bob arrived with a tiny portable tape recorder and told me he would transcribe my cassettes himself. At that point in my recovery, I could not have received a better gift.

At the beginning of the fourth week after the attack, my sister, Maria, arrived to spend her Easter break from New York University with me. Back in Brooklyn, Maria, too, had been put through an ordeal as a result of the attack. Day and night she had been on the phone, advising relatives and friends about my condition. During those first days and weeks very few telephone calls had been put through to my room. So *everyone* called Maria. Her life during those weeks was nightmarish. She tried to keep up with her classes but was bombarded with calls until late into the night, spending hour after hour trying to reassure everyone at a time when she herself badly needed support.

The family decided it would be best for her to join us so that we could all be together. Her presence and strength were a boost to the entire family. Now it was Maria, rather than my mother, who slept in my room at night. With our talking and laughing into the wee hours, we resembled two girls having a pajama party.

When I wanted to "write," Maria would prop the small recorder above my shoulder and turn it on. Then I talked into it for hours on end, trying to envision the people I was "writing" to. I hoped that some of them would be victims or their loved ones. For so long, I had been feeling terribly *alone* in my plight; although many people surrounded me, none of them had been attacked. As I spoke into my little tape recorder, I felt an almost tangible connection to others "out there" who had been through it too.

By early April, my release from Cedars loomed in the near future, and my family and I had to face the problem of where I would go for continued care and treatment. A recuperative hospital seemed the ideal choice, and we investigated a number of them. But we learned that my insurance didn't cover such facilities, and there was no way that my family or I could afford the expense of this kind of hospitalization.

Fred and I discussed moving into a new apartment and my going home with him. But he had to work all day, I was still far too weak and ill to function alone, and my insurance did not cover the costly services of a private nurse.

Flying east with my family could not be considered as a possibility either. I was in no condition to travel and had been advised that it was best that my medical care continue to be supervised by my L.A. doctors.

At a loss for any other safe place to go, we considered the possibility of my committing myself to Thalians Mental Health Facility, the inpatient wing at Cedars-Sinai. After all, I was unable to care for myself adequately. Where else did I have to turn?

So, in early April, Dr. Joseph escorted my parents and me across the street to Thalians. But even as we approached the building, my parents began to plead with me not to commit myself. In the elevator, on our way up to the locked third-floor ward, they reasoned that if I became a psychiatric inpatient, the stigma would follow me for the rest of my life. And they felt, with good cause, that I just didn't belong in a mental hospital.

Although I was far from decided, I argued that at least my daily psychiatric sessions would be paid for by insurance if I were an inpatient. I also pointed out that my release date from Cedars was just one week away; time was running out.

We got off the elevator and were met by the head nurse, who gave us a tour of the wing. As they wheeled me down the hall, I noticed the relative cheerfulness of the atmosphere. The color scheme was bright, and the walls were covered with artwork. The rooms, which were all private, were tiny but adequate.

However, I immediately began to see drawbacks: There was only one pay phone in the hallway, and patients lined up to use it. Most of the inmates seemed to be either loud, giddy teenagers or deeply depressed adults who, in some cases, acted overtly disturbed.

My parents' faces looked taut and anxious. The nurse rattled off a mind-boggling list of rules and regulations. Visiting hours were severely restricted and every moment of the day was regimented. The nurse made it clear that few, if any, exceptions could be made to the rules. With each passing moment my spirits sank lower.

Then, as we were about to leave, I noticed the window on

the door to one of the patient's rooms. A heavy grating criss-crossed it, gleaming with slats of thick gray steel. I looked at my parents and said, "Wait a minute, *I'm* not the one who should be in prison. This place isn't for me." We thanked the nurse and left quietly.

The decision had been made, and despite the still-present pressure of finding a suitable place, we were relieved. Even Dr. Joseph seemed silently glad that I had chosen not to live in Thalians.

I often look back on that day, thankful that I chose not to commit myself. But I realize that I was fortunate. For many victims, there is no other safe alternative. Until our society can provide a secure recuperative shelter for victims in their time of need, many will unnecessarily live under lock and key in mental hospitals because they simply have no other choice. One of my dreams is to build a haven for crime victims, where they can recover in a supportive, protected atmosphere until they are physically and emotionally ready to return home.

My family and I launched a telephone campaign to find an appropriate place for me. We called relatives, friends, friends of friends, agencies, etc., and explained the situation. Many of them responded by busily making inquiries in an effort to help us. We called, and we waited.

One evening a casual friend, Shelly D'San Juan, a costume designer with whom I'd recently done a play, stopped in at the hospital. She brought her boyfriend, Dr. John Lima. The moment I saw this kind man, dressed in his doctors' whites, my intuition told me he would have the answer to our problems. Amazingly enough, he did!

Dr. Lima explained that he was a physician at the Motion Picture and Television Fund Hospital in Calabasas, a suburb about an hour from Los Angeles. The hospital served only members of the film and television unions and their families.

At Motion Picture, there were cottages and lodges for the elderly who could still care for their own needs, and convalescent wings for people who required only minor supervision. Then there was J Wing, set up in two sections: one for the seriously ill who needed acute hospital care, and the other for patients who required skilled nursing care. This second section of J Wing sounded like exactly what I needed.

Dr. Lima stressed that the vast majority of patients at Motion Picture were elderly. But the young and infirm could also apply. Excited, we thanked the doctor for the news and asked him to speak to the hospital administrators about admitting me.

After Dr. Lima and Shelly left, a peaceful feeling came over me. Sheer instinct told me I would be accepted at Motion Picture. My good spirits were infectious, and Fred and my parents began to feel hopeful too.

Dr. Lima spoke to the Motion Picture Hospital administration and the very next day called to tell us that they would allow me to be admitted. Hours later, Cedars gave me a pass and I went with my family to see my new "home."

As we drove up to Motion Picture, I was impressed by the manicured, lush green lawn and the beautiful flowers. The grounds were exquisite. Dr. Lima came out to meet us and wheeled me into the main building.

As soon as we entered the hospital, we couldn't help but sense an atmosphere which can be associated only with people who are dying. As I was wheeled along, we passed patients walking with difficulty down the hallway, and saw others, clearly terminally ill, in their rooms. Without exception they were very, very old. Some were pushed in wheelchairs; others hobbled on canes or walkers; many moaned in their beds. My hopefulness turned quickly to despondency.

Dr. Lima led us to J Wing and introduced me to the staff. Most of them seemed brisk, businesslike, and aloof. I felt they looked upon me with disfavor, which confused me.

Weeks later the nurses told me that they had expected a spoiled, Hollywood starlet type, and they were not exactly looking forward to coping with the psychological problems of a stab victim. Most of them had worked professionally for years with geriatrics, but they had little or no experience in dealing with the particular needs of crime victims.

The head nurse, Jane Bladow, gave us a quick tour of the wing and rattled off a lengthy list of rules and regulations. The atmosphere at Motion Picture was no-nonsense, brisk, and systematized. In comparison, Cedars was a country club.

No one said a word during our long drive back. But the injustice of my situation struck me that evening. I had been stabbed nearly to death, put through indescribable physical torment, and was now being forced to live in an environment where I did not belong. I was a good, tax-paying citizen; I obeyed the law; I supported my country. Yet, in my role as innocent victim, the government had no place for me to go. Yes, the assailant was being given humane treatment. Nothing cruel or unusual was happening to him. But I had almost no support or assistance. Neither the state nor the federal government had a place for me, or for any of the countless others like me.

I did not expect a handout. If I had been able to live and work normally, I could have helped myself. But that was not possible. A crime had been committed and I had been the victim. And I felt that now *I* was being sentenced.

My unhappiness was exacerbated by still another blow: I had expected to continue my therapy with Dr. Joseph on an outpatient basis, once I'd been discharged from Cedars-Sinai. But shortly before my transfer to Motion Picture Hospital, I was presented with very upsetting news. Despite the progress I'd made while under his care, Dr. Joseph had been ordered to remove himself from my case. His superiors at Cedars had suddenly decided that handling the victim of such a horrendous attack was too complex for a resident who was not yet a full-fledged psychiatrist.

What galled me and my family was the fact that they had *assigned* Dr. Joseph to me and had kept him on my case for an entire month. Why on earth had they permitted this intense, prolonged period of therapy, only to insist later upon the young doctor's removal?

Outraged, I tried to have the decision altered, but I faced tremendous opposition. Dr. Joseph's superiors were adamant. Not wanting to hurt the young doctor's career at Cedars, I was forced to accept defeat.

Now, in addition to a drastic change of environment, I had to adjust to a new psychiatrist. Everything seemed to be against me. What was the point of making progress only to be knocked down by circumstances out of my control? I raged and wept. No one could console me. For two weeks I couldn't even bring myself to talk into my tape recorder. Everything seemed futile.

In our final session Dr. Joseph asked me what type of psychiatrist I would like to be paired with. I told him I had a list of requirements and asked him to write them down. My list read as follows: Wanted: psychiatrist. Must be young, male, Jewish, slim, attractive, sensitive, intelligent, creative, and nonjudgmental. In short, it was an exact description of Dr. Joseph himself!

We had a good laugh about it, but then the time came to say goodbye. Tears welled in my eyes, and he, too, seemed on the verge of weeping; we had been through so much together. I thanked him, gave him a quick hug, and turned away.

Later that same week I met with Dr. Peter Weingold. Amazingly, he fit my description to a T! At first I was somewhat defensive and resentful at having to repeat to him facts that Dr. Joseph already knew. But within just a few sessions I began to like and respect him, and responded well to him in therapy. Dr. Weingold nurtured and supported me. Without encouraging overdependence, he allowed me to rely upon him. We went through many stages of progress and regression and made steady strides toward health together. I feel that I owe my sanity, at least in great part, to the excellent psychiatric care I received from both these fine doctors.

One morning in April my moving day came, and I said a tearful goodbye to the people who had cared for me at Cedars-Sinai. I felt particularly thankful to Dr. Alexander Stein, and had a hero's trophy made up for him too. After all, if he hadn't agreed to operate on me on March 15, I would never have made it. It was an emotional parting. I gave him the trophy and a box of those sweets he loved to eat, and simply said, "Thank you." He had become not only my doctor but a trusted friend as well. On April 5, I moved into the Motion Picture and Television Fund Hospital. For security, I adopted an alias and became "Alicia Michaels." Even the plaque outside my room bore that name, and during the months that followed I grew so accustomed to it that, to this day, I still answer reflexively when someone calls the name Alicia!

At Motion Picture, my inpatient life-style was drastically altered. Order and discipline reigned supreme. On the one hand, the environment made me feel safe, protected, and well taken care of. On the other hand, at times it made me feel like a prisoner.

On J Wing everyone woke up early, and the day invariably began with a cacophony of moans and groans of pain and confusion. At breakfast I had to swallow a strong vitamin supplement which made me nauseous for the better part of an hour. By eight A.M., an orderly would wheel me out of my room to the first of two daily physical therapy sessions.

My left side and shoulder were weak and nearly useless from the pinched nerve incurred during the attack. It was almost impossible to move that side of my body because my arm was still in the heavy, bulky cast. I literally had to relearn the use of all the affected muscles.

My physical therapist, Phil, was friendly and dynamic. He often kept me laughing in spite of the pain. One morning he pointed out the very oldest man in the room (at least ninety years of age) and asked me how my date with him had gone that weekend. Another day Phil "scolded" me about the noise filtering downstairs from all those "wild parties" I had in my room.

After my arm cast had been removed, Phil began to guide me through the agonizing process of getting my damaged and swollen fingers to move again. At the start of each session he had me place my left arm in a whirlpool of what felt to me like boiling water. The heat sent spasms of pain shooting up my arm. After ten minutes or so, the temperature would drop enough to make it bearable. Then, forced to sit with my arm submerged for between thirty and sixty minutes, I grew bored to distraction and quite blue. The environment didn't help either. There, lined up before me, was a row of patients in wheelchairs awaiting their therapy. Many were senile; most had been made crotchety by pain or discomfort.

I tried my best to make friends with the elderly residents of the Motion Picture Hospital, hoping to develop a camaraderie. When I was a child and teenager, my best friend had been my grandmother. With her vitality, intelligence, and *joie de vivre*, she had taught me to love and respect older people. It had broken my heart when she died during my high school years.

But I found that many of the aged patients at Motion

Picture were turned inward to their own worlds. Pain, senility, and depression combined to make most of them virtually unreachable.

Now and then I would meet a feisty, talkative lady or gent who'd share with me stories of the years gone by when he or she had been in silent films or movie musicals. A few of them showed me faded but beautiful pictures of themselves in their youthful show-business days. Sadly, my contact with this kind of person was rare.

Once my arm had soaked, Phil worked me through many different hand and finger exercises. All of them hurt. I'm sure I disturbed a lot of patients with my howling and carryings-on, but it was better to howl and heal than not to heal at all. I kept hoping that I'd become immune or numb to the constant pain. But although I'd been through the most excruciating physical ordeals imaginable, I never lost my low pain threshold. If there was pain to be felt, you could be sure that I would feel every bit of it.

After my physical therapy sessions, I was supposed to rest quietly in my room, but I usually spent every second of the time on the phone. The beige telephone by my bed helped me to keep my sanity; it was my lifeline to the "real world." Whenever I felt lost or disconnected, I would call a close friend and take comfort in even the most mundane conversation.

At Motion Picture, my daily doses of painkiller were cut nearly in half. As the effects of medication diminished, my concentration improved so that once again I could read and enjoy books. I devoured them. They transported me out of the misery of my own life.

My friends Mayra Langdon and Michael Riesman, who'd flown in from New York to see me, gave me a copy of Norman Cousins' *Anatomy of an Illness*. As soon as I read the jacket I knew that this would be an important book for me. I practically inhaled it, reading it from cover to cover in one sitting.

Having gone through a near-fatal illness himself, Mr. Cousins made point after point that I agreed with wholeheartedly. I read the book over and over again until it was dog-eared, never seeming to tire of it or of its positive message. It fueled my desire to write a book of my own and reach out to people in ways that related to my own experience.

And so I returned to the writing I'd abandoned in my depression over the enforced change in psychiatrists. My right hand was no longer bandaged, so I could hold a pen again. Sitting in bed, I wrote reams and reams of thoughts, observations, and ideas, quickly going through dozens of felt-tip pens. Writing was wonderfully therapeutic; it gave me a sense of purpose.

Usually, in the early afternoon I was taken in a hospital car to Los Angeles for therapy sessions with Dr. Weingold or visits to other specialists on my case. The daily two-hour round trips exhausted me, but they were the initial steps toward my reintegration into society. I was forced to take elevators and sit in waiting rooms with strangers. A member of the hospital staff always accompanied me, but nevertheless, for me this simple, everyday activity was a challenge.

I was still terribly frightened and unnerved around people I didn't know. When I rode in the elevator up to Dr. Weingold's office, my heart would leap into my throat every time the doors opened and a new male passenger would enter. I knew *logically* that these men were just innocent workmen, doctors, messengers, and business people. But I was terrified that one of them would pull out a knife or a gun and attack me.

The only way to overcome these fears was to face them and to tackle them. And so, each elevator ride was another step forward. Getting *to* and *from* my sessions with Weingold were very much a part of the therapy.

When I returned from my L.A. commute, I was taken to the P.T. room for a second pain-filled session with Phil. By six o'clock, thoroughly exhausted, I crawled into bed and had dinner. In the evening, if visitors came, I was happy and "up." If not, I felt lonely and rejected.

Most people had taken my move to Motion Picture as a sign that I was "okay," and had either drastically curtailed or ceased their visits. This is a common pattern with friends of hospitalized victims. The irony is that, as drugged or pained as I was in the first days and weeks, I couldn't fully focus on the friends who visited. And now, in Motion Picture, when I was far more alert and in need of distraction, companionship, and support, I did not receive it.

I confronted many of my absent friends on the phone.

Some sounded guilty or sheepish, but they still didn't come. The worst were those who made promises to visit at specific times but neither showed up nor called.

Thank God for the few steadfast friends who did visit faithfully. I'll always remember them for their constant caring. They helped give me the courage and support to go on.

Not long after I had settled in at Motion Picture, my father and sister had to return home to New York. It was sad to see them leave, but they had to resume their own lives. My mother stayed on, living in a cottage which the Motion Picture Administration generously provided.

Fred visited every second day or so, but we had been growing further and further apart since the attack. He cared, he felt, and he hurt. But it was still locked up inside him. I suggested that Fred seek psychological help, but he adamantly refused. Every time he visited he seemed thinner and more depressed—locked in his own private hell.

Later, when I was well again, Fred told me some of what he'd been through in those days—his feelings of confusion, anger, desolation, helplessness. Then, too, he had his resentments: He thought that people ignored his pain and concentrated only on mine.

When I look back on it, I can see why he felt that way. Our *entire family* should have been in therapy, working out the various individual conflicts that arose as a result of the attack. We *all* needed attention and TLC. But at the time, only the most desperate and ill person received the attention: me.

Fred and I loved each other; we tried to make our relationship work. But we were trapped in separate, miserable existences we had done nothing to deserve. Enveloped in my insular world of fear and disability, I needed to put all my energies into healing. And Fred was too anguished and depressed to help and care for me. He visited; we talked. But we could never completely share our internal anguish. It colored every word we said, but it never overtly surfaced.

The more we submerged our problems, the more they festered. Fred was angry with me for changing, for withdrawing from him and clinging to my parents. I was angry at him for not being the Rock of Gibraltar. And we didn't have the presence of mind to see a marriage counselor. Later, after my recovery, when we sought professional help it was just too late.

Now, it is my recommendation to all couples whose lives have been touched by victimization that they *both* seek help in joint therapy sessions. The partner of the victim suffers intensely after an attack, and counseling is important, if for no other reason than to keep the lines of communication open. The victim needs to be helped to understand that his or her partner suffers too. Both partners must learn that no one, no matter how dedicated and considerate, can possibly be the perfect shoulder to lean on. I wish Fred and I had gone into therapy while I was still hospitalized. I believe it could have saved our marriage.

The sweetest and most thoughtful thing Fred did for me *ever* was to give me a tiny toy poodle puppy which we named Totsie. Because dogs weren't allowed in Motion Picture, we had to sneak her in and out of the hospital. I adored the puppy. Even on a part-time basis, it was so special to have a live little pet to love and care for. No matter how down I felt, Totsie's antics would always pick up my mood. I've since read some material on pet therapy, and I know it worked for me.

In the room next to me at Motion Picture was Mrs. Pat Gallant, a film industry hairdresser who was in the final stage of terminal cancer. At forty-nine she was the youngest person, next to me, on our wing.

Her husband, Tom, a location manager for the television program *Trapper John, M.D.*, visited constantly and was beside himself with despair over his wife's disease-ravaged condition. Although it was obvious that the end was near, Tom loved his wife too much to accept having to let her go. He willed her to live and desperately hoped for a miracle.

Pat Gallant was a courageous woman; she couldn't have been more aptly named. During our brief but intimate friendship, I learned a great deal from this highly intuitive, gentle woman.

Every day, I'd wheel myself or shuffle slowly into her room. Although she looked pale, gaunt, and emaciated, Pat somehow retained an ethereal, delicate beauty. On days when her pain wasn't completely unbearable, we had long, often serious talks.

She loved her husband, her children and grandchild, but life had become merely existence and she knew she would be leaving soon. Many times Pat told me she would welcome the release from constant agony. Pat had accepted death.

I sat at her bedside feeling unbearably sad at the inexplicable juxtaposition of our fates. There I was, terribly harmed and still quite ill. But I was going to survive. Each day I grew stronger. I was on the path to a full recovery. But before my eyes, Pat's life was ebbing away. We were both acutely, painfully aware of this bitter irony. Yet we became friends.

Pat taught me ways of coping with pain. She encouraged me to vent my anger and frustration. Most of all, she made me realize how important it was for me to make the most of my lucky survival: to take every second of life and live it to the fullest, and to cherish and embrace the gift of time. I try always to follow her advice.

On Pat's birthday, a warm spring Sunday, her entire family came to visit, including her year-old grandchild. My mother and I were invited over and, despite the hospital atmosphere, we all had a lovely party with a huge cake. Pat wore a pink lace gown and enjoyed every minute of the celebration. But she told me privately that she knew for sure this would be her last birthday.

While on a doctor's pass, I had bought ten small gifts for Pat's birthday. Every hour on that Sunday, I gave her one: a lace handkerchief, a tiny heart-shaped china box, a small bottle of perfume, and so on. She enjoyed each surprise and told me it felt like Christmas.

Patricia Gallant had been right. That Sunday was to be her last birthday. Not long after, she requested to leave the hospital. Her husband hired a beautiful chocolate-brown limousine/ ambulance and took Pat home, where she was cared for by a private nurse. I never saw Patricia Gallant again. She died in her own bed before my release from Motion Picture. I grieved for Tom, who had hoped for her recovery until the end. And I grieved for myself; I had lost a good friend. But I didn't grieve for Pat. She had accepted and welcomed death; the constant suffering had made life unbearable. I prayed for her to be happy and pain-free.

My victimization made me feel both isolated and alienated; at times I even referred to myself as a freak. I realized that I needed to talk to someone who had survived an experience similar to mine. I desperately wanted a role model: a recovered, functional victim who had returned to a normal, happy life.

Everyone tried to reassure me, saying that I'd make it through just fine. My psychiatrist, my family, and my friends all kept telling me how strong I was and that they *knew* I could do it. But none of them had been through such an experience. I needed *proof*.

Purely by happenstance, while on a pass from the hospital I met Miriam Schneider, a crime victim. She introduced herself, telling me she was a schoolteacher who'd been near-fatally shot in her classroom. She too had lived through a nightmare of physical and emotional pain. But now she was living a fulfilling life, teaching and raising her teenage daughter. Although Miriam and I had little in common as far as our day-to-day lives were concerned, we had plenty to talk about as *victims*. We poured our hearts out, comparing experiences, and soon realized that we'd been through many of the same problems, emotions, situations, and reactions. We exchanged phone numbers and said goodbye, but that chance meeting had a profound effect upon me. Miriam had survived; therefore I could survive too. The parallel was beautifully clear.

That same day, I formulated the idea for Victims for Victims, an organization in which crime victims could reach out to one another. I wasn't well enough to act on the concept, but I began to put my ideas on paper. Victims for Victims would not hold its first formal meeting for six months, but it was already very real in my mind.

My mother had been with me for eight weeks, sharing all my stress, fear, pain, and anxiety. She now looked drawn and exhausted. The pain had taken its toll, and I realized that she needed to be with my father in New York. It took a lot of courage for me to urge my mother to go back east. When we first discussed her leaving, she protested, fearing I wasn't ready. But after we talked it over for a few days, she agreed to go on condition that we make arrangements so that I would not be alone.

We turned to the Actors Fund of America, an organization dedicated to helping actors in financial need, and asked for their assistance. Mr. Iggy Wolfington brought my request before the board of directors. They graciously agreed to provide me with a full-time companion at their expense. A year later, they were reimbursed by the state.

Anna McDonald, a lovely actress who lived near the hospital, accepted the position, and after meeting her, my mother was satisfied that I'd be in good hands. In mid-May she returned to New York. Another milestone had passed.

For the first few days, I felt bereft without my mother, unable to sleep even with the aid of medication. But Anna was fun to be with, and we shared many of the same interests. I came to look forward to her visits, and my spirits began to lift.

Although I missed my mother a great deal, I realized that I had taken a giant step toward regaining my adult freedoms. "Mommy" was no longer there to buffer the pain.

By now, I'd become friendly with many of the nurses and nurse's aides on J Wing. As my pain lessened, my sense of humor returned in full force. There's no doubt that I kept the staff jumping: I created plenty of chaos on the normally sedentary J Wing—shrieking when I was terrified or in pain, roaring with laughter when I felt happy.

The stern-looking head nurse, Jane Bladow, turned out to be a terrific lady. Her brisk, no-nonsense manner belied her inner gentleness. As I grew healthier and more approachable, Jane seemed to take a special interest in me. Whenever she had a break, we'd get into long and intimate conversations. We discovered during our lengthy chats that we really enjoyed each other's company. A spontaneous, interesting friendship developed. The worlds of nursing and acting are far apart, but before long I learned that Jane and I shared a bond.

One afternoon a few weeks after my arrival at Motion Picture, Jane confided to me that she'd also been a crime victim. She described how her former boyfriend had beaten her and thrown her over a table, causing injuries that led to a five-month hospitalization. After Jane told me about this, we began to spend even more time talking together. We often discussed the many repercussions of victimization. After hearing of Jane's reactions to what had happened to her, and remembering the things that Miriam Schneider had said, I saw even more clearly that victims of violence go through many of the same problems. Jane thought my idea for a victims' organization was terrific, and she volunteered to help.

After Jane and I became friends, the rest of the staff really relaxed around me. They'd let me sit in the nurses' station at night (which was against the hospital rules) and I'd hang out with them, telling my film and theater stories and sharing in their jokes and laughter. I started to feel like "one of the girls," instead of just a loud and pathetic stab victim. And they began to realize that there was more to me than a big mouth and buckets of tears. I gained a true insider's view of the day-to-day problems that go along with the nursing profession. Once I understood the nurses and the difficulties they faced, I no longer felt that the staff resented me. Our misconceptions had been cleared up, and now they were all rooting for me.

The thought of being in the real world had always terrified me, but in June, during my final month at Motion Picture, I started to think, *Hey, maybe I can handle it out there!* I read even more books about others who had triumphed over adversity. Inspired by some of the people I read about, I threw myself with renewed vigor into my physical therapy program, and began to stretch and redevelop my seldom-used leg muscles.

It may seem trivial, but one of my biggest accomplishments was simply learning to feel comfortable in a restaurant. I was given dinner passes almost every evening, and would have a meal at one of the places nearby. I had to learn that not *everyone* in these establishments wanted to harm me or even to stare at me. Gradually I became less self-conscious and less afraid. I was even able to sit briefly at a table alone if my companion needed to use the phone or the restroom. Slowly, step by step, I readjusted to the outside world. I was given a number of all-day passes and did things like going shopping, visiting the homes of friends, and seeing movies. These simple pleasures thrilled me

My heavy medication was discontinued. I was learning to

deal with life on my own, weaning myself from the drugs that had sustained me during my darkest hours. When I felt like popping a tranquilizer, out of habit, or because I felt genuinely anxious, I played a game with myself, calling it the "Hold Out Game." It consisted of daring myself to "hold out" from taking pills for longer and longer periods of time. If I held out longer than usual without my "meds," I'd reward myself. Maybe I'd buy a new dress (on credit of course, my finances being what they were), or I'd let myself have a huge ice-cream sundae. At any rate, I'd find a way to treat myself to something special. It was a self-imposed behavior-modification plan. And it worked. I had relied on medication long enough. Now I needed to rely upon my own inner resources—even if I had to bribe myself to do it!

Dr. Weingold spent hours talking about and preparing for my discharge from the hospital. The thought of regaining my freedom began to give me a sense of excitement that grew day by day until at last I actually felt eager to leave.

On June 23, I said goodbye to the staff who had cared for me for so long. The past three and a half months had been a shattering nightmare, but it was time to go on. I walked out of the doors of Motion Picture Hospital and into the world again, ready to pick up the pieces and begin a whole new life.

CHAPTER 3

FEAR

Most of us, as children, go through phases when we wake up crying in the middle of the night about "monsters" or the "boogeyman." Our parents console us and tell us that we are safe, that there *are* no monsters. In time we become more secure, and our nightmares go away.

But what happens when we learn that, in a sense, the boogeyman we have feared since childhood really does exist?

It is difficult to put into words the uncontrollable, bone-chilling terror one is left with after a life-threatening attack. It is an insidious fear, awesome in its intensity and destructive power—hard to live with and harder still to break free of.

In the hospital, I was plagued by flashbacks which catapulted me backward in space and time and shook the bedrock of my sanity. Over and over I *heard* the attacker's voice, *saw* the blade glinting in the sunlight, and *felt* the knife being plunged into my body.

For many months after the attack, fear ruled my life. On some days it paralyzed me, and left me unable to perform even the simplest tasks. Often, I could not bring myself to take a walk down the hospital corridor, for I was convinced that there had been a security leak and that some unknown attacker was lurking nearby, ready to pounce upon me. At times I was reduced to a shrieking, sobbing, hysterical creature who, to all appearances, was losing her mind. Almost always, my fear led me to revert to a childlike, dependent state: too afraid to face the world, too afraid to be away from my parents, and much too afraid to be left alone—*ever*.

Some people felt that I *allowed* myself to give in to fear, to be engulfed by it. Their reaction confused and hurt me, because I desperately *wanted* the fear to go away. I *wanted* my freedom, control, and privacy back.

But my terrors were too strong to conquer simply by my *wanting* to. I needed to take slow, baby steps; I could not be rushed. And some of my well-intentioned friends tried to push me too far too soon.

For example, one afternoon in May my friend Carol drove me from Motion Picture to an appointment with Dr. Weingold. It was the first time I had gone to an outpatient appointment in a private car, unaccompanied by a member of the hospital staff.

After my session we stopped for lunch in the cafeteria of the building where my psychiatrist had his office. I had eaten there before with the hospital workers who normally escorted me, so I felt relatively comfortable. But in the middle of the meal, Carol stood up and said she needed to feed the parking meter. Startled, I blurted out, "Wait, I'll go with you!"

She paused for a moment, and then humiliated me by saying quite loudly, "Oh, Theresa, don't be ridiculous. You'll be fine—I'll be back in a second." Then she darted swiftly away.

People nearby who had heard this exchange began to stare at me curiously. There I was, gaunt, pale, helpless, my arm in a huge cast and sling, a hospital ID tag attached to my wrist. In my embarrassment I pushed my wrist tag up under my sleeve. I was shaking and on the verge of tears. After a moment or two, I couldn't bear the customers' eyes upon me any longer.

Slowly I eased myself out of my chair and walked stiffly to the ladies' room. With some hesitation I opened the door and was relieved to see a gentle-eyed middle-aged lady sitting on the sofa. I burst into tears and told the woman my situation. Luckily she was a kindly person and listened to me with sympathy.

Five minutes later Carol returned and found me in the ladies' room. All she had to say was: "Theresa, I thought it would be *good* for you to start getting used to being with strangers!"

Well, both then and today, I couldn't agree with her less. That humiliating experience did nothing to help me overcome my fears; on the contrary, because of that incident, it took me two more weeks to bring myself to leave the hospital without a security person.

Finding freedom from fear is a process that cannot be rushed. By trying to *force* fears away, you run the risk of cracking, falling apart entirely.

My case, of course, was extreme. I didn't just have a *feeling* that I would be killed if I was left alone—I was absolutely certain of it. And so, at the slightest sign that someone might leave me by myself, I rebelled vehemently—usually at the top of my lungs.

I know now that no real *physical* harm would have resulted if I'd been left alone, but most certainly I would have been in *psychological* danger. And I also realize that the emotions that prompted my terrified refusals to be alone were positive instincts growing out of a deep-rooted knowledge of my own potential breaking point. I believed that if I was left alone on the edge of my terror, I would go completely insane—or be driven to suicide.

And so, out of self-preservation, I insisted that a friend, a relative, or a hired companion be at my side day and night.

Many of the nurses and even some of my close friends reacted strongly—and negatively—to my becoming what one girlfriend termed "a prisoner of fear." They felt that I would end up unhealthy, unbalanced, and dependent on others for the rest of my life. They said things like: "Theresa, your fear will attract trouble and bring even more harm to you." Or they'd just say, "Stop being so scared. You're acting like a baby!"

I attempted to force myself to conquer my fears, trying repeatedly to stay alone. But each time, I ended up shaking, shivering, and on the verge of hysteria. These unsuccessful attempts at being alone made me feel even more guilty and miserable. It was clear that *forced* stoicism was not to be my route toward freedom from fear.

After talking to others who have survived similar attacks, I have learned that what works for one victim may not work for another. Some people *need* privacy, to prove to themselves that they are in control and that it won't happen again. They need time to think and they want to do it alone.

Ten months after my attack I appeared as a guest on a Boston talk show and spoke about my experience as a victim. After the taping, a lady named Karen approached me and explained that she had been sexually assaulted.

This fragile-looking, thirtyish woman told me that after the rape she had wanted time to rest and time to heal—all by herself. She moved from the apartment she'd shared with a roommate (the apartment where the assault had taken place) and took up residence alone in a new neighborhood. She broke up with her boyfriend and concentrated on solitary pursuits like needlework and oil painting. Now, two years after her attack, Karen was still living by herself. But she was beginning to seek out the advice and companionship of others.

Recently Karen had started therapy at a rape treatment center, and she told me that she preferred talking her problems out with her therapist rather than discussing them with friends or family members. Slowly, Karen's psychological wounds are healing, and she is especially proud that she accomplished most of the recovery on her own.

For Karen, solitude was the answer. Others, like me, need help, support, and companionship. Having people around me constantly was my armor against fear. The presence of friends, relatives, and companions gave me the sense of security I needed in order to endure the prolonged physical and psychological healing process.

But one unfortunate aspect of fear is its quality of contagion. People tend to be *afraid* around a victim who is frightened. Often they will not acknowledge their own fear. Instead, they belittle the victim's fears in an effort to squelch their own. It is common to hear visitors discouraging overt expressions of fear, saying things like "It's over. Stop worrying, for goodness' sake. Just forget it!" And why? Because *they* want to forget it; they are really talking to themselves.

This is an understandable phenomenon. When you are faced with someone who has been violently attacked (particularly if it was a random incident), you are also confronted with the possibility that the same thing could happen to you, or to someone you love.

Most of us, in rural and urban areas alike, go about our lives with a sense of invulnerability. This feeling of security allows us to ride subways, watch concerts in a crowd of thousands of strangers, and stroll with our children in public parks. It is basically a healthy and normal outlook, as it allows us to function in the society we live in.

But when we see someone who is hurt by violence, especially a friend or loved one, we are shaken. There before our eyes is shocking, terrifying *proof* that is impossible to ignore: Crime not only exists; it exists close to home.

Diane Craine, a fellow victim, told me that one of the most frustrating and upsetting aspects of her victimization was the total refusal of some of her friends to allow her to talk about her fear. Any mention of it, Diane found, made them uncomfortable, angry, and, she suspected, afraid for themselves.

Diane is a beautiful blond saleswoman in her twenties, living in the Midwest. She is highly successful, has a solid and happy relationship with the man she lives with, and is close to her family.

Two years ago she placed an ad in a local paper to sell her car. A woman named Amy telephoned and asked Diane to drive the car to Amy's home, claiming she was interested in buying the vehicle but had no transportation.

When Diane arrived at the address, a man answered the door. He asked her to come in and said that Amy was in the other room. Diane sat down in the living room and the man engaged her in small talk. But after fifteen minutes had passed, Diane grew tired of waiting for Amy to appear. She stood up to leave, but as she did, the man leaped behind her and put her in a headlock. He grabbed a rope, which he had hidden under the coffee table, and tied her hands behind her back. The man told Diane he was taking her car in order to get to

Kansas. She asked him please to remove a few of her belongings from the car before leaving. He then took a scarf and gagged her mouth.

When the man headed for the backyard, where the car was parked, Diane ran out the front of the house. But the assailant realized she had escaped and raced over to her, picked her up roughly, and carried her to the backyard. On the way, the gag fell from her mouth and Diane started to scream for help. She vividly remembers his words: "Shut up or I'll kill you."

Although Diane struggled and tried to fight him off, the man overpowered her, throwing her to the ground and putting a heavy iron gate over her body. When she moaned and whimpered in fear and discomfort, he gruffly warned her to shut up and stay absolutely still. Next, he bound her legs so tightly that her circulation was cut off.

Then, Diane describes her mind as "shutting off." She has no memory of any subsequent events until nearly two weeks later. The details of what happened to her were pieced together during the police investigation and told to her later.

The detective assigned to her case informed Diane that the assailant had beaten her severely with a large wooden board. Then, after throwing her bloodied, unconscious body into the trunk of her own car, he drove to a deserted area. There, he left Diane for dead in a ditch by a side road.

It is a miracle that two men came driving along the seldom-traveled route. They spotted Diane's body and called the paramedics. She was rushed unconscious to the nearest emergency room.

The attacker was later captured and incarcerated. The detective told Diane that the woman, "Amy," who'd responded to the newspaper ad had actually been the same man who captured and tried to murder her. Talking in a falsetto, he had disguised his voice on the phone.

Diane's physical injuries included a cracked skull, massive head injuries, and bruises and lacerations so severe that she could not walk, move, or feed herself. The assailant's brutal blows to her head resulted in irretrievable loss of Diane's sense of smell and much of her sense of taste.

Now, Diane is working again—and ranks first in sales for her company—but she is still living with fear.

Recently, Diane and I sat down over lunch and discussed our mutual post-attack terrors. Diane said that her fear compelled her to recount her nightmarish experience again and again. In fact, she was *driven* to talk, repeating her story in graphic detail to anyone who would listen. She even found herself telling it to strangers on buses or in other public places.

This kind of ventilation—the repeating of one's "story" over and over again—is common to many crime victims. Frequently it is short-lived. But for some, it remains a pressing need for weeks, months, even years. Ventilation can provide a comforting release of pent-up anxieties and terror. The sharing of fears with others can make victims feel less alone, less burdened, and—most of all—less afraid.

Diane found her friends resistant to listening to her saga again and again. Yes, they were willing to hear her out at first, particularly when she was bedridden. But as soon as she seemed on the road to recovery, most of her friends discouraged her from talking about it. Diane's feelings made them uncomfortable.

Just as my friends had done when I insisted that I not be left alone, Diane's friends told her she was "obsessed." They said, "It's over, Diane. Forget it." To them, her therapeutic need to repeat the details of the attack seemed useless and macabre—and, of course, it made them afraid.

One day, less than a month after the attack, Diane was out driving in the countryside with friends. Suddenly, panic gripped her. At first Diane wasn't sure exactly why she felt so afraid. But slowly she realized that they were only a few miles away from the site where she had been "ditched."

Diane launched into a recounting of the attack. She begged her friends to take her to the actual place where she'd been dumped. They became annoyed and told her she was being ridiculous.

Diane describes the terror she felt as a "fear of the unknown." It was so frightening to have been *told* the details of her attack and kidnapping, yet not to remember the events at all. She felt that seeing the site for herself would make it more of a reality than the nightmare it now was. Diane's imagination ran wild; her fantasies of the ditch and her abandonment were more terrifying than any reality could be.

Diane kept trying to explain her feelings to her friends, begging them to take her to the place where the attacker had left her, but the more she talked, the less her friends wanted to listen. They told her: "You're perfectly safe now. There's no reason to be afraid."

Diane's friends never took her to the site of her abandonment. And so she sat there in utter terror, alone and misunderstood.

Fortunately, Diane's parents and boyfriend *did* understand her, and they were patient enough to simply listen. So she was able to work out some of her fears through the process of ventilation.

After that incident in the car, Diane tried to stop talking about her attack. But when she kept her fears locked up inside her, tension and anxiety built up and made her feel as if she would explode.

So Diane talked, and talked, and talked, until gradually she started to feel "talked out." Eventually she was able to stem the flow of words that had sustained her for many months.

Even now, three and a half years later, Diane will occasionally feel the need to repeat the story of her attack, but she now *chooses* the people she confides in. Diane is healthy again, both physically and mentally. Fear is still a part of her life, but she has it under control enough to lead a happy, fulfilling life.

One of the most depressing things that can happen to a victim is to be abandoned by his friends. Unfortunately, the underlying reason for such desertion is usually *fear*—both the fear the victim feels (which is decidedly unpleasant to witness) and the fear it produces in those around him. A friend who abandons the victim no longer has to face either the victim's fear or his own.

Many people deserted me as soon as it was clear that while I was going to live, I was going to live in fear. They heard me talk about my fear of being killed. They saw me go through terrifying flashbacks. They saw the ugly wounds on my body—frightening evidence of my ordeal—and these people vanished. I think *I* was too scary for them! Both visually and emotionally, I was a frightening presence. And so they stopped visiting, went back to their own lives, and tried to put me and all that I represented out of their minds.

Once I returned to physical and emotional health, many of these people resurfaced. They'd seen me on a talk show or back at work, and they'd call and ask to get together. Sometimes they apologized and gave a wide variety of reasons why I hadn't heard from them in so many months. Sometimes they completely ignored the issue of their lengthy absence. And sometimes they told me that the whole incident had made them too frightened to cope. When they admitted their thoughts and were honest with me, I felt much better.

Ever since I was a child, I have been the "forgive and forget" kind of friend. It was never my way to hold a grudge. And so I said to myself now: *Look, who are you to judge, Theresa? They just didn't know how to react—it was all too weird for them. They're still your friends.* With these thoughts in mind, I decided to renew my relationships with the people I'd frequently thought of as "the deserters."

When I began to see them again, everything seemed fine, at least on the surface. We'd talk about family, music, auditions, theater, even my "remarkable recovery." But underneath our banter, something was wrong. I thought about these meetings often and discussed them with my psychiatrist, Dr. Weingold. Finally I asked myself if I *blamed* my friends.

My honest answer was no; although their desertions had hurt me, I couldn't bring myself to hate or blame them.

But I found that, much as I tried, I just didn't feel comfortable with my one-time friends anymore. How could I ever trust them to help me if another crisis occurred? When I had needed them most, they had allowed their own feelings of confusion, revulsion, fear, or—in some cases—sheer inconvenience to come between us. And so, not vindictively but sadly, I decided to stop seeing these people.

But throughout the post-attack period, my fear and pain were greatly eased by those friends who *did* stand by me, no matter how difficult it was for them.

In the very early days, there were times when friends would arrive to find me immersed in a terror so severe that it made me delusional. They would discover me staring at the wall repeating over and over the words *blood and knives, blood and knives.* Usually, when I sensed the arrival of visitors, I would be brought back to reality. But the friends who saw me in this condition, however briefly, were understandably traumatized.

Yet there was no limit to the love and compassion my truest friends showed me. They wept for me and with me, held my hand, consoled and watched over my family, and accepted me in spite of my physical and emotional scars. If I live to be one hundred, I will never forget them, and if they ever need *my* help I will be there for *them.*

In a sense, everyone in today's society is a victim of crime. The only real difference between the victim and the nonvictim is the violent act itself. But a basic, shared emotion is the *fear* of crime. An understanding of this common ground can effectively bridge the gap between victims and nonvictims and form a solid base of communication.

The first step toward overcoming fear is to recognize and accept its existence. But how do we do this?

Recognizing that you are afraid is usually not so difficult, since fear provokes tangible psychological and physical responses. You feel ill-at-ease, anxious, pensive, and "creepy." Your head may throb, your pulse race, your heart beat wildly, your skin become clammy, your eyes dart furtively. If we are attuned to them, our own symptoms can present us with a clear indication that we are frightened.

Accepting fear may not be quite so simple. Particularly in this era of self-reliance, we like to think of ourselves as very much in control. To acknowledge fear is to acknowledge a certain degree of helplessness. The realization that you are not 100 percent in charge of all that happens to you can produce a variety of responses: discomfort, distress, a sense of despair or loss, even a deep depression.

In learning to accept fear, it helps to realize that you are not alone, that you are not a weakling because you are afraid, and that many before you have conquered or learned to live with fear.

If you think of accepting your fear as a *constructive* act—a vital, necessary step toward health—it will be easier to achieve.

The first and most important person you must deal with—even if you are in a situation where no one else around will accept your fears—is yourself. And although you may feel incredibly weak, if you try to *be easy* on yourself (in other words, nonjudgmental), you'll feel a lot better.

Try writing—or saying aloud—the words: "I am afraid, and that is *normal,* under the circumstances." Simply expressing that unpleasant feeling lurking inside you is a form of release in itself. It is also a verbal statement of the *reality* of your feeling. Once you've been honest with yourself about your fear, you are armed with a strong weapon—acceptance of the truth—and you can get on with ways of coping with it.

THE COPING MECHANISMS

Once you've accepted the fact that you are afraid, the next step is to take action. Of course it's impossible simply to wake up one day and conquer all your fears in one fell swoop. But you can chip away at them, even when they seem overpowering. We have many tools at our disposal to help us dispel fear. Some of the most useful are: *Humor, Reaching Out to Others, Forward Thinking,* and *Therapy.*

We human beings are hardy creatures; getting through a violent crime *at all* is in itself proof of one's strength and endurance. These very qualities that enabled us to survive can also be at the core of our battle against fear.

Humor

Almost every crime victim I interviewed said something like "I couldn't have done it if I'd lost my sense of humor." I, too, can vouch for the amazing healing powers inherent in simple laughter. For what is the act of laughter if not an exquisite form of release?

It's true that in the aftermath of a crime, joking and having fun may be the furthest things from your mind. But over the past few years, I've come to see that even the direst circumstances have their bright side. The way we *perceive* what we are going through is really the key.

When I first discovered that I was hooked up to various life-support systems, my initial reactions were shock, discomfort, and a certain fascination.

But as the hours ticked by and these machines became an unpleasant, annoying part of my life, I started to resent them. When I sensed that my anger at being hooked up helplessly to these devices was building steadily, I realized that I had two choices: to glare at the machines daily, hating them, fearing them, and perceiving them as ugly and unnatural—*or* to see them as rather odd but *funny* pieces of equipment that were, for the time being, attached to me.

I looked at the tubes, the wires, the dials, the gauges, the monitors, and thought of them as sci-fi futuristic devices designed to ship me into outer space. When a nurse would come and push a button or peer into a monitor, I'd think, *Ready for blastoff!* and giggle to myself—while she looked at me as though I were loony.

Sometimes I'd lie there and make believe I was a robot—a special, life-size mechanical doll whose function was controlled by the various machines I was connected to. The "Theresa Robot" of my fantasy had been created by Dr. Stein, and unlike other mechanical creatures, she could also think and feel.

I'd make the nurses laugh by affecting a metallic, grating "robot voice" and saying, "I am Theresa the Robot. I am here to do your bidding. Would you feed me a nice pain pill now?"

Imagining what life would be like as a robot "living" in a world of humans amused me for hours. If the people who attended me were gruff or thoughtless, I'd think to myself: *Poor things, they're only human!* And it cheered me up.

These fantasies may sound silly—or simplistic—but they really worked, transporting me out of my miserable reality and into a brighter, though distinctly imaginary, world.

When faced with a seemingly untenable reality, the choice is ours: We can embrace the grim side or the bright side. I won't be like Rebecca of Sunnybrook Farm and say that you can *always* be cheery and funny in the midst of despair—*I* certainly wasn't—but I will say that *some* of the time we can get ourselves and those around us to laugh through our tears.

Shaina, who works for a bank in San Francisco, rides the bus to and from work every day. She is a feisty brunette in her mid-thirties. Slightly more than a year ago, she boarded the bus on her way home. Seeing that there was a strange-looking man in the back of the bus, she sat in the middle. The other passengers included six youngish men and a middle-aged woman. At her stop, Shaina got off the bus and immediately sensed that someone was uncomfortably close behind her.

As she tried to move away, Shaina felt a knife plunge into her back. Before she could draw another breath, the blade pierced her body again and again. As she fought with every ounce of her strength, Shaina glimpsed the face of her assailant and realized that the knife-wielding attacker was the "strange" man who'd been on the bus.

Luckily, the bus driver rushed to her aid and pulled the assailant away from Shaina, allowing her to stagger to safety. The paramedics arrived swiftly and Shaina was rushed to the hospital, where she was treated for four knife wounds in her back and one in her arm.

It took the emergency room doctors all night to finish stitching up her injuries. Shaina remembers lying there joking with them about what color thread they were using to sew her up.

When I asked her why she felt like cracking jokes after this brutal attack, Shaina said it had just seemed natural. "After all," she explained, "in a way, it was absurdly funny. *Life* is funny. I mean, there I was on my way home from my boring job, in a great neighborhood, when a complete *nut* goes crazy and stabs me for no reason at all. It was a totally depressing and terrible situation, but at the same time it was so bizarre that it made me laugh. Plus, I was *very* glad to be alive. When he stabbed me, I could easily have been killed. So I felt like I had *plenty* to be happy about."

Shaina spent five days in the hospital and underwent microsurgery to repair cut nerves and tendons in her arm. The hospital staff was amazed at how rapidly she recovered and how "up" her spirits were. Shaina kept joking, mainly saying things that were funny in a "weird" way. She referred to the attacker as "that creature" and to her arm sutures as "track marks." She called her cast "the club," and her pain medications "my fixes."

You might think this was a temporary, even an hysterical, reaction, which Shaina used to submerge her real feelings and that eventually she would break down and crumble. But the amazing thing about Shaina is that she still refers to the whole event with humor—and she has made a great recovery physically and emotionally.

Shaina regained full use of her hand (to the surprise of her doctors, who had predicted limited use at best), returned to work, and saw a psychiatrist only a few times before realizing that she really didn't need therapy.

Yes, Shaina is still angry, but she believes that looking at her situation from a humorous standpoint helped her then and continues to help her now.

If you are a victim and you don't consider yourself or your perspectives to be inherently funny, it is still possible to benefit from humor. You can make it a point to invite as your visitors the friends who know how to make you laugh, or your favorite aunt or uncle who can always tease you into a smile.

If you are not lucky enough to have amusing friends or relatives, you can turn to professional funny people by playing a tape or video of your favorite comedian. Then, too, there are plenty of books around that are both humorous and uplifting.

The trick is to find out what makes *you* laugh. Even if you are weepy or depressed most of the time, you can draw up a contract with yourself, agreeing to laugh or at least see the lighter side of things for one hour out of the day. You can include your family and friends and ask them to help you. Some of the things you might try are: renting a film of your favorite movie . . . buying comic books . . . playing a harmless prank on your favorite nurse (or the one you don't like *at all!*) . . . painting your face like a clown . . . buying a dirty joke book.

As you begin to feel better, you can change the contract with yourself so that you spend two hours, three hours, or even longer, actively taking part in pastimes that bring you joy. Hopefully, after a while you'll become so accustomed to adding laughter to your life that you will no longer need to have a contract at all.

My puppy, Totsie, was a never-ending source of laughter for me. Her antics cheered me even when I was in terrible physical pain. I hid her under my bedclothes and watched her play with my bandages, or with the equipment I was attached to. I dipped her paw in red ink and had her "sign" my cast. Watching her wobble about on her rubbery puppy's legs and flop down exhausted after a race around my IV pole was pure fun. It didn't erase my terror or pain, but it helped.

At Victims for Victims, I'm often with people who have been violently attacked in a variety of ways. It may seem odd to outsiders, but we sometimes sit around and crack jokes about our assailants, our injuries, the justice system, and so on. We can be very serious about it, too, but it'd be a pretty dreary group to belong to if all we did was cry.

Many of us have derogatory but comic names for the people who attacked us: "Mr. Mad," "Jerko," "The Weird Machine," "Ugly Face." We ask one another: "When is *your* weirdo getting released?" We call the prisons they're in "summer camps" or "country clubs," and we joke about the *true* lunacy of rewarding these vicious felons by giving them "time off for good behavior." We figure that if we didn't joke about it (in addition to working toward changes in the system), we'd go off our rockers.

Those of us who are public speakers refer to ourselves at times as "professional spokesvictims." We try to help others (nonvictims) to get past the taboos about crime victims, to make them realize that we can joke and laugh and be happy again, even if we have been stabbed, shot, raped, or beaten. One of our members, who is paralyzed because of a shooting attack, christened her motorized wheelchair "Speed Racer," and gives little children rides on it all the time. She has lost neither her love of laughter nor her zest for life. Staying in touch with humor helps us to confirm what's great about the present—the very fact that we're *alive.*

The atmosphere in the clubhouse where we meet ranges from the very somber to the positively silly. We try to balance our emotions, and to hear each other out when one or more of us is "down." But we still try to evoke every bit of shared joy available to us.

Reaching Out to Others

When people are afraid, they often turn to others for support. As we've discussed, this is a valid and healthy response. But in addition to receiving aid *from* those around us, there is another very effective way of coping with our fears: giving our help *to* others.

You may be thinking: *I'm terribly depressed. What on earth could I do for anyone else?* The answer is—plenty!

Almost any victim feels better when he realizes that he is not the only one who is afraid. A victim who decides to reach out to others often finds that the very act of helping someone else to cope with fear lessens his own feelings of anxiety, isolation, and terror. Fear is far less consuming when we channel some of our energy outward, rather than focusing it upon ourselves.

About three weeks after my attack, Dr. Stein told me that the fifty-five-year-old businessman in the room next door to mine, Mr. Bluestein, was to have heart surgery the next morning. The staff, as well as members of the Bluestein family, were very worried that he would not survive the operation. Their concern was not primarily based upon his physical condition, but upon his emotional state: Mr. Bluestein was terrified.

It's natural for anyone who faces major surgery to be frightened. But Mr. Bluestein's fear had escalated beyond what could be considered "normal," or healthy. His terror was so overwhelming that it completely prevented his adopting a positive outlook about his survival, and this actually weakened his overall physical and emotional condition. Mr. Bluestein was convinced he would die on the operating table—and everyone around him knew that his terror and negativity could lower his resistance and his will to live. In short, Mr. Bluestein was in danger of literally scaring himself to death.

When Dr. Stein asked if I would speak to Mr. Bluestein and try to help him, I was quick to agree. So many people had been helping me for weeks—now it was time for me to come out of my shell and do the same for someone else.

Looking around my flower-filled room, I chose a beautiful bouquet of roses and tucked them under my arm. I had no idea what I would say to the frightened stranger, but I was determined to help. Taking a deep breath, I headed out the door.

Mrs. Bluestein, a slender, gray-haired lady with an Eastern European accent, greeted me, ushered me into the room, and left. Huddled in the bed was Mr. Bluestein, his eyes wide, his face chalk-white, his covers drawn up to his chin. He stared out at me, panic-stricken, and tried to speak. "H-h-hello" was all he could manage.

When I started to put the roses into a vase on his night-stand, Mr. Bluestein shook his head, protesting the gift. But I launched into a description of my room as "the flower shop" and told him he *had* to accept the roses. I joked with him and said things like "I have about a *million* of them and I never liked flowers anyway. It takes me hours to water them. In fact, you'd be doing me a favor to take them off my hands."

He seemed to relax somewhat and looked at me quizzically. He was probably asking himself what on earth this chatty, pigtailed, pink-robed creature was doing in his room, waving her arm cast around and cracking jokes.

After a while I asked if I could call him Mr. B for short. He smiled ever so slightly and said the secretaries in his office had been calling him Mr. B for years.

Then I told him why I'd come and what exactly had happened to me. I described my own thoracic surgery and showed him my surgical scar (or "zipper," as many veterans of heart surgery refer to it). I admitted to him that in the emergency room I, too, had been afraid—and still was.

Mr. B was quiet for a moment, then said, "You've been through so much worse than I—I feel embarrassed."

I told him that *embarrassing* him out of his fear was the last thing I wanted to do and asked him to tell me how he felt. Slowly he began to confide in me, describing the visions of death that plagued him. I was amazed at how much his terrors were like my own and pointed out the similarities in the way fear had gripped and weakened us both.

As we talked, our camaraderie grew and I implored him to use me as an example. I told him I knew *he* could pull through just as I had—the proof was as tangible as the stitches in my chest.

Looking straight into his eyes, I said, "Listen, Mr. B, you can't *stop* being afraid any more than I can, but you can say to yourself the same things *I* say when I'm scared: 'Okay, I'm afraid. But I'm also alive, strong, loved by my family, and a basically healthy person. I refuse to let fear take me over and make me even sicker. I will accept it and deal with its side effects, but I am not going to let fear kill me.' "

I told Mr. B that once the operation was over, he'd hurt for a while and be afraid to do many of the things he'd done before surgery, but that in time his fears would diminish.

During our entire visit, I did my best to move about in order to look as physically recovered as possible. I wanted to show him the strength I'd regained in only three weeks.

I even turned his bedside radio on and danced to a pop song for a minute. (I ached all night because of these antics.)

Mr. B shook his head in amazement at my sprightliness. When I invited him and his wife to go out disco dancing after we were released, he seemed tickled at the mere thought.

Suddenly he murmured, "Maybe you're right, girlie." An idea struck me and I headed for the door, saying, "Mr. B, wait right there." This prompted a laugh and a big grin that seemed to say "Where else could I go?"

I went to my room, gathered up four more bunches of flowers, and brought them back to him. Then I said, "Now, Mr. B, you'll have to get out of ICU and come back to your room very fast, because you're going to have to water these flowers—I can't take them anymore!" With that, I winked at him and left. Mr. B was still huddled in his bed—but *laughing*.

The next morning at seven A.M. my family and I prayed for Mr. B. During the lengthy surgery I tried to send him good thoughts and courage. I watched TV but couldn't concentrate. The day crept by as we awaited word on his condition.

Finally Mrs. Bluestein burst into the room. Her eyes were wet, and for a moment I imagined the worst. Then she said, "He's awake. The surgery went great. The doctors say he's doing very well." I gave her a big kiss and then she said,

"His first words when he woke up were: 'Tell that girl thank you.'"

I still get teary-eyed just thinking about that moment. Helping Mr. B had a great effect on *me* too. Mr. B's survival gave me courage. It took away some of my feelings of uselessness and despondency.

I'd seen just how detrimental the effects of fear had been upon Mr. B, and the way his outlook improved when he decided not to let fear completely overtake him. And now, I needed to live up to my own words and apply them to my situation. I'd helped Mr. B a lot, but I'd helped myself even more.

The chance to aid another person may not present itself quite so soon after your own attack. But even the thought of eventually reaching out to others can give you a goal. Regardless of your predicament or your physical and emotional condition, there will inevitably be a time in the future when you can use your experience to advise and support someone else.

In Victims for Victims and other self-help groups, the basic concept is "people helping people." Time and time again I see peer counselors (those who help others who've been through a similar experience) benefit from their work with recently victimized clients. At first it can be scary to share your fears with someone who is even more afraid than you are. You may worry that hearing about his or her intense feelings of panic and anxiety will trigger your own fears and make them worse. Well, to be honest, this does happen sometimes. But far more frequently, when you reach out to someone whose fear is greater than your own, you see immediately how much progress *you* have made.

Of course, not everyone who is victimized will go into victim advocacy or peer counseling, but there are other ways of coping with fear by reaching out to others. Volunteer work with children, the elderly, or the handicapped can give you a firm grasp of your own strengths and capabilities. It's hard to feel consumed by terror when you use your energies to aid the truly helpless. And in the meanwhile, you have the gratification of knowing that you're performing a valuable service by caring for the needy.

Learning to overcome or live with fear is a lengthy process that causes us pain, but also deepens our understanding of human nature. If you use this newfound knowledge to reach out to others, you will receive a twofold reward: a lessening of your own fears, and the gratitude of those you've helped. And it makes you feel *wonderful!*

Forward Thinking

It would be impossible for me to guess how many times people have asked, "How did you *survive*? Not just the attack, but all those months after that?" In the earliest days following my release from the hospital, I developed a number of somewhat general replies: "Oh, you'd be surprised how tough human beings are!" Or, "Well, I really had no choice." Or, "I owe it to my family." Or, "I took it one day at a time."

Usually, after answering, I would quickly change the subject. But later on, when I was alone at home, I'd wonder what the real answer to this question was. Why *had* I lived through the deadly attack and the sheer, unabated agony of my recovery period?

As I thought about it, the one thing that had seemed to help me most of all throughout the experience was my steadfast belief that *This is not forever.* I thought and spoke this phrase whenever things were really rough. In times of fear, pain, and anger, I often kept from going mad by insisting to myself that the problems that plagued me then would be *over* or *lessened* in the future. If I firmly believed *This is not forever,* I could cope with almost anything.

In addition to my constant affirmation that my troubled state was transitory, I developed a "game," a technique that took me out of my misery. At a loss for what to call the process, I came up with the term *forward thinking.*

In looking back, I realize that I *instinctively* used forward thinking immediately after the attack, when I lay on the verge of death on the floor of my apartment. My physical and emotional agony was so severe that the only way I could bear it was to envision a time in the future when the pain would be over. Somehow I was able to hold on to the last shreds of life and hope by thinking even as I lay there in an ever-widening pool of my own blood: *This is not forever.*

During the recovery period, if I was frightened, enraged, in pain—or even just bored—I mentally transported myself out of the reality of my unbearable present and into an imagined lovely future. How? Actually, it was wonderfully easy. I'd think of a time in the future—perhaps a week or two away, or as far off as six months or even a year—and I'd envision myself whole, healthy, and free of whatever problem I now had.

This "game" was often helpful when I was afraid. Sometimes, when I had a terror-stricken reaction to a specific occurrence, I was able to calm myself by recognizing that the fear was *temporary*, and by gazing mentally into the fearless future of my imagination.

One day, while on a pass from Motion Picture Hospital, I went with my mother to a nearby store, hoping to buy gifts for a few of the nurses. It was not my first time out, and although strangers were about, I scanned the aisles for a few minutes with relative peace of mind, placing a few interesting items into a shopping cart. Suddenly I sensed that I was being watched. Glancing warily to my right, I spotted a boy in his mid-teens, dressed in a black leather jacket and torn jeans. He stared at me unabashedly. My brow beaded with perspiration. What did he want? Where was my mother? What could I do? I felt frozen to the spot and unable to catch my breath. I believed the boy would lunge at me any moment. I *ran* out of the store as though pursued by a maniac. I'm sure anyone who saw me believed I'd lost my mind completely, and with my big metal brace on, I must have looked ridiculous racing down the aisles and out the door. Panting, I arrived at the hospital van, where an attendant awaited me. He gently helped me into the vehicle and asked what had happened. I just stared ahead.

Seconds later, my mother, puzzled and concerned, joined me. She, too, wanted to know what had happened. I shook my head silently, but by now my mother had come to recognize the distinctive look of fear that clouded my eyes after a frightening incident.

For thirty minutes I sat in the van. I was shaky, unsettled, and still afraid. Rationally, I knew that the boy had either seen me in an acting role, or was just a brazen, rude brat. But I was still unable to shake the fear.

I said to myself: *Theresa, it's been only three months since you were hurt. You have a right to be scared. This is not forever.* And I speculated about what a similar shopping trip might be like a year from that day.

I imagined the following scenario: I enter Bullock's, a department store, with my sister. Maria wanders over to the cosmetics department while I linger at the jewelry counter and look at some delicate pearl earrings. Feeling that I am being watched, I look up and see the very same youngster. For a moment my heart pounds wildly and I start to quiver. Then, I think to myself: *Wait a minute. This kid is fifteen years old. His mother is probably buying him some school clothes. Maybe he's just a fan.*

I swallow hard and give the boy a little smile and a look that says "You don't intimidate me." Suddenly the boy stares down at his sneakers, shifts uncomfortably, glances back at me, and blurts, "Hey, are you in the movies or something?" I give him a big smile and say, "Yes."

Instantly he seems to turn into a little boy. He gushes, "Wow, I knew it!" and races off to tell his mother. I breathe a sigh of relief and ask a salesgirl to show me the earrings.

My projection of a future shopping trip was not *unrealistic*— not a fairy-tale dream about a blissful, rosy future that might never come true. It's important to envision a future you realistically believe is possible. That's the key to successful forward thinking.

Back in the van, I felt much better after my little mind-trip into the future. It eased my anxiety to picture the teenager as a harmless kid. I believed that in time I would learn to handle this kind of situation in the way I'd *imagined*, rather than the way I'd actually dealt with it.

One of the nice aspects of forward thinking is that it allows you to perceive time as your friend. During tedious hospital stays or periods of deep depression, it is comforting to know that time *does* march on. And with each day that passes, it's possible to make strides in our physical and emotional healing.

Envisioning a positive, brighter future is a way of setting

goals. If we want these "visions" to become real, we have no choice but to *work* toward them. The majority of the victims I interviewed who are now functional, happy, and mentally sound practiced some form of this forward thinking.

Shaina (the lady who was stabbed five times when stepping off a public bus) had won two tickets to Hawaii just a few weeks before her attack. While she was in the hospital recuperating from surgery she kept picturing herself relaxing on Maui, basking in the sun, sipping piña coladas. Shaina knew she'd have to recuperate for weeks before returning to her job at the bank. What better place could there be to rest and regain her health than an exotic tropical isle? So Shaina not only *envisioned* the future but asked a girlfriend who was going to Hawaii with her to confirm their reservations.

Today, Shaina remembers how much easier it was to deal with the discomforts of medical procedures, stitches, physical therapy, and the like when she could think to herself: *Three weeks from now, girl, you'll be dancing the hula!*

In the meantime, the technique helped Shaina deal with her assailant's pretrial hearing. While sitting in the courtroom, Shaina used forward thinking to calm her nerves. When her attacker's appearance made her feel faint with fear, Shaina calmed herself by thinking: *This will be over within one hour. Then I will meet my boyfriend and we'll have lunch at my favorite restaurant.* That is exactly what she did. And a few weeks later, she *was* on that beautiful Hawaiian beach she'd envisioned during those dreary hospital-bound days.

Of course, not every victim has two free tickets to the tropics tucked in her purse. But Shaina, in those frightening and chaos-ridden days after her attack, might easily have made the decision to forget the trip to Hawaii or postpone it until a much later date. She could have allowed post-attack depression to engulf her so that a vacation would have been a physical or emotional impossibility. She could have given the tickets away or sold them to help defray her medical bills. But instead, she used her imagination and forward thinking to help her get through the roughest period.

Shaina left for Hawaii with a *huge* cast on her arm. (I saw it and I can say it was bigger and more cumbersome than most.) The cast encased her left arm from just below shoulder level, bent at the elbow, and covered all her fingers. There, on that breathtakingly beautiful beach, the cast itched intolerably and it was unbearably hot. Shaina had to be careful to prop her injured limb up in a certain way, and her throbbing, sweating arm detracted from her overall enjoyment of the pleasures of Hawaii. But Shaina refused to let her discomfort ruin her vacation. She allowed her thoughts to drift toward the future, imagining how lovely it would be when she could rub soothing oil over the itchy, swollen arm. And she told herself again and again how lucky she was that her cast would be off in only a month.

One of the best ways of checking on your progress in forward thinking is to use a tape recorder. For instance, if you were robbed and assaulted in your car and feel that there is no way you will ever drive again, simply set your machine on Record, state the date, and talk out your feelings. For example: "I am terrified. I don't think I'll ever drive my Camaro again. I'm scared to get into a car." Then envision yourself in the future, come up with a reality you think might be possible, and speak it into the tape recorder: "Six months from now I would like to be alone behind the wheel of a car. I see myself driving to my favorite restaurant to meet my husband, and celebrating my brave 'solo ride' with a bottle of fine champagne."

Six months later, you may play back that tape and find that you've made your forward thinking a reality even sooner than you'd imagined possible. Or maybe along the way, you will have made the decision to sell your beloved Camaro because it brought back scary memories. You may be driving your teenage daughter's beat-up Volkswagen instead. Your hands might get clammy and your pulse might race during the first few trips alone. But it is quite likely that if you work hard at it, you'll be able to conquer your fears and actually *live* those forward thoughts.

There are many whose serious injuries and disabilities are, at least within the limitations of today's medical knowledge, permanent. Even for them, forward thinking can be a helpful tool. It may mean envisioning a time in the future when they will *cope* with their disability better, accept it more, and learn to perform great feats anyway. There are quadriplegics who paint and write with a pen in their teeth, paraplegics who are great wheelchair athletes, cancer-ridden individuals who help others and live out their lives productively. Human beings are so adaptable that virtually all of us can learn to take a horrible present reality and turn it into a productive and fulfilling future.

In addition to projecting your thoughts forward to a time when you will cope with your disabilities better, you can also envision the possibility of major advances and discoveries that medical science may make in your lifetime. It's entirely possible that, sometime in the near future, researchers will perfect techniques for repairing severe spinal injuries, curing diseases we now consider terminal, and correcting even the most extensive scarring.

It may seem terribly difficult to forget your disastrous present circumstances, to tell yourself *It's not forever* when everything seems bleak and horror-filled. But if you keep in mind that others have faced and conquered dire conditions, you'll realize that you can escape the present by mentally creating an image of a better tomorrow and working toward it.

Therapy

I would be lying if I said that today my life is completely free of fear. But I have learned to face my terrors, analyze them, and cope with them. While fear remains a part of my life, it does not control me as it once did. For me, therapy was the tool I needed in order to come to grips with an existence radically altered by violent crime.

I discovered the value of therapy firsthand after my attack, and in my work over the past number of years, I've seen its effectiveness for other crime victims. If patients and their counselors (or psychiatrists, social workers, etc.) are paired well, therapy can be healing and beneficial for the victim, his family, and important others as well. It is especially effective during the post-attack period when emotions are in conflict and everyone involved is frightened and confused.

I do not mean to imply that *all* therapists are good for *all* victims, or that therapy is some magical cure-all that can wipe away fear and place the victim back on his feet in a matter of days. On the contrary, for many victims a successful recovery from the effects of terror is an arduous, grueling battle filled with many tiny steps forward and an almost equal number of retreats and regressions.

No mental health professional can be expected to do all the work for you. He is there to guide you and to be leaned upon during the rough times, but the victim himself must play the most active role in his own emotional recovery. Hard work and personal effort can do a remarkable job of speeding one's release from post-attack terror.

As a result of post-traumatic stress, the syndrome that plagues many crime victims, I was hypervigilant for many months. Even strolling down the street in a fine neighborhood was as frightening to me as a walk through a mine-filled war zone.

When I discussed my fears with Dr. Weingold, he always understood—on both a human and a clinical level—what I was going through. He explained *why* my anxiety level was so high, and made me realize that my reactions were normal, in light of the circumstances. This support and encouragement from a professional lessened my fear that I was "going crazy." Being given an actual diagnosis—post-traumatic stress—was a great relief.

Dr. Weingold played an active role in my journey back to mental health. We discussed various methods of dealing with terror. He never looked down upon my needs, but instead encouraged me to feel that I had the right to be frightened. At the same time, he managed to make me see that there was hope at the end of the tunnel. Again and again he explained that the terror I felt was very real but also—at least in part—temporary. I often asked him: "But *when* will I be able to do something alone? When will I feel less afraid?"

And he'd say, "When you feel at ease enough to let go of some of your fear, you'll just *know* it."

Whenever I made some progress on my own, I looked forward to reporting it to my psychiatrist. During the Christmas holidays, I visited my family in New York. The streets of Manhattan can seem frightening even to someone who has never been a victim. To me, of course, they were terrifying.

But it had been nine months since the attack on my life, and I was *tired* of being afraid. I was determined to make progress during my holiday visit home.

One clear, cold afternoon, I was walking in a residential East Side area with an old friend, Bob Arcaro. By now, everyone I was close to knew that I needed to be accompanied from one destination to the next. They had not only heard me talk about my fear, but many of them had experienced it firsthand, especially when they were out with me in public.

I looked ahead at the quiet tree-lined street and felt an uncontrollable desire to walk it—alone. I said, "Bob, meet me at the corner."

My friend looked at me with concern and said, "Are you sure?" At my insistence he headed for the corner, casting looks back at me over his shoulder. As he got farther and farther away, goose bumps appeared on my flesh. I kept glancing furtively around, shaking whenever anyone walked past. But I knew I wanted to conquer that street and overcome a part of my fear.

I stared ahead and saw Bob at the end of the block, waiting for me. And for the first time in nine months, I walked in public alone.

At first I could hardly put one foot in front of the other, and moved forward as though in slow motion. My fists were clenched so tightly that my nails dug into the palms of my hands. My breaths came so quickly that I almost hyperventilated. I tried to convince myself: *You can do it. You can do it—go! Go! Go!* I forced my leaden feet to quicken their pace. The cool air made my hair fly back over my shoulders. My face felt tingly and ruddy. The space around me and the absence of a person at my side made me feel lightheaded. I thought to myself: *You are free!* And then I broke into a run.

Seconds later I was in Bob's arms. We hugged each other quietly and together shared the importance of that moment. The triumph I felt after walking that street alone elevated my mood for days. The following week, when I told Dr. Weingold, he was excited for me but not surprised. After that, I began to tackle my fears with renewed enthusiasm.

It is possible that I would have conquered my fears on my own, or with only the support of friends and relatives. But I honestly don't feel that I could have done it without professional guidance. It helped me so much to have a person outside my inner circle of family and friends who could—without bias—assess my feelings and actions.

Because Dr. Weingold was being paid for his services, I was never afraid of burdening him or hurting his feelings. I felt he genuinely cared about me as a person but that his concern was tempered by his professionalism. Our sessions were also a frame of reference that documented and pointed up my progress. I knew that from one week to the next I was going through changes—usually positive ones.

When I was terrified, hysterical, or out of control, I or my family could call upon Dr. Weingold for help. We came to trust his judgment and usually acted upon it. I was in therapy with Dr. Weingold for only about a year, but by the end of it he'd helped me to become functional and self-confident. I feel that I was lucky to have found such an excellent psychiatrist, but I've seen that there are *many* professionals who have both the expertise and the compassion necessary to treat and help a victim of crime.

There are many kinds of therapists, and it's vitally important for the victim to find the proper person as well as the best *mode* of therapy for him and/or his family. But how does one go about doing this?

Recommendations of friends or trusted medical doctors will often be of value, but your own instincts are usually your best guide when finding a therapist who is right for you. If a victim is too physically or emotionally incapacitated to seek therapy on his own, then it is up to those around him to see to it that he receives help.

At the initial counseling session, it should be made clear that *this* counselor (or psychiatrist or social worker) is not the only possible choice. If, for any reason, the victim feels uncomfortable with or disquieted by a particular therapist, then it is best to interview others before deciding which person to work with. Frequently, victims are so grateful for help that they are able to relate to and work with almost any good, accredited mental health professional.

A victim's personal preferences, financial situation, and

geographic location all contribute to the selection of the kind of therapist he will work with: psychiatrist, psychologist, social worker, counselor, peer counselor, crisis worker, volunteer, and so on. The most important factor is that the therapist be a positive, action-oriented, and caring individual. Rarely does a college degree *alone* determine the overall worth and helpfulness of a mental health professional. What is most important is good chemistry between therapist and patient.

The attitude of those around a victim toward his therapy can play a part in how well he responds. Encouragement is so important. A frightened victim needs to know that his loved ones consider therapy an acceptable way to regain his emotional equilibrium and free himself from fear.

I personally find it amazing that in many hospitals and police stations across the country, psychological help is neither suggested nor provided to crime victims as a matter of course. While it is true that, on an individual basis, victims are frequently given recommendations to seek therapy, these suggestions are piecemeal and sporadic. Some victims hear nothing at all about psychological help from the law-enforcement officers or hospital personnel they come into contact with. And so, many victims continue to live in fear.

Because of the turmoil surrounding victims and their families following an attack, the idea of seeking psychological help may simply not enter their minds. Most people involved are too busy dealing with the physical and financial repercussions to worry about professional counseling for the emotional ones. The advice of an outside party is often necessary. If the suggestion comes from an authority figure, such as a hospital worker or law-enforcement officer, it will usually be looked upon with respect and consideration.

We can only hope that, as the value of therapy for victims and their families becomes more widely recognized, the *suggestion* that victims seek professional psychological care will—without exception—be made by hospital and police personnel. Ideally, I believe that the assistance of mental health professionals should be routinely made available to victims in need.

Good, early psychological help can mean the difference between a victim who lives in fear for the rest of his life and one who goes on to recognize this feeling, analyze it, work through it, and eventually conquer or cope with it.

CHAPTER 4

ANGER

When people came to visit me shortly after the attack, I think they expected me to be swathed in spotless white bandages, lying pale and lovely on my bed of pain, and somehow managing a beatific smile of gratitude—the gratitude of a "lucky girl" whose life was spared despite the incredible odds. In short, they expected to see "Saint Theresa." Now it's true that my survival was described by doctors and laymen alike as near-miraculous, but nevertheless, my experience did not turn me into a paragon of otherworldly virtue. My visitors, to their dismay, found themselves confronted by a seething, snarling, wailing, yelling, vehemently angry victim.

Whenever that fact embarrasses me, I remind myself that it would be difficult to conceive of a human being who did *not* experience anger after being attacked. Let's face it, being stabbed-shot-raped-beaten-threatened-kidnapped *should* make you mad.

When another human being forces himself upon you and hurts you physically and/or emotionally, you would have to be *numb* not to react with either open or internalized rage. Being interfered with, harmed, abused—*altered*, against our will—puts us in a position of helplessness. It makes us angry at the world, the attacker, life, God, the system.

Because I was an invalid after my attack, it was especially hard for me to find an outlet for my rage. I couldn't:

kick—my legs were bandaged;

cry—the sobbing hurt my injured lung;

throw things—my arms were splinted;

scream—my chest would rip apart.

My boiling anger was bottled up inside, and my only possible release was verbal. I am thankful that no one tape-recorded the horrible things I uttered over and over again during that time. Although I am far from proud of what I said—much of it not unlike the ravings of a lunatic—my endless stream of profanities, suicide threats, and other ugly utterances helped me to unleash my terrible rage.

Some of the nurses chastised me for my outbursts, told me I should count my blessings, and "tsk-tsked" to each other about my bitter diatribes. Their disapproval made me feel guilty and embarrassed. But, in looking back, I must forgive myself for those loud, lengthy, and offensive tirades. For when I ask myself now if I had a choice, the answer is no.

ANGRY . . . BUT ALIVE!

The *good* thing about anger is that it is an emotion infused with life. The experience of anger can be *comforting* to a victim. It lets him know that he is still alive—kicking, yelling, snarling, fuming, sulking, but *surviving* too. Feeling angry is a million times better than being dead and feeling nothing.

I remember worrying most about myself on days when I felt apathetic—emotionless, adrift. I was so disconnected that I was unable to click into feelings of any sort. On those days I was grateful if someone or something provoked me—positively or negatively.

*   *   *

Anger comes in many shapes and sizes. It can lie dormant within you, so quiet you hardly know it is there. It can be like a tiny itch that grows a bit more bothersome each day, making you tense, edgy, and churlish. It can be maddeningly, embarrassingly apparent to all, exploding in a seemingly endless stream of outbursts. Or it can be a deep, unchanging, brooding sensation—an unpleasant feeling that doesn't grow but doesn't go away either.

Many victims act out or deal with their anger soon after their attacks. Others have a temporary sensation of peacefulness and/or a feeling of gratitude at being alive. But often this is the proverbial calm before the storm. Although the timing and scope of the anger varies from one victim to the next, it will surface eventually. And when it does it should not be ignored—for left unattended, it can eat away at you until you become an embittered, negative human being.

The victims who seem to make the speediest and most thorough recoveries are those who recognize their own anger and *deal* with it. I'll go a step further: It is perfectly fine to embrace your initial anger and think of it as one of your "vital signs"—tangible proof that you are alive and responsive to your situation.

CLEAR AND PRESENT ANGER

Am I angry today? My answer is an emphatic yes. But it is a different anger from my intense, often out-of-control feelings of two years, or even one year ago.

Nowadays I usually feel quite *level*. I stay extremely active and involved and try not to dwell upon painful thoughts and memories. But sometimes physical reminders of my attack rear up and provoke me unexpectedly.

When the weather changes and my permanently damaged fingers become cramped and painful, drawing themselves into an ugly, clawlike position, I get angry. I remember how gracefully elegant and pain-free my fingers used to be, and the familiar bubbles of rage begin to percolate.

When I try on clothing in a department-store fitting room and am confronted by the scars on my body, harshly illuminated by the fluorescent lighting, I get angry. And the rage I feel is sometimes compounded by the shocked, pitying stares of the salespeople.

Yes, shopping for clothes—much as I love it—is still an activity that pushes my "anger buttons." I have, of course, been forced to adapt my style of dress to cover my scars (which, after plastic surgery, are much less noticeable than before but are still visible unless covered by pancake makeup).

As I go through the racks of clothing, it has by now become second nature for me to seach for fashions that will cover the scars but will still look stylish and attractive.

When I try on a great-looking, trendy outfit and realize that, although it looks fabulous in every other way, the neckline is too low-cut for me, I get angry. When I see row after row of pretty little bikinis which I can never wear again, I get angry. And, when I see the strapless evening gowns I used to adore, I do get *angry*.

At times like these I console myself by trying on the many fashions that I *can* wear. And then I remind myself often that I very nearly went—to coin a term—to that "great big shopping plaza in the sky."

For the most part, I am still able to have fun at my favorite boutiques. And on days when I find myself feeling more anger than pleasure during a shopping expedition, I drag myself away from those sales racks and do something else instead.

The shopping malls of New York City and Los Angeles are not the only "anger triggers" for me. Almost every day, I include a dance class as part of my routine. Sometimes I take ballet; sometimes it's jazz, tap, or aerobics. I love both the artistic satisfaction and the physical release of the rigorous dance workout. But often I am faced with a painful dilemma when I take these classes.

Most dancers wear low-cut V-neck or scoop-neck leotards, which are less restricting and give a lovely visual line to the upper torso. Since the attack, I've managed to find pretty modern dance wear with high-cut necklines which are not overly confining.

Although I'm comfortable in my brightly colored leotards, there are times when I look around at the other women lined up at the barre and cannot stop my eyes from being drawn to their necklines. I become riveted by the smooth, unmarred line between each dancer's exposed collarbone and upper torso—such a beautiful part of a woman's anatomy. And I start to *reel*. It is not envy of the other girls' lovely bodies that boils inside me, but sheer rage at what the attacker has done to my own.

During these moments, I find myself gripping the practice barre and clenching my teeth. More than once, the sight of all those smoothly delicate necklines and cleavages has left me on the verge of fainting. I then try to summon all my inner strength, concentrate on the exercise we are doing, immerse myself in the music, and allow the action of dancing to transport me into a better frame of mind. Sometimes it even works.

WHEN NOTHING ELSE WORKS

Although I try my best to put my anger to constructive use whenever possible, there are days when I look into the mirror and see in my own eyes the suffering that I can never put completely behind me; when I realize that my body will never be as it was before; that my naïve, guileless trust in people has been taken away forever by a madman; and that this was neither nightmare nor fantasy, but hard, cold, and—worst of all—*irrevocable* reality.

At times like these, pure, unadorned rage sweeps over me. If I'm unable to circumvent it or redirect it by throwing myself into an activity to refocus my energy, I end up succumbing to it. I find myself a private, secure place and I act out my anger, giving in to it and letting it—*temporarily*—flood my senses.

What I do in those moments varies. Usually I have an old fashioned blowup, throwing pillows, kicking couches, screaming and yelling, weeping with frustration, and crying out against the fate that's befallen me. I let myself go on and on until I'm thoroughly exhausted. As soon as I've done that, I feel much better and it's usually *months* before I feel such a strong need again.

But what can you do if an overwhelming need for an angry outburst comes over you when you are *not* in a proper place to do anything about it? Well, after embarrassing myself on many occasions by launching into screaming tirades in such inappropriate places as restaurants, airports, and business offices, I came up with something I call my "angry book." In my purse I carry a little memo pad. If I'm *bursting* with rage—and I want to spare those around me from my wrath—I practice writing out my anger. I just whip out that notebook and scribble furiously every mean, black, awful, nasty, terrible thought in my head. By the time I've finished writing down what's going on inside me, I am usually calm enough to comport myself until I get home. Then, if I'm *still* itching with anger, I let it out with a roar!

Recently I had an emotional outburst which was prompted by another woman's pain. Through my work in Victims for Victims, on any given day I learn of many new cases of victimization. Over the phone, or in person, I hear tale after tale of rape, robbery, mayhem, and murder. I feel empathy for each person involved, but I have had to develop a certain method of distancing myself from their pain so that I can be strong and clear-thinking enough to help *them* while still maintaining my own equilibrium. But there are times when hearing the story of just one more victim makes me see red.

Just a few weeks ago I spoke to Bernice, a woman in the Southwest whose former boyfriend had attempted to murder her by attacking her savagely with a crowbar. Through her own heroic efforts and will to live, Bernice managed to escape with her life. But her physical injuries and disfigurement are extensive. A large portion of her face is permanently paralyzed, and the blows to her head were so severe that she was literally scalped.

Bernice has had major plastic surgery, but her hair, which she told me had been her "most beautiful pride and joy"—a thick, lustrous black mane—may never grow back on a large part of her head, and since the attack she has been forced to wear a hairpiece.

Bernice is extremely depressed, finds it hard to motivate herself, and has deep suicidal feelings. Her ex-boyfriend is now in jail but will be up for parole in a few years. She told me she is so certain that her ex-boyfriend will stalk and murder her when he gets out—he has sent messages through his relatives to this effect—that she is tempted to kill herself "painlessly." At times Bernice feels that she would rather put herself to sleep quietly and peacefully than die the bloody, violent death she feels this deranged man has in store for her.

After my conversation with Bernice I was so overcome with anger that I could barely put my phone on the hook. I pounded on the walls again and again, venting my fury against their cold, unyielding surface. Questions flooded my mind: Why does this poor woman have to live in such abject fear and misery? Why is her vicious assailant being released so soon? Why do people maim and kill each other so senselessly, so violently? There were no answers immediately forthcoming, so I just kept punching away at the walls until I fell into my bed in an exhausted heap.

Although this kind of behavior may seem immature, most mental health professionals feel that acting out anger is, at times, an effective and healthy way to rid oneself of angry demons. If you hurt no one, and simply provide yourself with this occasional release, it can help you to clear yourself of "angry energy," so that you can get on with everything else in your life.

POSITIVE OUTLETS

Of course you have to seek *positive* outlets for rage. You can't hurl verbal abuse, kick and break objects, or generally behave like an ogre forever. No matter how awful a situation is or how bitter you feel, there will come a time when that constant acting-out of rage begins to seem—even to the angriest victim—repetitive and fruitless. Eventually we tire of living with and listening to our own rampant rage. If you cannot seem to break a long, continuous cycle of uncontrolled bursts of anger, it would be wise to seek professional help.

Once you have decided that simply *venting* rage is no longer therapeutic, you will deal with the question "Now what do I do with all this anger?"

I've often wished I could put my anger in a box and lock it up someplace deep inside me. Perhaps once a year I'd go off to a mountaintop and release it, letting it rip out and howl itself into infinity.

You might wonder why I don't wish to have all my anger disappear forever, rather than keeping it locked up inside me. Well, I feel that one of the reasons I'm here today *is* my anger. I believe that my rage gave me the drive to keep fighting death, pain, and the sick wishes of the person who harmed me. And if I hadn't been so angry about the way victims are treated in society, I wouldn't have formed Victims for Victims or become so involved in victim advocacy. Without question, my anger has had some positive results.

Leadership and Rage

There are many outstanding examples of people who have channeled their rage constructively:

• Martin Luther King and other civil rights leaders were angry over the injustices suffered by blacks.
• The forerunners of the women's liberation movement were angry because of society's treatment of women.
• Members of the organization Mothers Against Drunk Driving (MADD) were angry at the intoxicated drivers who killed their children.

The leaders of these movements didn't merely scream about injustice. Rather, they took their intense, burning anger and focused it, using it to work toward a better society.

You might say, "Well, that's just fine for Dr. King or Gloria Steinem. They are extraordinary people. But I'm not into social activism—and I certainly don't want to be a political leader. So what can *I* do with all my rage?"

The answer can be put into one word: DISTR/ACTION.

Distr/action

What is DISTR/ACTION? It is simply doing *something*—anything—that serves to direct your energies *away* from your anger. Since letting blowups be the only way of dealing with anger would be unhealthy and unfeasible, the key is to balance these occasional emotional explosions with alternative ways of handling your rage.

When I feel a storm of anger brewing inside me, I ask myself: *Theresa, are you in the mood for another blowup?* More often than not, the answer is *No*. At this point my general rule is: Get out of the house! Why? Because being cooped up or walled in can compound feelings of rage and frustration. Your environment often presents you with reminder after reminder of the very reason you're angry in the first place.

Sometimes a simple change of scenery will help to redirect your energy and emotions.

As a teenager, when the pressures of math exams, dates for the prom, and finding a summer job came down upon me, I took myself to a local theater and sat through a double feature. Now I find I can dissipate my anger in the very same way. So when I start to feel irritable and furious, and I want to avoid a blowup—or a costly shopping spree at a mall—I take myself to the movies.

Whether I watch comedy or heavy drama, I find that seeing a film is one of the quickest and least expensive ways to help me forget my problems. I just sit there and immerse myself in the lives of the characters who flicker before me. Munching on a big bucket of buttered popcorn is also comforting, reminding me of all those Saturday afternoons at Loew's Alpine Theater in Brooklyn.

Another way in which I practice DISTR/ACTION is by taking myself to a museum. One of my favorite haunts is the Metropolitan Museum of Art in New York City. I find it incredibly soothing to drift from one exhibit to the next, gazing upon magnificent paintings or sculptures and immersing myself in their beauty. The highly visual—and emotional—experience of viewing fine art can almost always transport me out of even the darkest state of mind.

I sometimes comfort myself with the knowledge that many of the great masters, as well as some of our contemporary artists, used the expression of their artistry as a way of releasing their pain, their rage, even their madness. It makes me feel as though the artist and I are, somehow, kindred spirits.

A visit to the Met provides me with a *physical* release as well as a psychological one: The place is so enormous that simply walking through its many grand hallways or climbing its ornate marble stairways is in itself a mildly stimulating physical activity which, by the end of the day, leaves me feeling pleasantly tired and relaxed.

Of course your own tastes and preferences will dictate what little tricks you find to soothe your angry feelings: physical activities like sports and dancing, visiting galleries or museums, reading racy novels or great works of literature, building a table in the garage, talking things out with a friend, or treating your favorite niece to lunch at a grown-up restaurant. What you *do* isn't as important as how it makes you *feel*.

The method of dealing with rage that has worked for me and lots of other victims is: *Use it!* Take the power and adrenaline it gives you and channel your rage into ACTION.

The very same coping mechanisms we used in dealing with fear—namely humor, reaching out to others, forward thinking, and therapy—can also be applied here. With anger, however, you're already one step ahead: Rage is an intense, power-charged emotion and possesses a much less "mysterious" inward nature than does fear. Therefore it is easier to identify anger, to come to grips with it, and to learn how to redirect the energy we put into anger toward positive, creative action.

What's So Funny About Being Mad?

Did you ever watch the behavior of people who are really *angry*? Even when the *cause* of their rage is quite serious, there are times when their antics can be pretty funny.

Think about it for a moment. What do you do when you are hopping mad?

Pace like a caged animal?

Pull your hair?

Pout like a baby?

Jump up and down?

Stuff vast quantities of chocolate chip cookies into your mouth?

Scream?

Rock back and forth?

Keep everything inside?

Sometimes when you are in the midst of demonstrating your absolute fury, you can turn your own emotional tables around in a split-second. How? Well, take a look at yourself— just for one tiny moment—and see if you can find the humor in your own behavior.

Are you ripping a box of Kleenex to shreds?

Is your face an unbecoming shade of purple?

Are you baring your teeth like an angry little ferret?

Have you wept yourself into raccoonlike rings of mascara?

Or are you sitting on the floor kicking and fussing like a two-year-old?

Even if the laughter your own behavior provokes is bitter, dark, or begrudging, at least it will give you a momentary respite from the rage. You might even—at least temporarily— laugh yourself out of your foul mood.

Have you ever had an argument with a friend or lover in which you allowed your disagreement to escalate to the point of yelling and running around the room? Then, suddenly, one of you looks at the other and at the silliness of your mutual behavior and, even if the argument is over a serious issue, has a case of the giggles? Soon the other person, more than likely, chimes in and the fight dissolves.

Sure, both of you still feel strongly about whatever the subject of the dispute was, and it will need to be resolved somehow. But at least you've seen the funny, human side of your behavior.

Well, it may take two to tango, but it doesn't always take two to laugh. A solitary case of the "screaming meanies" can often be cured with the remarkable tool of humor. It's quite simple: All you have to do is picture your angry antics in your own mind's eye.

I remember an incident at Motion Picture Hospital when I was still wheelchair-bound. My left arm was encased in plaster and I was unable to roll myself around the hospital without help. Because I could push only the right wheel with my free hand, the chair would spin in circles rather than moving forward.

I'd been up since six A.M. and was depressed, crotchety, and bored to distraction. Finally eight o'clock rolled around, and it was time for me to be taken down to physical therapy. Although the exercises were painful, I looked forward to breaking the monotony of sitting in my dreary little room.

By eight-fifteen the orderly hadn't arrived to bring me to P.T., so I rang for the nurse. She came by for a moment and told me they were short-staffed and I'd have to wait.

My mother was in the cafeteria eating breakfast, and I was trapped. I sat there helplessly as the minutes crawled by. Eight-thirty came, then eight-forty-five—and still no orderly arrived. Again I pushed the call button. A terse voice snapped over the intercom: "Theresa, you will just have to wait!"

I felt like a caged animal. Anger churned inside me, and I told myself I would not sit there like a vegetable—I'd get to therapy myself.

And so I started to push my wheelchair with my right hand. The chair lurched to the left. Then I reached across my body with my right arm—which caused me considerable pain—and gave the left wheel a push. Now the chair lurched to the right.

I pushed right, then left, right, then left, again and again. With each push my chair moved forward a few tiny inches. After thirty minutes, I'd managed—with much huffing and puffing—to roll myself out of the room and a few yards down the deserted hallway. The P.T. room was still three corridors away, an elevator ride downstairs, and then two more long, winding stretches from that point. Sweating from the exertion, I took a breather and calculated that at the rate I was inching along, it would take about four hours to get to the P.T. room. The thought made me livid, and I just lost it! I banged on the arm of my chair, grabbed the right wheel, and pushed it angrily again and again. My chair circled to the left and I spun around in dizzying, rage-filled circles. Again I pushed—again I spun. And so I circled around and around in the middle of J Wing's corridor like a madly spinning top.

Then, during one of those dizzying turns, the thought struck me: *God, I must look a riot.* As I stopped in my tracks, convulsed with laughter, I realized what a ridiculous form my anger had taken. I imagined the spectacle I created—a wheelchair-bound whirling dervish, brow furrowed with rage, pink nightie flapping in the wind, wasting my time and energy in a silly-looking fit of pique.

I doubled over with laughter and looked up to see four white-capped ladies peering at me from the nurses' station. Seconds later an orderly walked up to me and said, "Are you ready to go downstairs now?" I nodded and burst out laughing again. The orderly said, "Hey, you're in a cheery mood this morning," and he rolled me away.

If I hadn't caught myself and recognized my behavior as silly—and laughable—before that poor orderly arrived, I probably would have snapped at him and burst into tears. Instead I described what had happened, and we had a few chuckles. He was sorry for the delay, but explained that two orderlies were out sick. An unnecessary blowup had been avoided.

One can't expect that *every* attempt at seeing the funny side of anger will work. But it certainly is worth a try.

Victims, as well as those who are seriously ill or handicapped, often have feelings of angry helplessness about their plight or lack of control over their own unfortunate situations. This anger may be evidenced by a bitter, nasty disposition, by chronic complaining or bemoaning one's fate, by terrible fits of rage. But there are also those individuals who learn, frequently by trial and error, how to express their anger through humor. They amuse themselves and others with sardonically funny references to their appearance, their attack, the cancer cells eating at them, their limited marriage prospects, their useless limbs, or anything else connected to their plight. They find that laughter helps them—and others—to deal with rage. I am, at least some of the time, one of these people. So is my friend Frank.

*   *   *

Frank Garrett is a funny, funny guy. A former dancer with a ballet company, he is now an aspiring director/writer. He is also a victim.

In August 1984, Frank took the F train to Bergen Street as he did each morning, en route to his "survival" job as a cabdriver. He left the subway station and began to walk the two short blocks that led to the taxi company garage. Daylight was just beginning to break.

Frank had walked scarcely ten yards when he heard the metallic jingling of keys just behind him. The sound signaled the beginning of a nightmare.

Frank tried to turn around to see who was behind him, but a kid in his late teens stepped swiftly to his side and held a pistol to his temple. For a few seconds Frank felt someone at his back, rifling through his pockets. Then—BLAM! The gun exploded.

Frank found himself lying on the ground. There was no pain. No feeling at all from his neck down. *Oh, my God—I'm paralyzed,* he thought. Frank felt something wet trickling down his face. A voice inside him said: *I'm dying. I'm going to die on Bergen Street.* The certainty of his death was as hard and cold as the pavement he lay upon.

Suddenly Frank felt an urgent need to *move.* In a trance-like stupor he managed to struggle to his feet. He realized that he wasn't paralyzed after all—just strangely numb and tingly.

A man appeared at his side and took his arm, saying, "Take it easy. My wife called the police." Frank stared un-blinkingly at the stranger. The man was kind, but it was clear that he was fighting to control his revulsion at the sight of the tiny, deadly bullet hole in Frank's head. Blood was everywhere.

Frank leaned upon the man and staggered forward. He'd walked only five or six steps when the police arrived. Then the mad race began. The officers in charge rushed Frank to the hospital. Minutes later they pulled up to the emergency entrance, sirens screaming.

Frank *ran* in with a policeman. His rubbery legs seemed to move of their own accord. So did his mouth. He couldn't stop talking. "Call Helen," Frank repeated again and again. "Call Helen. I'm not dying, am I? Call Helen." Frank talked and talked as he was stripped and catheterized, hooked up to IVs, and X-rayed. Over and over he cried out: "Call Helen."

Finally Helen arrived, like a piece of some puzzle from the past—from the life he'd lived before the bullet struck. They'd been involved for over eight months, practically living together, deeply in love, and growing closer each day.

Frank clung to her desperately. "Am I dying, Helen?" The girl was pale, tense, damp-eyed. She held him like a baby and crooned, "You're going to be all right." Frank tried to believe her.

The neurosurgeon arrived, introducing himself as Dr. Isaacs. He seemed kind and honest. Frank asked, "Where's the bullet?"

The doctor answered, "We'll see," and ordered a CAT scan.

After the tests, as they waited, rushes of emotion raced through Frank. He felt physically strong, powerful—wired— resilient. But his head felt "spacey and airy," as though his mind were on a different plane.

The X ray was brought in. Dr. Isaacs pointed to a clearly defined white spot, saying simply: "That's it."

Frank stared in disbelief. The room was silent. Grim, unspoken terror filled the air: A bullet was lodged squarely in the center of his brain.

Frank heard his own shaky voice asking: "Can you get it out?"

The doctor's answer came ringing back out at him as if from an echo chamber:

Noooooooooooooooooooooooo
Noooooooooooooooooo
Noooooooooooooooo

Dr. Isaacs explained what would happen next. Surgery. Not to remove the bullet—it was too deeply imbedded for that. But, as Dr. Isaacs told Frank, when bullets enter skulls, pieces of bone, hair, and skin get dragged in too. The purpose of the operation was to clean as much of that out as they could.

Ten A.M. Four hours had gone by since the bullet had crashed into Frank's brain. His head had been shaved. It felt cold and numb.

Frank lay in pre-op, squinting wearily up at the anesthesiologist.

"What are my chances?"

"About seventy-five percent."

"Oh, God."

The anesthesia began to take effect. Frank looked around at the people in the room. He felt an incredible love for them and sensed they were rooting for him, willing him to live. He swallowed hard and said, "I wish you all good luck." Then he was out.

Many hours later Frank woke up, surprised to have made it through. And so began a week of hospital life. Helen was there night and day, like an angel, a gift from God—kind, loving, supportive. Friends came, all of them stressing how "lucky" Frank was.

But the doctors were candid about Frank's chances: It was possible that he could live to be a hundred, with few if any side effects or painful symptoms. But if an abscess formed, Frank could be dead any day. "So little is known about the brain," they sighed.

All the doctors could do was hope that the bullet wouldn't move and that no infection would set in. All Frank could do was work toward regaining his strength and try to adjust to his new reality: There was a bullet in his brain that would not go away. His life could end tomorrow—or today. Nothing would ever be the same.

Frank's post-attack existence was tough, grim. But two things kept him alive and fighting: his anger and his sense of humor.

Frank was filled with bitterness over what had happened and over the terrible uncertainty that ruled his life. He railed against the gunman who'd cut him down. He was given to sudden, uncontrollable outbursts of anger, which left him weak and trembling with exhaustion.

But he quickly realized that his anger and pain were difficult for people to deal with. He saw that it was a lot easier on himself, on Helen, and on others if he interspersed his fits of rage with just as many bouts of laughter. When Frank began to laugh in spite of the pain, he realized that he hadn't lost everything. He could still think, could still take joy in life, could still touch people with his raw, biting wit.

Frank had always enjoyed playing pranks. And he could

still think of some wild ones. A young nurse entered Frank's room one morning carrying a little black plastic bag. Quietly, and rather covertly, she placed it in his bedside-table drawer. Curious, Frank took out the sealed bag, which was imprinted with his name. Tearing it open, he found mounds of black hair, which he recognized as his own. He burst out laughing and said, "Is this a joke?"

The nurse said, "No."

Frank asked, "What's it for? In case I die, will you glue it back on for the funeral?"

The young woman shifted uncomfortably and mumbled, "Well, to be honest—yes!"

At this, Frank roared. He also decided that if he did die, he wanted to go out with a laugh. So he persuaded Helen to buy and bring him a blond wig. Then he cut off its tresses and put them into the plastic bag in place of his own.

Explaining it to me recently, Frank said, "Well, I had one death to die. Why not die it as a blond?"

Once Frank learned that those around him were more comfortable with him and with his injury if he made them laugh, he set out to become "the funniest victim in Manhattan." And he became very good at it. In fact, he couldn't remember ever having made people laugh as much—not even during his brief stint as a stand-up comic when he was in his teens.

Frank's brand of humor was decidedly black, and often tinged with bitterness, but it made him feel vibrantly *alive*. It quieted his seething rage—and kept him from sinking into suicidal despair over his precarious hold on life.

Frank came up with strange nicknames for himself and references to his injury. He began to call himself Bullet Brain. And he persuaded Helen to have one of his hospital gowns imprinted with the words HOLE IN THE HEAD. When people teased him or a nurse annoyed him, he'd say, "Hey, don't treat me like that! I've got brain damage!"

One day Carla, a friend of Frank's who is a Nichiren Shoshu Buddhist, called and chatted for a moment. Suddenly she said, "Look, I'm with friends—we're coming there to chant for you. You need it!" Before he could respond, Carla hung up. The fact that Carla hadn't bothered to ask him if he'd like them to chant made Frank angry. And he wasn't in the mood to listen to the dronelike chanting of *"Nam, myoho renge kyo."*

Frank sat there fuming for a while. Then he had a great idea. The man in the bed next to him had been in a coma for two weeks. He never moved, and appeared to be sound asleep.

When Carla arrived with her friends, they came to Frank's bedside, took out their beads, and prepared to chant. But Frank shushed them with an air of deep concern and whispered, "Carla, the man next to me has been in so much pain, he hasn't rested in weeks. This is the first time he's been able to sleep. Please go and chant for me at home."

Understandingly, the would-be chanters nodded and tiptoed out of the room. When they were gone, Frank chortled merrily to himself.

Recently, Frank told me that he would have become completely embittered if he hadn't maintained his sense of humor. For a while after his release from the hospital, he became so full of anger and despair that his humor temporarily deserted him. But after he'd worked through his pain and survived the crisis, Frank's effervescence, exuberance, and sense of humor returned in full force.

Today, Frank often jokes about the shooting and about the bullet lodged in his brain. And to tell the truth, it helps all of us who know him to be able to release some of our pain and anger at his unpredictable condition by being able to laugh with him.

One day soon after we met, Frank called me at home. I asked who it was, and when he answered, "Frank," I acted momentarily confused. Then he said, "You know me, Theresa. It's me—Frank Bullet-in-the-Head Garrett."

This type of gag is so acceptable and offhanded with him that many of his friends—including me—feel comfortable enough to say things like "Look, Frank, I know you have a bullet in the brain, but that's no excuse for being forty minutes late!"

Retaining his humor kept Frank from cracking up, and today it helps him to deal with his still-present anger about the shooting, his precarious hold on health, and about his assailants, who have never been caught. Frank's still here, still sane, and still able to enjoy life filled with at least as much joy as pain.

Shared laughter can help to ease the pain, the anger, the alienation, of being a victim. Somehow when we acknowledge together the ironic humor existent in almost every situation, it is easier to share and understand the experience of rage. Tempering anger with humor works; even an uneasy laugh is vastly preferable to the dead silence that often follows an outburst of anger.

Over the past few years I've trained myself to see the lighter side of anger. Almost always, I'll follow an explosion of anger and yelling with laughter or a joke.

Recently I heard that a victim/friend's case had been postponed for the fourth time. A group of us had arranged to be in court with her the next day. Some had requested a "sick day" from work. We'd set up a car pool. We'd notified the press. And at five P.M. the evening before, during a Victims for Victims board meeting, we were told of the latest continuance.

Wham! I picked up the nearest nondangerous object—which happened to be a Victims for Victims T-shirt—and flung it across the room, where it landed upon my tiny four-pound puppy. Totsie yelped and ran scurrying for cover. I roared with laughter and told my fellow board members: "We should make up a T-shirt for Totsie: I AM A VICTIM OF VICTIMS FOR VICTIMS." The quip eased the tension in the room; we each wrote down the next trial date we'd been given—knowing it would probably be changed yet again—and we went back to our business.

Reclaiming your sense of humor may not be easy. You may have to prompt and prod yourself to go after it. You may need to apply some concentrated energy. You may even have to *learn* to laugh again.

After a tragedy, we spend so much time crying, mourning, and suffering that we can forget how to have a good time, how to enjoy a well-timed joke, how to revel in the everyday pleasures of life. We simply get out of practice.

No matter how terrible your trauma has been, you can give yourself permission to have fun again. You can take the time to look for a funny twist, a piece of ironic wit, a brighter side to the darkness. You can turn some of those howls of rage into peals of laughter.

Humor won't take the pain—or the anger or the bitterness or the grief—away like magic. But it can give you more and more moments of solace until eventually you will find that joy has once again entered your life.

Reaching Out to Others

You might think that an angry person wouldn't be a suitable helper for someone else. But anger can motivate us to become terrific helpmates and champions for the rights and needs of others.

Often, anger fills us with an almost unbounded energy. It can make us feel "antsy," edgy, restless, in need of an outburst or release. If we take these sensations and *direct* them, we can do ourselves a lot of good while at the same time performing much-needed and appreciated services.

Frank Garrett found that, despite his sense of humor, he was still seething with rage. Soon after his release from the hospital, his girlfriend, Helen, unable to handle the stress of the situation, broke off their relationship. She was frightened by the life-threatening bullet in Frank's head. She loved him, but she couldn't deal with the changes the shooting had produced in their lives.

Frank's spirits plummeted and rage engulfed him. He had lost his health, his job, his happiness—and now Helen. Often, he flew into solitary rages in his apartment. Within a few days, he'd destroyed every breakable object he owned. Bills came in every day. He had no insurance, no life savings, and no credit. Problems pressed in upon him—and he no longer had a woman to share his feelings with.

Frank ranted on and on, at the top of his lungs. He howled like a wounded animal. He wept for hours. The attacks of rage exacerbated his condition and brought on mind-boggling headaches.

The police called and said they hadn't found the gunmen yet and there were no leads. Frank fantasized hunting his assailants down, holding a gun to their heads, and then terrorizing them until they smelled their own deaths. He hated those animals—hated them. He thought about them, cursed them, and became obsessed with them.

All Frank's energies went into lashing out verbally and emotionally at the gunmen. But it was fruitless: The criminals were free, probably roaming the same streets in search of more victims to torment or kill.

Frank felt trapped at home amidst his own spiritual debris, screaming into a vacuum. But he hated inflicting his rage upon those who came near. So he tried to withdraw, telling his friends that he needed solitude.

A few really close buddies refused to let Frank isolate himself. Despite his protests, they kept dropping by and calling him. Frank tried to joke with his visitors, to fool around as he'd done in the hospital. But they all saw that things were radically different: Frank's post-attack humor had included a fierce—if rather wild—element of joy. Now it contained not even the slightest hint of optimism or good spirit. Frank's sense of humor had become far blacker, more sinister, more tinged with violence and hatred. Frank was a changed man. An angry man. A vengeful man.

His friends began to worry about him, and Frank started to worry about himself—he didn't even *like* himself anymore. He abhorred his own behavior and the bitter taste of anger which was with him night and day.

One lonely morning Frank found himself, for the first time, seriously contemplating suicide. In the midst of his grim thoughts, a voice within him said: *Frank, call Bill.*

Bill Trump, one of Frank's best friends, is a Vietnam veteran who became a paraplegic when he was injured during the war. Yet for years Bill has trained and worked with both disabled and able-bodied veterans in an acclaimed improvisation troupe. He is the bravest individual Frank has ever known.

Frank's longtime buddy became his role model. They talked for hours that first morning. Then, Frank visited Bill almost every day. Bill understood his friend's rage and despair. He reminded Frank that his life was far from useless, that there was still much he could do. The bullet could kill him tomorrow, or he could live to be a hundred—no one knew. But Bill told Frank to think about *today*, to get back into physical and emotional shape and use what he'd learned during the nightmare he'd survived. "Get out there," Bill urged. "Work with kids, addicts, veterans—whoever! Share your life force, man. Don't waste it smashing china. That attack happened. The bullet's in there. But you're alive. Don't let that anger eat you up—get back into *people* again!"

Before the shooting, Frank had been involved in a number of reach-out programs: drug rehabilitation, finding shelter for street people, counseling troubled teens. He hadn't done that kind of work for a while, since his hours on the job were so long and his relationship with Helen had taken up so much of his free time. But some of the people he'd worked with still kept in touch. Many were off drugs and holding down jobs, partly as a result of his efforts. The more he thought about working with troubled people, the more appealing he found the idea. He had both the time and the incentive. And that bullet in his head wouldn't make a damn bit of difference to someone who needed help.

So Frank decided to go for it. He vowed to get back into a program of helping others. But first, he needed to get back on his feet again.

Frank began to take better care of himself. And within a few weeks his strength started to return. The anger attacks stopped entirely. He even went out and bought some new dishes!

Frank went on a job hunt and, after only two interviews, landed the perfect "survival" job as a telephone salesman. It would pay the rent, but it wouldn't be too taxing. He'd still have plenty of time to work with others and take good care of himself too.

Frank was now ready to go. He weighed his options: Should he work with drug addicts again? The handicapped? Children? Teenagers?

Frank wandered around his Lower East Side neighborhood and checked out the various bulletin boards. He pored over the little local handout newspapers. He even read the help-wanted sections. He compiled a list of places and people who needed assistance—there were literally dozens of possibilities. Frank thought he'd visit the homes and centers and see for himself where he'd best fit in.

When Frank was in the midst of his search for the program or group that would most benefit from his work, the movie *Victims for Victims* aired on NBC-TV. Frank had never heard of me, or of my attack, but the blurb in *TV Guide* sparked his interest. He watched the film. And the moment the closing credits began to roll, he called Victims for Victims—the organization—to volunteer. We met at the first meeting of the New York chapter, and I immediately sensed his dedication and energy. So we put him to work.

Within two weeks Frank was on the steering committee of the New York chapter. And he now heads the Victim Rep Network, which provides telephone and in-person reach-out services to victims. His energy and enthusiasm are boundless and infectious. Frank stirs everyone up and makes us all work harder.

Since joining the organization, Frank has counseled both male and female victims, as well as family members. His clients have all remarked on his positive energy, his concern, and his wonderful sense of humor.

For the first time since the shooting, Frank feels strong, useful, and healthy, and he believes that he gets as much help from his clients' courage as they get from his.

Frank says, "Reaching out to people who've been hurt like I have has made me stop lashing out with complete, utter futility. Sure, I'm still mad about what happened—I'm disgusted that those creeps were never caught! But I don't spend so many hours each day wasting time thinking about *them*—they don't *deserve* my attention. Instead, I focus my energies on people who need my help and my support. Plus, I have the friendship and concern of the other volunteers. We really understand each other.

"The bottom line is this: If I can hold a person who's been shot, stabbed, or hurt by a criminal and tell them they're not alone—that they can make it through like I did—then it makes my life worth living. If that bullet moves, and it zaps me tomorrow—at least I'll go out doing something decent!"

Frank Garrett was lucky enough to have had a great role model in his friend Bill. But some of us have to convince *ourselves* that we should start reaching out to people.

When we are angry and embittered, the thought of dealing with and helping others may be the furthest thing from our minds. We may want to recoil from people entirely, to refuse to risk being hurt again, to distrust people in general. We may feel angry not only at the world but at everyone in it. I myself felt this way for a long, long time.

If you feel you're just too angry to have purely humanitarian, noble thoughts about helping others, try a different approach: Decide to reach out—but do it for *you*. Simply take the position: *I am reaching out to others because it will help me to get out of my own problems, to channel my rage constructively, and to gain more self-esteem.*

Having an attitude like this at the outset can take away the onus of becoming an instant volunteer or "do-gooder." And it eliminates the pressure of having to be a *perfect* example. One thing to remember: *Any* sincere help you offer to those in need is appreciated—no less so when it also helps you. And chances are that when you see the response of the people you've helped, you'll want to keep doing it for *them* as well as yourself.

People sometimes ask me: "How can you devote so much time and energy to the cause?" My answer is: "Because it helps *me* too." Yes, I am proud that my work touches people's lives and gives them strength and courage, proud that I can be a role model for other victims. But I am not a martyr to the cause. I *love* what I do. It makes me feel good; it provides an outlet for my anger; it gives meaning to my life; it helps me fight depression; it gives me a sense of purpose; it provides me with daily challenge.

Working with victims directly and fighting for victims' rights have helped me to achieve total health. And the work has changed my life for the better. Yes, it helps others. But it also helps me.

Peer counseling or personal assistance may not appeal to you. Perhaps you are just too angry to handle direct contact with strangers. If so, you can get involved in behind-the-scenes activity. Any work you do for a nursing home, a hospital, a youth center, or any understaffed charitable group—even if it means typing, phone work, soliciting donations, cooking a meal, or planning a social activity—still translates into helping people. You can touch many lives indirectly with services rendered.

Perhaps you are more interested in social or legislative changes than you are in caring for people's emotional or physical needs. Keep in mind that making changes in our society—and in its laws—can greatly improve the lives of human beings. The rewards are different in this kind of work, but they are just as great.

I've learned over the past few years that social activism can be the perfect outlet for an angry victim. You can reach out by seeking rights for:

the elderly

the handicapped

the poor

the homeless

the veterans

Try getting behind a cause you really believe in and using your own rage to fight for an ideal. You don't need to be up on a podium giving speeches or talking into a microphone at press conferences and demonstrations. There are plenty of less-visible jobs—including research, drafting proposals, making phone calls, writing articles, doing office work—which can be invaluable to a vast number of groups.

Any kind of reach-out plan you devise for yourself must be tailored to your own needs, interests, and timetable. Here are a few suggestions:

If you	Volunteer at a
are a feminist	women's center
know sign language and need practice	school for the deaf
love children	youth center or children's home

If you	*Volunteer at a*
want to learn about gerontology	retirement home
adore politics	legislative group
want to help other victims	victims' organization

This list could go on for many pages. Rest assured, you can find any number of ways to volunteer that would be beneficial, interesting, and enjoyable to you.

You may not, at this point, be able to spare a large amount of time. That is absolutely fine.

Making the decision to reach out to others doesn't mean you have to give up your *life*. You can choose to take on as much or as little as you like. It is best not to overextend at first, but to start with a few hours a week and build from there, depending on your desire and ability. Don't think of reaching out as making a sacrifice. Think of it as adding something new—and positive—to your own life. And as a way to let go of some of that seething, churning rage.

If you think you'd like to reach out to people but you feel uncomfortable or even frightened about doing so, it may be helpful to start by working with people who tend to be non-threatening and thankful for much-needed attention: the elderly, the infirm, or the very young.

I, for one, find it hard to resist children. No matter how angry I feel, it is soothing to me to spend time with youngsters. Kids respond so openly and warmly to attention.

Often, when I feel as if I'm about to explode, I go off and spend the day with my four-year-old godson, Luke. The energy I would have put into a blowup, an angry depression, or an argument gets rechanneled into a long walk in the park, a visit to a nearby zoo or museum, a carrousel ride at the local pier. Luke's enthusiasm and bubbly charm win me over every time.

If there are no children in your family and you don't know anyone who'd like a free babysitter for a while, you can seek the company of children who live in youth centers and children's homes which are found in almost every town. The kids who live in places like these *need* attention and could greatly benefit from a caring adult who wants to spend a bit of time with them. In fact, these children are hungry for attention. Some of them may themselves be victims—of child abuse, incest, or various other crimes. Sharing a few hours a week with a lonely youngster—and helping him to deal with his rage and confusion—is an excellent way to redirect your own anger.

If working with others on a one-on-one basis does not appeal to you, you might prefer to reach out through a group effort. There are many glee clubs, choirs, and amateur acting troupes which give performances at rest homes, hospitals, and community centers. Their audiences are *very* responsive and these groups are often hungry for new members. If you're not interested in the performing aspect, you can still join a group like this by doing technical or administrative chores. They are usually more than happy to provide you with on-the-job training.

Again, the important thing about reaching out is not what you do, or whom you do it for, but that you make a decision—and *do* it.

Forward Thinking

Learning to see our emotional turmoil and rage as finite is a major step in dealing with anger.

If I hadn't practiced forward thinking—and convinced myself that there was a future beyond my current state of consuming anger—it would have been nearly impossible to get through the period following my release from the hospital.

My sister, Maria, and I had a full but often tedious schedule. Our days were long and exhausting, involving two doctor visits on the average. There were long, uncomfortable drives to various medical offices, endless hours in waiting rooms, and all kinds of tests and procedures to endure.

In addition to hating the miserably repetitive and frustrating daily routine, I was angry and depressed about my disintegrating marriage, the upcoming trial of the attacker, the further surgery I'd have to go through.

Maria was just as wretched as I. She missed friends and

family in New York and was depressed about missing grad school and teaching. She, too, was sick and tired of endless rounds of doctors and hospitals. And she was angry.

At times Maria's annoyance seemed to be directed at me; after all, she wouldn't be miserable if she hadn't volunteered herself as my companion. But in reality she knew it wasn't my fault, and so she tried hard not to resent me.

We were two angry ladies. If we hadn't constantly reminded ourselves—and each other—that our miserable state of affairs was temporary, we *both* might have gone off the deep end.

I trained myself to look to the future and to have faith that everything in my life would eventually change for the better. When I felt blinded by rage, I'd say to myself: *Theresa, a few months from now you are still going to feel angry about all this. But you won't feel as angry. It will not hurt as much. You will not have as many outbursts. Time is going to help heal all this anger.* I only half-believed these self-administered pep talks, but I needed to look forward to something.

Maria's personal style of forward thinking was mainly exhibited in her writing. Hour after hour she scribbled in her diary. She took that book with her everywhere—and I mean *everywhere*. In it she described not only the events that were taking place now, but also her plans for the future.

Maria stayed sane during what she often refers to as "the worst time of my life" by drafting an intricate, detailed ground plan for the coming winter, when she would return to New York. Whenever Maria made an entry, she would write, "Only —— days to go." I'm surprised she didn't count the *hours* too!

She gave herself specific goals—for instance, that she'd have a job within a month of her return to New York. And, while still in L.A., she took steps to make her future wishes a reality. She typed up draft after draft of her résumé until she was 100 percent satisfied with it. She had copies made and sent to New York, where a girlfriend submitted them to various schools that needed midwinter teacher replacements. Eventually one of those résumés led to a job offer—which came even sooner than her desired goal!

Maria even wrote down her plans for the Christmas party she would throw for her friends in Brooklyn upon her return.

On a swelteringly hot August day I found her sitting in a doctor's waiting room, writing down the items she needed for the holiday celebration. I shook my head in amazement as I read it: mistletoe, poinsettias, Santa suit, eggnog, pine wreath . . . That party seemed many moons away, but making those early, specific plans helped Maria out of her current unhappiness. (And it turned out to be a good party too!)

Maria wrote most when she was really mad, like after we'd had an argument or after I'd had a loud and ugly blowup, or after we'd learned I'd need more surgery (which meant she'd have to suffer through still another recuperation with me).

Both of us shared lots of *verbal* forward thinking too. When things were really rough, I'd say, "Cheer up, Maria. Only —— months to go."

We even made up a game called "One Year from This Day," which was our joint effort at forward thinking. Whenever either or both of us felt furious, we'd grit our teeth and say (or sometimes snarl): "One year from this day ——." Then we'd fill in the blank with what we hoped—or actually believed—we'd be doing. My sister would say, "One year from today I'll be giving an English test and all my students will pass it"; or I would say, "One year from today I will no longer need to go to physical therapy." This simple game helped release our anger and tension and kept us from turning against each other.

One day when Maria was fuming about always having to drive me everywhere (my hand was still in a brace), I said, "Maria, a year from now I'll pull up in front of NYU when your class gets out. I'll be in a Rolls-Royce, with chauffeur, and we'll drive you all over the city." It sounded like a grandiose, unrealistic scheme, but as it turned out, it virtually came true.

A little over a year later I was promoting a project in New York and the company gave me a stretch limo and driver for the day. I immediately picked up my sister in Brooklyn, took her to a Broadway matinee, and then out to dinner at Joe Allen's. Maria loved it: The chauffeur drove the whole way!

One day Maria and I visited the prosecutor on my case, Mike Knight, at the Santa Monica courthouse. He explained to us that even if the man who had attacked me was given the maximum penalty possible by law—twelve years—he'd actually be out in six. In fact, unless my assailant seriously misbehaved in prison, he would—under California's determinate sentencing laws—be automatically released on August 7, 1988. Neither a parole hearing nor evaluation of any kind would be required.

Both my sister and I saw red. We were furious, confused, and filled with contempt for the system. Yet the law was the law. Even if it could be changed, it would not be retroactive. We drove back to L.A. in stony silence. Our forward thinking seemed pointless. Why bother to play "One Year from This Day" when all we could fill in the blank with was "Jackson will have served one sixth of his term"?

We'd been home about an hour when the man who would later produce the movie *Victims for Victims* called. After my conversation with him, I turned to my sister and said, "Maria, a year from this day, my story will be made—or in the process of being made. I will insist that they expose the ludicrousness of this sentence. A year from this day, *millions* of people will have an awareness of how much injustice there is in our system."

It didn't make us happy, but it did make us feel better. This forward thinking helped to focus our anger upon a very *possible* future goal.

In November 1984, the epilogue NBC ran at the conclusion of the film made millions aware of my attacker's sentence and the complete injustice that it represented.

Janet Kiley was introduced to me in December 1984 at our annual Victims for Victims Christmas party. A tall, attractive twenty-six-year-old, she sat in a wheelchair, flanked by her mother, Vera, and her best friend, Ann. The first things that struck me about Janet were her broad, inviting smile and the feeling of warmth and optimism she exuded. Yet Janet had been the victim of a shooting attack which left her paralyzed from the chest down. That night she told me the entire story.

Janet had always led a happy, healthy, physically active life. She held a full-time job as a bartender at Las Casas, a pretty, music-filled Mexican restaurant frequented mostly by families and couples. Customers at Las Casas were friendly and the tips were good.

In warm weather Janet also worked part-time as an aerobics teacher, and during winter months as a ski instructor. She adored skiing and felt most alive when she was whizzing down the snowy slopes. On March 7, 1984, Janet and her friend Rose left the house at ten-thirty P.M. and dropped in at Charlie's, a local pub/disco they frequented. Rose's boyfriend was there with a friend of his, so the four of them shared a table. They had a terrific evening and danced nonstop for two hours to the top-forties tunes that played over the sound system.

Exhausted, drenched with perspiration, Janet finally left the dance floor. All she wanted to do was rest. As she made her way toward her table, a wiry, intense-looking red-haired man approached and asked if she wanted to dance. Janet politely explained that she was tired and needed a break. Then she re-joined her friends.

After a while Janet noticed that the man who'd asked her to dance was seated at a table directly across from hers. He kept staring straight at her. Janet saw the man's friends making faces at him; they seemed to be teasing him about something. She wondered if the guy had made a bet with his friends that she would accept his invitation to dance.

Janet and her friends made plans to go out for a late-night "breakfast." She now believes that the man at the next table—and his four buddies—overheard the conversation. At about 12:45 A.M. Janet saw them leave the bar. Fifteen minutes later, she, Rose, and the two young men they were with headed for Rose's car.

The moment she walked outside, Janet heard the man yell, "Hey, take this, you f——ing bitch!" She stared in the direction of the voice and saw the redheaded man and his pals in a nearby car. The man who'd asked her to dance was in the back seat, holding a gun pointed straight at Janet. Terrified, she turned and ran. A shot rang out. It ripped through her spine, right between the shoulder blades. She fell to the ground. Another blast from the gun hit Janet's right calf. With a screeching of tires, the gunman and his buddies drove away.

Janet lay there. She couldn't move. Couldn't feel. She was

confused and thought they'd shot her with an elephant tranquilizer. People poured out of the bar.

Minutes later the police arrived, then the ambulance. They
quickly placed her in the vehicle and raced toward the hospital. The ambulance attendant asked if she was allergic to anything. "Yeah—cats," Janet replied.

"Hey," said the attendant, "I see you haven't lost your
sense of humor."

"I guess not," said Janet.

In the emergency room they began to cut off her clothes so
they wouldn't have to move her. "Hey," Janet begged them.
"Don't destroy this outfit. It's my favorite." The nurses looked
at her in disbelief.

They inserted a chest tube because the bullet had pierced
Janet's lung and it had collapsed. Spinal fluid was coming out
of the bullet hole in her back, but the doctors were afraid to
operate. They said the fluid might stop on its own.

The fluid did stop—three days later. The doctors told
Janet her spinal cord was severed at level T-6 and that she
would never walk again.

Janet had little reaction to the news because of the power-
ful medication, which made everything seem hazy and unreal.
Her three days in General Hospital passed in a dreamlike blur.
She remembers almost nothing about those seventy-two hours.

Janet does vividly remember a visit from the detective on
her case, who asked, "What kind of gun was it, Miss Kiley—a
revolver or automatic?"

"I don't know. I'm not a gun expert," she replied.

With that, the detective pulled out his own gun, right
there in ICU, saying, "Did it look like this?"

Janet stared at him, her face contorted with rage. Then,
she ordered him out of the room. It was the first time she'd
felt anger—or much of *anything*—since the shooting.

When she was out of danger, Janet was moved to Long
Beach Memorial. At this hospital Janet found herself surrounded
by negativity. She was told she had less than a 5 percent
chance of walking. The nurses, doctors, even the staff psychiatrist assigned to her said, in effect: "You must adjust. You will
probably never walk again."

Janet responded, "You don't know *me!*"

The negativity surrounding her confused—and enraged—Janet. She thought to herself: *How am I supposed to get better if all they do is knock me down?* She sank into a deep, engulfing depression.

Janet thought of committing suicide. She knew she was capable of doing it; after all, she could still move her arms. "Without my family and friends, I would've killed myself for sure," Janet says today. "They—especially my mom—held out hope. And I didn't want to hurt *them* by taking my own life."

When the initial heavy doses of medication were reduced and Janet finally took in the reality of her condition, her first thought was: *Oh, my God, please let me ski again!* And no matter what the doctors said, she refused to give up hope for the future: first, to walk. Then—to ski! Forward thinking kept Janet alive then, as it does now.

"At first," says Janet, "I set unrealistic goals for myself. Like, I said I'd walk by my birthday. Then, when that day came and I wasn't on my feet, I got depressed. So now I aim for steady day-to-day progress. I look forward to each new sign of improvement."

At Memorial Hospital, Janet worked fiendishly, tirelessly, in physical therapy. But even her physical therapist discouraged her from dreaming of really walking again. Janet sensed that they wanted her to acquiesce, to give up. She railed at them and said, "No way—I'm a fighter!" The angrier Janet became at their negativity, the more fired up she felt about proving them wrong.

Day or night, when Janet felt hysterical, enraged, or hopeless, she'd call her mom on the phone. And Mrs. Kiley was there for her daughter, with her own brand of forward thinking.

"You're gonna walk again, Janet. I know it. You're gonna be my miracle baby. And on that day, we're going to tell all these people, we told you so!" Mrs. Kiley was angry too. She knew her daughter needed encouragement and motivation, not a constant dampening of her spirits.

Janet begged the doctors again and again to take a CAT scan. She was sure it would show she had some spinal cord left, that it hadn't been completely severed. The doctors at Memorial refused to order it, saying that the regular X rays showed them all they needed to know. Janet's spinal cord was severed. Nothing was left.

Janet was infuriated. She knew that she herself couldn't order the CAT scan. But she set herself a future goal: to find a doctor out there who *would*.

After one month and two weeks, Janet was released from Memorial. She and her mom searched high and low and found a chiropractor they trusted and respected. He was, thank God, an optimist. The chiropractor, Dr. Lomax, ordered a CAT scan, and to everyone's joy, it showed that 50 percent of Janet's spinal cord was left—some on each side. The bullet had passed right through. But the spinal cord was not severed. There was *real* hope.

When Dr. Lomax had done all he could for Janet, her brother Daniel found a place where she could get physical therapy five days a week, seven hours a day: the Gibbs Institute. Janet says now that the Institute and those who work there have given her support, hope, motivation, and courage. They, too, practice forward thinking right along with Janet. Her therapists constantly say, "Janet, I can't wait to see you really walking!"

Shooting Janet was the gunman's first offense. He was let off early, convicted only of attempted manslaughter. He received eight years, and will most likely serve only four. The thought that this man who senselessly gunned her down will be walking free in so few years enrages Janet. "I try not to dwell on it too much. When I get depressed and think that he'll be out in a few years while I'll still be in a wheelchair, I stop and tell myself that I will overcome this. I *will* be walking before they let that criminal out. I'm not letting him take away my dancing, my skiing, and my mobility forever. No way! I'm too much of a fighter for that."

Janet says, "The way I keep myself going is by refusing to be defeated. I do not accept the doctors' depressing diagnosis as law. I'm telling you, they say I won't walk again—but other people like me have proven doctors wrong. And I'm going to do it too. The mind has so much to do with the body, I'm convinced that if I keep thinking positively, good things will happen. Gibbs has given me hope and I've made real, chartable progress there. Those therapists believe in me and I'm going to show them how right they are. Every week, I tell myself I'll make a little more progress. And I always do."

Janet and her boyfriend, Joe, will have been together six years this coming April. He has been wonderful, standing by her throughout the ordeal. Forward thinking, in a way, has helped to *postpone* their wedding plans. Says Janet: "Joe keeps asking me to marry him, but I'm asking him to wait awhile. Oh, I plan to marry him for sure—but I'm telling you I am going to *walk* down that aisle at our wedding!"

Janet's plans for the future are not just idle, wishful dreams. She is working slavishly to achieve them. Her therapists at Gibbs say she is one of the most highly motivated, goal-oriented, hard-working patients they've ever had. And they believe that although the odds would seem to be against Janet, given the severity of her injury, there is still hope. With her combination of positive energy, hard work, and the spinal cord she still has left, the people at Gibbs believe there is a possibility that Janet can achieve her goal.

Janet began her therapy at Gibbs in May. By December, all kinds of progress had been made: She had learned to sit up without assistance and to stand with her knees locked straight up and down (before, they'd been like Jello). She had learned to contract her leg muscles and they had become clearly defined. And finally, her nerve tracks were feeding the muscles—though not quite enough to hold her up. "*Yet*, that is!" Janet said that night. This young woman had made a tremendous amount of progress in only seven months' time.

Janet's full day of therapy at Gibbs cost $700. In early December her insurance company forced her to visit one of their doctors, who reported that she needed therapy only three days a week, two hours a day. This doctor denigrated the progress Janet was making as "insubstantial" and insisted that no matter how much therapy she received, she would never walk again.

So Janet was forced by the insurance company to cut her therapy back to three days a week. But thankfully, although insurance pays for only two hours each day, Gibbs gives her a full day of therapy anyway. Janet says now: "Sure, I'm mad. I hate sitting home when I could be there at Gibbs making progress. Now the insurance company says they are cutting me down to two days. And after May—nothing at all. I'm really angry at that insurance company, and I'm getting a lawyer to fight for me. But in the meanwhile, just being angry doesn't do me any good. It's more important for me to focus my mind and my energy on getting to *move* again. Then, when I'm walking, I will *show* these insurance people how wrong they were. I plan to walk into their offices on my own two feet one day—and I hope they're embarrassed to tears that they didn't help me."

If that's not forward thinking, I don't know what is.

Therapy

A good therapist can be a tremendous asset when we're learning to work through our anger. He or she can suggest ways to express rage, to channel it, and even to use it to our advantage.

Because many people—including our best friends and closest relatives—do not react well to rage, it helps to have a place where we can go and openly discuss, analyze, and even act out our anger. And a therapist can also help us learn to cope with *other* people's reaction to it.

In therapy we don't need to deny or suppress our rage. We don't need to apologize for it. We don't need to smile sweetly and say, "Don't worry, I'm fine." What we *do* need is to work on our anger constructively. A good therapist won't try to *erase* anger instantly, but will encourage us to confront it, explore it, accept it, and work through it.

Without the help of my psychiatrist, it would have been nearly impossible for me to get through the summer and fall following my attack. The anger that engulfed me made me feel like a walking time bomb.

In June 1982, after I was released from Motion Picture Hospital, my husband, Fred, and I decided upon a trial separation to give us both time to think.

My sister, Maria, and I moved in with a close friend, Maria Smith, and her two-year-old boy, Luke, who is my godson. It was wonderful to be out of the hospital. I felt elated by my newly regained freedom, and eager to be a part of the real world again. But I was in for a rather rude awakening.

The six months that followed proved to be one of the most

difficult—and anger-filled—periods of my life. Building up my strength and continuing to work toward complete recovery were no easy tasks, particularly without the shelter and protection of hospital life. The world was soon slapping me in the face with harsh, cold reality.

Many people couldn't understand the anger that poured out of me. After all, they said, I was out of the hospital, my health was returning, and my sister was there to help me—my life was on the upswing, wasn't it? In response, I'd shake my head and vow to keep my anger a secret. But then I felt stifled, miserable—and even angrier than before.

I was locked in an emotional battle against my altered life and body. Acceptance was still a long way off and I needed to lash out and talk about my anger. But people were tired of listening.

This disapproval of my rage made me even madder. I would sit and fume for hours, resentfully thinking to myself: *If they got stabbed ten times, if they were scarred for life, if they had a lunatic who wanted to kill them, they'd be angry too!* I felt completely misunderstood, confused, and even guilty.

In therapy I found a place where my anger and pain were accepted and understood. Where my emotional turmoil was deemed a justifiable, appropriate response to my circumstances.

Dr. Weingold repeatedly said I had every right to be filled with rage; that I wasn't a baby, wasn't a brat, wasn't "crazy" to feel as I did. He encouraged me to talk about it, to express my rage, both with him and with others who were able to make an effort to understand. And he helped me to have faith that in time my anger would lessen greatly. But first I had to work through it.

Dr. Weingold encouraged my interest in working for victims' rights as a way for me to express anger constructively. He listened to my ideas on how to deal with my rage and gave me some of his own. Dr. Weingold's was an eclectic, supportive approach. He didn't mollycoddle me, but he gave me enough security to embrace and accept my own rage.

Many things contributed to my feelings of anger during the period immediately following my hospital discharge, but what made me angriest of all was the way people dealt with and looked upon me on the outside.

During my last weeks in the hospital I'd appeared to be (and often felt) physically strong in comparison to the other patients. But here in the real world, people treated me like a weakling, a frail little flower, an invalid. I began to see myself as others saw me: pale, gaunt, and slow-moving. I still wore a huge, curious-looking metal brace on my hand and arm, and my torso was encased in a bulky pressure device designed to keep the scars from further growth. The combination of the brace and the pressure device made it impossible for me to move or walk about normally.

I was not exactly a healthy-looking specimen yet. And the people who gawked at me open-mouthed, whispered or commented to each other—even giggled or laughed out loud—never let me forget it. I wanted to scream at them: "Leave me alone! Don't stare at me. For God's sake, go away!"

Once, in the ladies' room of a restaurant, a young girl stepped up to me boldly and asked, "Hey, what's wrong with *you*? Did a dog bite you?" Then she burst into shrieks of nervous laughter. Tears of rage and humiliation flooded my eyes. I had an impulse to slap her—to strike back at her and at all the others who were unkind and insensitive. But I just stared at the girl silently until she left the room. I managed to pull myself together and return to my table, keeping my anger inside until I got home. Then I unleashed it in a fit of hysterical crying that lasted long into the night.

By the time I'd been out of the hospital for a month, I'd already suffered through quite a number of such encounters. And I began to panic, becoming unnerved whenever I knew I'd have to confront a group of strangers.

Doubts about my ability to function in public clouded my mind: What if someone was especially cruel and I became so angry that I actually *did* hit her?

I wondered if I should hide myself away somewhere until all the braces and devices had been removed from my body. But I knew that was nearly a year away. And I felt that sequestering myself would make me even more a prisoner of my fate than I already was.

My psychiatrist and I discussed the predicament. I sensed that Dr. Weingold, too, was concerned about how strangers treated me and how I responded to their reactions. I was still

quite delicate emotionally and he didn't want to see me regress or lose my hold on mental health. And neither of us really
wanted me to retreat to a hospital or some other "hide-out."

There was no way for Dr. Weingold to sweeten reality for
me, but he did manage to help me understand the reactions
of others. He talked to me for hours about the tendency
people have to stare, to gawk, to whisper, to pass rude remarks about the handicapped. And he explained that generally this behavior grew out of the fact that *they* had a problem:
These people had little or no exposure to those who were
"different." They didn't *know* how to act or what to say. They
didn't realize that you can treat someone in a wheelchair,
brace, or body cast as simply a *person*. For the most part, the
insensitivity I'd encountered had been more the result of ignorance than cruelty.

During our sessions Dr. Weingold suggested ways in which
I could deal with people's inappropriate responses. Surprisingly, he encouraged me to be blunt and straightforward. He
reminded me that I had every right to let others know that
their behavior made me angry. Dr. Weingold explained that
the object of a direct approach with these people was *not* to
embarrass them or to retaliate. Rather, the main point would
be for me to express my own anger directly—for the sake of
my own emotional well-being. In addition, telling these people
how their behavior affected me would *educate* them: It would
let them know, in no uncertain terms, that their behavior was
rude, inappropriate, and infuriating.

So I took Dr. Weingold's advice and began to apply it.
One evening, at a social gathering, a middle-aged woman
openly stared at me for over an hour, speculating in an audible
whisper about who I was, what had happened, what the
purpose of that metal contraption could be, and so on.

After a while, I'd had enough. I marched over to the lady
and said loudly, "Please, ma'am, try not to stare at me so
much. It makes me very uncomfortable. And if you have any
questions about me—or about this brace I'm wearing—I'd be
more than happy to answer them for you."

The woman, flustered, apologized quickly and darted away.
I shrugged my shoulders and returned to my friends. Nothing

further occurred, and I was able to relax and enjoy the rest of the party.

The direct approach really worked. When people saw the devices I wore, they frequently urged me to "Sit, dear, sit." Now I learned to say with a smile: "No, thank you. It's my arm and my chest that are hurt, not my legs."

While waiting in the greenroom to appear on a talk show one day, I was confronted by a blustery middle-aged man who made his way over to me, drink in hand, and said, "My God, that's a strange-lookin' piece of paraphernalia you got there, heh-heh. Looks like a bear trap to me!"

I flinched for a moment—as did some of the other guests who'd overheard. Then I looked him straight in the eye and said tersely, "No, this is obviously *not* a bear trap, and I am even more obviously not a bear. You, however, are a very rude man and I suggest that you learn some manners before you inflict your senseless remarks upon someone else!" With that, I turned on my heel and walked away. The man grew beet-red under the stares of those who'd been listening, but I felt fine.

Before Dr. Weingold's suggestion to handle people like this man firmly and directly, I would have submerged my feelings, done a shaky interview, and gone home to cry for hours or to take out my anger on my poor sister. Instead, I expressed my anger and disapproval to the person who deserved it. I'd dealt with my rage directly and appropriately. And I was free of it right there on the spot!

Hidden Anger

For the most part, I've always tended to express my anger freely and overtly. It is right out there for me—and for everyone else—to see. But for many others, anger can lurk inside so quietly that they don't even know it's there.

Donna Evans is a beautiful, intelligent New York actress with a flourishing stage career and a rapidly growing film career. She is a strong, independent lady and one you'd probably describe as fearless. In 1979 things were on the upswing for Donna. She was working steadily, she'd just redecorated her lovely Manhattan apartment, and she'd recently met a handsome and talented young actor named Ed, who would later become her husband.

One evening, as Donna was entering the lobby of her apartment building, she was accosted by two knife-wielding teenagers. Donna's mind spun around. She was afraid they would stab her to death. But she tried to appear cool and collected.

The teenagers made lewd gestures and seemed intent upon hurting her, or raping her. She tried to talk them out of it by reasoning with them. It is possible that talking to the assailants saved her life, but it did not prevent both young men from sexually assaulting her. After the rapes, they left as suddenly as they'd appeared.

Donna remembers the period after the attack as one of profound conflict. Her primary feeling was one of *guilt* and not anger. She never railed against or felt hatred for the young rapists. Donna felt that the *real* reason for the sexual assault upon her was that the boys were socially and economically deprived. After filing a police report, she worried that this one criminal act on the part of the teenagers might destroy the rest of their lives. The only anger she felt then was toward society, for making these boys what they were.

Donna did not have an hysterical or highly emotional reaction immediately following the sexual assault. The only change in her life was in how she related to men; more and more often, she found herself provoking complete strangers by telling them about the rape and making *them* feel guilty.

But she pretended to be blasé, nonchalant about what had happened to her. Her new boyfriend called a week after the rape. When Ed asked her "What's new?" she breezily responded, "Oh, I just got raped."

Donna went on with her life. Things quickly went back to normal. She felt fine and in control. No terrible rage or anguish surfaced. She felt she had survived a potentially lethal altercation, and she truly believed that she had psychologically adjusted to it.

Two months after being sexually assaulted, Donna left New York City to perform a leading role in a classical play with a major repertory company. She was excited about the job and launched into rehearsals with great energy and enthusiasm. But the rehearsal period had barely begun when Donna started to black out.

For days the fainting spells continued. Donna went to the hospital and to various private doctors for tests, but no one could find a medical reason for the unpredictable blackouts. Each day, Donna felt more and more out of control. Her entire life seemed to be crashing down around her.

Ellen, an old friend from high school who happened to live in the area, got in touch with Donna. When they got together, Donna told Ellen everything that had happened in her life during the past few months. It turned out that Ellen had been doing volunteer work at a nearby rape treatment center which was considered one of the best in the country. She suggested that Donna's current problems might be directly linked to the sexual assault. Donna was not at all sure that this was true, but she agreed to call the center and make an appointment.

Donna was assigned to an excellent therapist, Jean Craig. A clinical psychologist, Jean had worked with rape victims for many years and was a dedicated, tireless counselor.

Beginning therapy caused an explosion of anger to erupt from Donna. It was soon clear that powerful, gut-wrenching, unresolved rage over the rape was the direct cause of her recent lapses of consciousness. The anger inside Donna had lain dormant for too long. It needed a release, and so it found an outlet in the ultimate act of utter loss of control: blacking out or fainting. Despite her months of seemingly perfect adjustment, the psychological effects of the sexual assault had been festering in Donna's mind all along.

Five days a week, Donna worked with Jean. They talked about the rape itself, Donna's subsequent guilt, and the intense anger that was causing her to black out. Donna found in therapy an outlet for the rage that churned within her. She abandoned the habit of making light of the rape. With her counselor's help she began to recognize the sexual assault for what it really was: a horrendous, painful, unjust attack upon both her body and her mind.

Hour after hour, Donna talked to Jean. Slowly she released herself from the grip and burden of guilt. Donna began

to see the teenaged rapists for what they were: young criminals who, despite their poverty-stricken upbringing, were still
responsible for their violent acts and must therefore suffer the
consequences. She also learned to direct her bitterness at the
assailants, rather than blaming and "punishing" *all* men for
the crimes committed by some.

As Donna progressed in therapy, the blackouts diminished and then disappeared. She retained some of her anger
but learned to cope with it and express it safely. To this day,
Donna credits therapy for her recovery from the delayed but
extremely potent emotional response to the trauma of rape.

Again, I don't believe that therapy is a cure-all, but for
many of us who have been victimized, the help of a therapist
can lead us to identify and understand our rage; to uncover a
variety of workable, appropriate ways of handling our justifiable anger; and to progress toward better emotional health.

CHAPTER 5

PAIN

I can well understand why snakes are often used to symbolize that which is evil or deadly. During the nightmarish days following my attack, images of coiled, sharp-toothed, slithery creatures wafted in and out of my consciousness.

I remember the pain of those days as quiet, lethal, menacing—*serpentine*. Its sinister presence engulfed me, grasping me within its powerful jaws and threatening to swallow me whole.

Pain was everywhere. It didn't stop at my outer layer, but sank into my pores and bored its way down through layer after layer of flesh, bone, muscle, and nerve. And the viperish agony did not stop there; it dug its way still deeper, far beneath and beyond my physical being, until it sank its sharp fangs into the center of my heart and soul.

The inner recesses of my mind were fertile ground for hideous hallucinations. Tiny serpents appeared out of nowhere, their pointed tongues aimed directly at me. Eerie little voices jeered, "You will die of pain. We are pain and you will die." Then they slithered away, screeching with bizarre high-pitched laughter.

There were many moments when I believed those evil, taunting voices. My agony was so intense that I began to feel that even if the pain didn't *kill* me, it would surely drive me to insanity.

I was most vulnerable during that final half-hour before another pain shot could be administered. "I can't take this pain. I'm going crazy," I wept, rocking my head back and forth and shrinking away from the serpentine creatures, which seemed to be everywhere.

Powerless, I lay there, waiting for the visions to vanish. As the frightening images finally slid away, I peered out of my blackened, sunken eyes, relieved by the comforting sight of my mother keeping her silent vigil by my bedside. We stared into each other's eyes, locked in the grip of shared agony, and prayed for respite. Eventually, it would come in the form of a shot of Demerol. I often wished they'd give my mom a shot too. But even that potent narcotic could hardly have touched the hurt that lay deep inside her.

> Into all lives some rain must fall;
> Into all lives some pain must fall.

Once the drug had taken the edge off the pain just a bit, this singsong rhyme spun round and round in my head. The chant became a sort of lullaby. As the drug enticed me into still another brief but welcome nap, I often closed my eyes and silently sang myself to sleep.

My misery knew no bounds. I thought of my eyes as "hellholes" from which I peered out of my wretched world of inner and outer torment. But my agonized glimpses into the land of comfort and normalcy were hardly a consolation. All that I could see seemed distant, removed from my own horrific, viper-infested world.

And thus I lived for many days. There was nowhere to run, no way to hide from the pain. And so, for a while, I let it claim me. Unblinking, I stared at the serpents. I accepted them and the spasms of pain which shot through my body. Then, I closed my eyes and lost myself in my dronelike chant:

Into all lives some rain must fall;
Into all lives some pain must fall.

Alcoholics Anonymous has a wonderfully effective philosophy: "One day at a time." Alcoholics endure their painful withdrawals and their subsequent abstinence by focusing only upon each twenty-four-hour period. Thinking of all the difficult days that stretch ahead would make the task seem insurmountable.

During my worst, most painful period, I virtually lived three hours at a time, getting from one soothing injection to the next by the skin of my teeth. I'm certain that if I had allowed myself to think much further than my next pain shot, the prospect of the weeks and months of suffering awaiting me would have been unbearable.

And so, by living three hours at a time, I was able to survive until the viper of pain began to loosen its nasty bite.

The following, prolonged phase of suffering proved quite different. Gone were the visions; gone were the eerie, wretched little voices. Now, pain entered my life on a more tangible level.

In some ways, it was a relief to wake up from the drugged nightmare with my faculties intact. But in other ways, it hurt even more keenly. Because my senses were sharper, I felt the pain more intensely. But I had no choice. I no longer confronted a painful dream, but an equally pain-filled reality.

Many crime victims find themselves tossed into a world where pain rules and comfort takes the back seat. It is a state made even more awful by the fact that you are there through no fault of your own.

For many victims, pain of mind and pain of body become interlocked. Even when a person's body is not harmed during the course of the actual crime, the emotional anguish suffered after a victimization is often physically debilitating.

And so, victims of crime have a rough time ahead of them. There are no easy ways out. Perhaps the most encouraging thing I can say is that many thousands of victims have managed to live through even the most hideous and prolonged suffering. Frequently, the progress has been halting and piecemeal. But, through trial and error, we discovered what helped—and what hurt—when dealing with our own suffering.

No two people are alike in their perception of and tolerance for pain. Therefore, those who are hurt must seek and pursue that which specifically helps *them* to alleviate and live with their suffering.

I've often heard people say, "You can't really *remember* pain once it's over." I have found that to be utterly false. I *can* remember how every part of my body hurt and how much pain filled my heart and soul. In fact, I try not to think about it too often, because even the *thought* of all that suffering hurts.

Many people have said to me: "There's no way I could have endured the pain that you did. I would have gone nuts, or killed myself." All I can say to them is: "I would have thought so too. But when you're forced into a terrible situation, you find you can deal with a lot more than you'd ever thought possible."

After the attack, my mother was in an understandably anxious state. She remembered that ever since I was a tiny girl, I'd always been much more sensitive to pain than my sister, my cousins, or other kids my age. A tiny bruise or scratch sent me into hours of agonized weeping. Whenever I had a dental appointment, I was miserable before, during, and after the procedure. I screamed like a banshee at the very *sight* of a needle and had to be physically *dragged* into any doctor's office or emergency room. It was clear that I had very little tolerance for pain of any sort.

During my teenage years, and into adulthood, this situation grew no better. If anything, it became worse. I was such a baby about pain, it was downright embarrassing.

When I was twenty, my agent recommended that I have my teeth capped. I had my heart set on a film career, and the thought of a dazzling smile appealed to me. So off I went to Dr. Gregorio, a renowned "dentist to the stars."

Well, that man had never seen the likes of me! I hadn't been in a dentist's chair since I was about twelve years old. The minute he moved toward me with his little steel picks and prongs, I began to shake like a leaf. Tears ran down my face, and I moaned and wailed piteously as he took care of a few minor cavities. He was puzzled and concerned by my extreme reaction—I'm sure he feared that I'd drive his patients out of the waiting room—but he explained that he didn't believe in laughing gas or other anesthetics. Then he suggested that I take a mild tranquilizer before my next visit, when he would begin the process of filing down my front teeth to little points in order to place temporary crowns over them.

One week later I arrived with a friend, feeling pleasantly groggy from the mild sedative I'd swallowed. But the moment the drilling began, I started to shake, sweat, and weep. Only this time it was much worse. Chills shot down my spine and I literally began to *scream*. The doctor could not get me to stop. As he continued to drill, I grew closer and closer to hysteria. Although he'd planned to do four of my teeth, he hastily finished up just one, capped it with a temporary crown—and gave me another doctor's business card. Still racked with sobs, I stared down and read DR. HARRY HAMBURG, DENTISTRY UNDER GENERAL ANESTHESIA. Gulping and hiccoughing, I thanked Dr. Gregorio and slunk out of his office. The other patients stared at me, shaking their heads.

So I began having my teeth capped by Dr. Hamburg, a jovial fellow whose walls were covered by framed book-jackets of his recently published *The Joys of Anesthesia*.

Every two weeks, I went to Dr. Hamburg's office to have a few more teeth capped. There with me in the waiting room were others who could not bear the onslaught of an ordinary dentist's drill. Some, like myself, were simply phobic about pain. Most, however, had some sort of serious physical or emotional problem that made ordinary dentistry impossible.

When it was my turn, I climbed onto the long operating table, rolled up my sleeve, and watched as Dr. Hamburg inserted an intravenous needle into my arm. Soon, sodium pentothal was surging into my veins. I tried counting to ten, made it only to four, and passed out. Each time I regained consciousness, I had two more shiny white caps in my mouth.

It was natural, then, after the attack, for my mother to worry that the pain would make me crazy or suicidal. I'd hear her whispering tearfully to my dad: "Tony, I don't know how she can get through this—she could never even stand a little scratch.''

The hard, cold fact of the matter was: *I had no choice.* In the past, when pain was before me, I'd found various and sundry ways to avoid or lessen it. But after my attack, I was trapped there in that bed, forced to bear with the results and repercussions of multiple stab wounds and painful medical procedures.

If I tried to *deny* the pain, or fight it fruitlessly, I surely would have been driven crazy. You really can't deny reality and still stay in the real world. What is, is. And that pain *was.* I instinctively knew that the only way to live with my pain and eventually learn to cope with it successfully was to *accept* it as real. And I did exactly that. It hurt like hell. It made me weep with misery. And it drove me to terrible depths of suffering. But I refused to deny it. I accepted it, felt it, and even hated it. But I allowed it to be there. I held fast to the knowledge that what the doctors and everyone else said was true: Things *would* get better, and so would the pain.

Time and again, I had to battle with the weak little voice inside me that squeaked and quaked: *I can't get through this. It hurts so much.* And I said to myself: *Yes you* can. *You can and you* will.

As the days went by, I learned through trial and error that I did have some power over the pain—and that this power was in my *mind.* I found that the intensity of my suffering could be altered, depending upon my attitude or perception of it. When I looked at the pain with a resentful, negative eye, it hurt all the more. But when I saw it as a sign of progress and healing, it didn't bother me quite so much. The hurt didn't go away, but its hold upon me was greatly reduced. In effect, I was learning to control *it*, rather than allowing it to control *me.*

I began to face the frequent, painful medical procedures with an entirely different attitude. I endured the injections, the burning medications, the removal of literally hundreds of stitches, the blood tests, all of it, by thinking to myself: *It hurts, but I can take it. All of this is helping me to get better.*

Of course I didn't automatically master this way of thinking. There were still many days when I couldn't muster the strength to control my perception of pain—when my mind would simply rebel against all the negative things that were happening to me. At times like that, I would howl and rage and fight the pain. And, unfortunately, this made it hurt even more.

I had to learn to work just as hard at coping with my emotional torment as I had at dealing with the physical suffering. The wounds in my head and heart could not be denied any more than could the deep gashes that marred my body. But learning to handle the pain in my body took away some of my anxiety. Regaining control by consciously altering my perception of the pain in both mind and body had a dramatic effect upon me. My overall condition—and state of mind—improved by leaps and bounds.

I found it helpful to be active, both mentally and physically. When my mind and—to a somewhat limited extent—my body were engaged in some productive activity, my focus was drawn away from the pain.

One of my most effective pain-relievers was the telephone. By speaking to a fresh voice (preferably a person completely disconnected from the world of hospitals and illness), I was, for a while, able to project my thoughts and concern into *their* reality. Sometimes, casual chatter was a pleasant and effective diversion. On other days I preferred to discuss business with my manager or agent, or to talk shop with actor friends.

Though I'd never been an avid television viewer, during my recuperation I found the "tube" could sometimes help me to re-direct my energies away from what hurt me. During those tedious hospital days, I often watched both the morning and the evening news programs. They helped in three ways: They took my mind away from my own troubles; they kept me abreast of what was going on "out there" and made me feel I was still a part of society; and they made me aware that *many* human beings—even entire nations—were suffering at least as much as I.

In the early days of my recovery period, when those empty hours stretched endlessly before me, I longed to read stacks and stacks of books—to lose myself in the world of literature. But unfortunately, in the early post-attack days the combination of drugs and pain made it extremely difficult for me to read. I asked my friends or family to read aloud amusing short stories, poems, or articles they found in current magazines and newspapers. When people discovered stories they thought I'd like but which were too long to read to me, they often clipped them out and placed them in a folder I kept for just this purpose. Then, when I was finally able to read on my own, I had quite a lot of interesting material to begin with.

Simple games were also diverting. I especially liked to play board games like Parcheesi or Scrabble, and card games like rummy or hearts. Instead of holding my "hand" in a fan, as one normally would when playing cards, I'd place them up against my arm cast or against one of my stuffed animals. When there weren't any visitors, I'd entertain myself with game after game of solitaire.

None of these little mental diversions was complicated; my mind was still too muddled for anything requiring lengthy, focused concentration. But the trick for me was to be able to direct my thoughts away from my hand, my chest, my head, or whatever else ailed me.

Soon after I was moved from ICU into a regular room, I began to regain a modicum of self-sufficiency. But it was limited by the physical pain which was now a ruling factor in my life; almost every part of me *hurt,* and as a result, my mobility was severely impaired.

There were many activities that would be impossible for me to do on my own for a long period of time. But there were still things I *could* do, right there and then, in spite of the injuries.

Trying to do even the most mundane, everyday tasks for myself became a challenge. My left arm was totally immobilized, and my right index finger was rather awkwardly splinted and bandaged. But with a lot of practice and patience (which, for me, have always been in short supply), I learned to use the four unharmed fingers on my right hand with remarkable dexterity.

When I needed a second "hand," I used my mouth to grasp objects like bobby pins or pencils. I had read books and seen movies about paralyzed people who had learned to be adept at all sorts of activities despite a nearly nonexistent level of mobility. And I found myself doing exactly the same thing. If my right hand was throbbing badly, I would use my mouth to pick up and hold various objects. If, when I did this, visitors looked at me with pity, I felt embarrassed, branded as a cripple. But *doing* for myself far outweighed my concern about what I looked like—or what anyone else thought about it.

Besides, the more I worked to accomplish physical tasks without assistance, the less time and inclination I had to give much thought to the pain itself. Engaging my mind and body in the process of retraining kept my pain and suffering level *down*.

Soon I'd learned to brush my hair and my teeth, apply makeup, dial and handle the telephone, button and tie my own pajamas, and cut my own food. And I felt elated. It was wonderful to perceive myself as functional, rather than as completely dependent.

As early as three weeks after the attack, I felt the urge to exercise. Because I've studied dance all my life, my leg muscles have become very developed. After a few weeks in the hospital, I noticed that the muscle tone in my calves and thighs was disappearing. Disliking their flaccid appearance, I asked Dr. Stein if I could do some moderate exercises. He quickly gave his approval but, with a twinkle in his eyes, warned me not to try leaping or pirouetting down the halls, lest I knock over some of the less agile patients.

So, right there in bed, with my arm still suspended in traction, I began to do a twice-daily series of leg exercises. In only a few days I saw a noticeable difference. And it made me feel great. As the weeks progressed I increased the number of repetitions of each exercise. In addition, I began to work out my right arm as well, flexing the upper-arm muscles, lifting small objects, and carefully rotating the arm as I'd learned to do in exercise classes.

When I exercised my legs and arm twice a day, I found that my overall physical pain and suffering was greatly diminished. Working on my body and coaxing it back toward health made me feel capable—in charge—and functional. In addition, the mild, pleasant physical exertion gave me a spiritual and emotional uplift. Moderate exercise was powerful medicine! I would later learn that by exercising I was forcing my body to release endorphins, which work as effective combatants to pain.

When my heavy cast was removed, I consulted with my

hand doctor and he approved a set of very mild exercises for my left arm. Because the muscles in that arm had atrophied from disuse, I initially did the exercises under the supervision of Phil, my physical therapist. In a short time, however, I was proficient enough to be trusted to do them on my own.

Once I was able to stand and walk steadily, I began to exercise in my room. Although Dr. Stein had approved of my regimen, I was afraid that the staff at Motion Picture would not. And so I did my exercises in private, closing the door and having Fred or my mom stand guard.

Fred even brought my leotards, dance slippers, and music tapes from home, and I began to do simple ballet warm-ups, clutching the back of a chair and using it as my barre.

I let my body be my guide and was careful not to jostle or disturb the injuries, which were still extremely sensitive. But these little private "classes" made me feel stronger, happier, and more at peace with myself.

I continued to dance during most of my stay at Motion Picture and thought of my ballet practice as a delicious secret. When Fred or my mom rapped on the door sharply two times, it meant "Someone's coming." Hastily, I tossed on my robe and popped into bed, covering my slippers with a blanket. None of the nurses ever saw me doing a single plié or stretch in my room, though a few of them commented on my sudden, prolonged passion for classical music.

By the end of my stay at Motion Picture, I had regained plenty of flexibility, muscle tone, and strength, particularly in my legs. And I felt delighted that I'd done it clandestinely. Then, my nurse and friend Jane handed me a goodbye note as I left the hospital. A few hours later, during my flight to New York, I read: "Theresa, J Wing will never forget your laughter, your big mouth, or your Jane Fonda-style workouts!" I had a really good laugh at that one, but I was touched that, for all those weeks, they'd let me do my exercises without badgering or teasing me.

As I look back now, I realize that after the hideous stabbing, I made an important choice: to embrace life and sanity rather than death or madness. And in so doing, I chose a path strewn with pain. But, at every point along the way, I knew that, no matter how hard it was, IT WAS WORTH IT.

I felt as though I'd won an important victory. I had certainly learned a great deal in the process. I saw that there was within me a well of human strength which, for lack of need, had been untapped. And I began to draw upon it every day.

I turned to God in prayer; I turned to friends and loved ones for support and encouragement; I leaned upon the comforts of pain medication; I sought the help of my psychiatrist; I tried methods that others who were traumatized had used; I devised various personal coping mechanisms of my own—and I lived through more pain than I had ever thought was possible.

Given my low tolerance for pain, which still plagues me to this day—ask my dentist!—I believe that if *I* can learn to cope with severe and prolonged suffering, just about *anyone* can.

THERAPY

Recently I had the privilege of meeting simultaneously with three experts in the field of pain management: Dr. Michael Scolaro, director of the Pain Rehabilitation Program (also known as "the Pain School" or "the Pain Center") at St. Vincent's Hospital in Los Angeles; Dr. Tom Kappeler, his associate at the clinic, whose background is in psychopharmacology (brain chemistry) and neurobiology; and Dr. Marjorie Toomim, director of the Biofeedback Institute in Los Angeles, California.

Dr. Scolaro began by giving me some background information about the Pain Rehabilitation Program: "It is a comprehensive, full-time, three-month program which treats chronic pain sufferers and helps to redirect them to a functioning, productive life. Patients at the center generally spend the first week in-hospital, and go through the remainder of the course as outpatients."

We agreed not only to discuss the specific methods of therapy employed at the clinic, but also to talk about pain itself: its physiological and psychological causes; its varying effects upon different individuals; and the cultural, sociological, and environmental factors that contribute to the experience of pain.

At the Pain School, it is part of the therapy to *learn about* pain. When patients develop an understanding of pain, they become much better equipped to learn to control and diminish their suffering. The program is specifically designed to treat chronic pain sufferers, people for whom the experience of pain and preoccupation with the illness, injury, or assault has become so intense that they are unable to function on a productive level. As soon as I heard some of the ideas and techniques employed by Drs. Scolaro and Kappeler, I realized that their methods could be beneficial for anyone who must live with some degree of temporary or chronic pain.

As soon as I met Dr. Scolaro, I understood why his patients respond so well to his advice and ministrations. A sprightly, energetic man, he radiates a sense of genuine interest, concern, and compassion for the people he treats. But I sensed that Dr. Scolaro is also a strong, firm leader who tempers his regard for his patients with the expectation that they will work tirelessly under his supervision.

His vast experience has taught him that people who are in pain have developed an attitude of helplessness and hopelessness about their plight. "Frequently," he explained, "they are so depressed about their greatly impaired physical abilities that they have stopped trying to perform even the most basic skills. Motivation is minimal, or even entirely lacking."

When patients first arrive at the Pain Center, Dr. Scolaro tells them, in no uncertain terms, that *they* must now become responsible for their own progress and recovery. Yes, they have been through a terrible ordeal—whether as the result of an illness, accident, or violent assault—but the fact remains: They are in pain, and only *they* can learn to work through it and go on with their lives. In order to do this, they must learn to help themselves.

Hearing Dr. Scolaro describe the importance of self-reliance in pain-management, I remembered that, back in the hospital, when I was in extreme pain, I felt a gnawing resentment toward others who were healthy. I wanted *them* to help me, to take care of me. Deep down, I believed that because I'd been so horribly and unjustly attacked, the world *owed* me something. My situation was unfair, the pain was miserable, and I wanted others to take it away or to do everything in their power to make life easier for me.

This seems to be a very common feeling among pain-sufferers. But according to Dr. Scolaro: "It's very important for people who are in pain to learn to accept their conditions, and then to recognize that, whether it is fair or not, they must learn to help themselves."

Dr. Scolaro continued: "The very first thing we tell patients, loud and clear, is that, no matter what agony they've been in—whether they've suffered for six months, two years, or even *ten* years—there is *hope*. There's life at the end of the tunnel. There's a window about to open.

"We tell them: 'You've been through a situation that has put you into a state of helplessness. You've reached your lowest ebb. And now, we represent another approach: an approach of *hope*. It's possible for all of you to learn to manage your pain and build your lives again.'

"It is really amazing! Sometimes, just holding out a verbal ray of sunshine and hope to an individual who has grown accustomed to negativity and helplessness can almost make the pain go away in a matter of moments."

Dr. Scolaro began with the *causes* of pain, saying: "Most of the time, people in pain can point to a specific physical cause [e.g., the actual accident, attack, or disease]. But in addition, cultural, sociological, and environmental factors may also be aggravating the condition. Because of this, patients at the Pain School are taken as a *whole*; their pain is looked at not only from the perspective of the original cause, but from that of all the other contributing factors as well."

When I asked Dr. Scolaro how doctors can judge a specific level of pain—severe, moderate, low—he told me that the major consideration at the center is: "How much does *this person's pain* disable, incapacitate, and emotionally debilitate him? How overwhelming is it? How far-reaching are the implications?"

At this point, Dr. Kappeler joined the conversation. His primary responsibility at the Pain Center is the evaluation of the biological functioning of each patient's brain, and its relationship to pain, anxiety, depression, and—ultimately—recovery.

Dr. Kappeler stressed the need for early intervention and psychological management—even if it is simply in the form of advice or a consultation—because it can make a dramatic difference in whether or not a given patient later becomes a chronic pain-sufferer. "It is important to address the issue of a given patient's pain and stress," Dr. Kappeler stated, "as well as how it makes him feel. Then, some sort of viable, personal way of coping with it on both a short-term and a long-term basis should be explored. If this is done soon after the attack or injury, the risk of his becoming a victim of chronic pain later on is greatly reduced."

The doctors pointed out many times that pain is really the sum total of many factors, and however it all adds up will determine the degree of suffering of an individual. Yet, how often have we heard people say things like "Oh, she's going on a bit too much about that arm of hers. When *I* broke *my* arm, I just put it in a cast and carried on as if nothing happened!" Or, "He is so ridiculous. He has a *cold*, not pneumonia." Or, in the case of a crime victim, how often have we heard remarks like, "For goodness' sakes, it's been *three years* since that attack. Don't tell me she's *still* agonizing over it!"

Dr. Kappeler addressed the issue of the added stress felt by victims of crime. "An unanticipated, vicious attack," he said, "is extremely stressful and can often lead a person to start living in a submissive state, or perhaps an anticipatory state, where they partly *expect* that something bad will happen. This condition lowers the pain threshold. Then, too, a person may begin to *hold on to* physical and psychological pain, in order to remind himself to stay alert and to guard against attack."

He made me remember my first weeks after my release from the hospital, when I once again began to walk out on the city streets. With my heart beating wildly and my thoughts racing, I walked quickly, clutching my bad arm stiffly to my body. Consumed with anxiety, I peered frantically in all directions, convinced that it was possible—or even likely—that I would be attacked at any moment.

My mind *and* body were tense, strained, and pain-filled. I was *on guard* with every muscle, nerve, and thought. As a result, any pain I felt—whether it was in my aching hand and fingers, my still-healing wounds, or my bruised and battered psyche—was greatly magnified.

Even in retrospect, it helped to hear that a reaction like this is common after a severe trauma like mine. Perhaps, if I could have examined my behavior at the time with this insight, I might have been able to adapt to it—or at least understand it—more readily.

Next, the doctors raised an issue I hadn't known was especially relevant to the experience of pain: philosophy. Most of us here in America have a decidedly Western philosophy. We tend not to accept things as they are, but to go out and change them. We are taught to believe that there are always many options open to us. We believe we can exert a strong element of control over our destinies, in matters great or small.

People who are raised under the influence of Eastern philosophy are often taught that only through *acceptance* of what happens can you learn to control your situation. The basic idea is that one changes the *self* in adaptation to circumstances, rather than trying to change the external world.

Dr. Scolaro said, "We've come to believe that because of this tendency to accept and adapt, an Easterner's tolerance for pain is often much higher than that of the Occidental. The Easterner feels his pain, accepts it as an unavoidable reality, and takes steps to adapt to it.

"When a Westerner is violently attacked, he quickly learns that there is absolutely no way to change what has happened; he has become a victim. There was no choice in the matter; no options were offered. There is no way to avoid or erase a certain degree of physical and/or psychological pain. Suddenly, the basic Western philosophy of 'If you don't like it, you can change it (as long as you work hard to do so)' is rendered invalid.

"The result is often an acute state of depression. And, in this weakened condition, we lose our tolerance for pain. Even relatively minor suffering becomes a psychologically significant reminder of defeat. And, as such, it hurts even more."

At the Pain Clinic, Drs. Scolaro and Kappeler force their patients to accept the trauma, to stop trying to deny it or make it disappear. The program is totally reality-oriented. Patients are constantly confronted with *the way it is*. They are not permitted to run away from obstacles, or to avoid tackling them. At the Pain School, coddling is not permitted. Patients are taught: "If you don't like something, you must change the way you *perceive* it—and then, make the best of a tough situation." In other words, the focus shifts to reducing their suffering by changing *themselves*.

There is no way a victim can control what has already happened. But he *can* control the degree to which he allows it to devastate him *afterward*. He can triumph by being active in his own rehabilitation and by refusing to give his pain the power to destroy his life.

Goal-setting is an important part of the Pain Rehabilitation Program, and can especially help people who must struggle on their own through a period of suffering. It can also help a pain sufferer to avoid the development of learned helplessness.

There are an unlimited number of goals a person in pain can choose to work toward. He can decide to regain the use of seriously damaged limbs, to go back to college in a wheelchair, to write a collection of poetry about his experience, to get active in his church or community, to do volunteer work, to adopt a pet and care for it himself, to be fitted for a prosthetic limb and wear it faithfully, to work with a seeing eye dog.

When a person sets a goal and begins to work toward it, he regains some control over his life. He accepts that he cannot change the past, that he can't make the trauma disappear. But he also takes on the challenge of rebuilding his mind and body in the aftermath. Goal-orientation serves to boost self-esteem and to increase the level of pain-tolerance because it takes the focus away from the pain and places it on the task at hand.

Dr. Toomim, director of the Biofeedback Institute, is a psychologist who believes in an integrated approach to therapy. She uses biofeedback and, when called for, psychotherapy, in the treatment of pain and stress disorders. Although her practice at the Biofeedback Institute includes a wide variety of clients, Dr. Toomim has had a great deal of experience with pain-sufferers and with crime victims who come to her with problems resulting from their attacks.

Dr. Toomim pointed out that "by using biofeedback instruments, a patient can *see* as well as feel the results of his efforts to relax muscles, dissipate spasms, and control the way he moves his body.

"Using biofeedback properly can give a person a sense of control over the body. And the equipment itself is merely the apparatus one uses in order to learn which techniques suit an individual best. Once a patient learns which methods help him most, he can then practice without the aid of the instruments."

As I learned during my own recovery, when a victim's mind is consumed by his trauma—the resultant pain or thoughts of the perpetrator—it becomes even harder for him to make a physical and emotional recovery. Biofeedback can give a victim a completely new focus by directing his attention to a living graph of his own tensions and body functions. Then the victim can begin to concentrate upon achievement and positive results in the present, rather than on the unpleasant and disturbing past.

Dr. Toomim explained: "With the help of the biofeedback instrumentation, a patient can learn to notice when he is excited or agitated, as opposed to being relaxed. Then the patient can train his body to produce a different appropriate response, just as we learn to type, swim, or do anything else. He can learn to use healing and relaxation techniques to reduce both stress and suffering.

"Moderate exercise can certainly be very beneficial for pain patients," Dr. Toomim said. "But it helps to use biofeedback to determine how *much* exercise is beneficial for an individual patient. When muscles aren't strong enough and are suddenly overworked, they can go into spasm. The result will be even more pain. If a patient is monitored, he can learn to move very slowly and gently up to the point where he's about to go into spasm. Then, when he sees his stress level rising, he can stop, stretch, and perhaps work it just a bit more.

"It's important to work with a pain patient on both a physical *and* emotional level," she continued. "As we help him learn to be able to think of his trauma and yet keep relaxed, the patient can actually *see* the results on the monitor and say, 'Wait a minute—my hands got cold when I talked about that issue. Let me go back and try again. What can I do to make it different? How can I control it?'

"So, essentially, we're using the body to decondition fear, stress, and pain. Some of it is simple behavior modification and some of it is altering how you *think* about it in order to reduce suffering."

*   *   *

During my attack, I'd incurred a pinched nerve which later caused a great deal of pain, stress, and tension in my neck, back, and shoulders. I could never seem to get completely comfortable. Even today, my neck and shoulders still tend to be stiff and tense. Often I roll my head from side to side or massage my shoulders with my fingertips in an effort to soothe the soreness.

Dr. Toomim noticed me doing this and offered to give me a biofeedback demonstration. She placed me in a comfortable chair, rolled out the equipment, and attached little sensors to both sides of my neck and shoulders. After turning on the machine, Dr. Toomim pointed out the areas we would concentrate on and showed me the numbers that indicated the stress levels on those parts of my body. Not surprisingly, the level of tension there was quite high.

Next, she asked me to roll my head around, doing the exercise I did frequently to try to release the tension. *Up* went the numbers: The feedback clearly showed that rolling my head *added* to the stress. Dr. Toomim told me to try moving my head back and forth *slowly*. I did so a few times and the stress numbers decreased. It was quite exciting to see exactly how my body was affected by my actions.

Next, I tried massaging my shoulder. As I did, I noticed that I was pressing my shoulder *up* against my fingers. And once again, as I performed my customary "pressure-relief" action, the tension level shot way up.

"Well, I guess I'm doing everything wrong," I said.

"That's true, but up until now you didn't have any proof, did you?" Dr. Toomim replied.

We tried a few simple shoulder exercises and found that what worked best for me was to press my shoulders *down* and let my arms dangle loosely.

Next, we tried the technique of visualization in an effort to get my neck and shoulder muscles to relax. First, Dr. Toomim told me she wanted to show me how energy would affect my muscles.

"Think of something absolutely terrible," she said.

The first unpleasant thought that jumped into my head

was *I have to do my taxes this week.* Ouch! I felt a twinge in my neck, and the numbers on the monitor started to creep upward.

Dr. Toomim said, "Think of something even *worse.*"

And so I thought about the fact that the man who stabbed me will serve only six years in prison. Eyes squeezed tightly shut, I fumed to myself: *It's disgusting! It's just not fair.* Then I heard Dr. Toomim say, "My! You're very angry about something. Look!"

I opened my eyes and saw that the stress numbers had *rocketed.*

"Okay now," said Dr. Toomim, "let's think of something *nice.*"

Gratefully, I focused my thoughts on pretty trees, flowing brooks, grassy slopes. The numbers scarcely moved. Dr. Toomim shrugged. "Try again."

Thinking that my mental images might be too general, I closed my eyes again and thought of one of my favorite places on earth: the Villa D'Este in Tivoli, Italy. I imagined myself standing there amid the splendor. The beautiful fountains and rushing water were everywhere. A soft breeze tickled my face. The sun warmed the top of my head. It was heavenly.

Dr. Toomim murmured, "Look at the numbers now." I glanced up and saw that the stress levels had dropped at least ten points in each of my "trouble areas." I was amazed.

"Hey, this is fun," I said.

"Of course it is," she answered. "All the patients like it. It's hard to feel helpless when you're seeing proof of your own power right in front of you, isn't it?"

I couldn't agree more. In just a few minutes, I'd been able to see what worked for me—and what didn't. The process was simple and pleasant, and the results were utterly concrete. There was no hocus-pocus; the numbers on the monitor didn't lie!

It felt wonderful to have proof that positive energy *works.* And, for a victim who's feeling helpless and depressed after an attack, I truly believe that biofeedback would be an excellent therapeutic tool.

Next on the agenda at my meeting with the "pain professionals" was a discussion of endorphins and how they affect one's level of pain tolerance. Endorphins are one of a group of opiatelike substances produced naturally by the body in the central nervous system. They raise the pain threshold and produce sedation and a sense of euphoria.

For each new patient who enters the Pain School, the goal is to increase the production of endorphins in order to decrease the patient's suffering. Drs. Scolaro and Kappeler explained that during the physical trauma itself, and directly after it, a person excretes and utilizes endogenous morphine compounds, which protect him from acute pain and acute psychological suffering. His level of tolerance for pain, therefore, is greatly increased. As production of endorphins and adrenaline escalates, his concentration is primed for *survival*. Vigilance and ability to think quickly are greatly increased.

Later, when the crisis is over, there is a major change. As the victim feels his plight and his pain, and realizes that his circumstances are inalterable, his pain tolerance level declines. Even his immune system will be in a state of stress. He may develop infections or see himself as "falling apart." He may be unable to sleep or to eat.

The disease or injury may now be medically quiescent— meaning that the patient will not die from the trauma and that his medical condition is under control—but nevertheless, he may be experiencing severe, crippling pain.

At this point, the patient is most depleted in endorphins. He doesn't have the neurobiological chemicals he needs in order to sleep well, eat well, have a normal sex life, and experience hope and joy. This state of depletion is accompanied by severe depression; the patient may see no end to his misery, may feel totally without rewards, and completely helpless. In this condition, he will have far less tolerance for pain.

Dr. Kappeler believes that depression can be seen as much from a biological or neurobiological perspective as from a psychological one. "Most patients upon admission to the Pain Program are not producing endorphins," he said. "So, from a physical, medical-biological, and psychological perspective, we try to *in*crease their endorphins in order to *de*crease their pain. This is done in a variety of ways.

"Patients are encouraged to be active in their physical and

emotional rehabilitation, to meditate, to learn about the body and its functions and to exercise vigorously each day."

"When a pain sufferer is forced to *move*," interjected Dr. Toomim, "a certain degree of discomfort is to be expected. And in response to that, the body is forced to develop endorphins."

Every patient at the clinic participates in activities like bicycling, walking on treadmills, and playing active games. The patients are told that what they're doing is as important as preparing for the Olympics. And it actually *is*.

"We tell our patients," Dr. Scolaro explained, "that there *is* an escape hatch or window open to them—a way out of their pain. But in order to get to it, they must make a major, concerted effort toward physical and emotional rehabilitation.

"One of the things we know about opiates," he said, "whether they are internal [e.g., endorphins] or external [e.g., morphine] is that people get tolerant to them very quickly.

"In order for a natural opiate to work, it must be able to attach to a nerve cell, which will be its receptor. The nerve cell adapts to the endorphin very quickly. Therefore, the endorphins work only for a few hours or days, and then your capacity to deal with pain in that manner peaks."

The process of endorphin production is important to understand, for it reminds us that there *is* a biological factor involved in severe, chronic pain. But we must also put efforts into beginning active psychological intervention too.

"Another factor in pain management which is almost universally accepted," said Dr. Scolaro, "is group dynamics. Pain patients share a common bond and—à la Alcoholics Anonymous—can offer each other support and advice based on their own personal experiences with pain."

Dr. Toomim agreed and added, "It's *very* important to reinforce *well* behavior rather than pained behavior. All steps toward activity and wellness should be responded to with positive, enthusiastic support.

"A *good* response on the part of a pain patient's friend or relative would be: 'Hey! It's wonderful you got out of bed today. Why don't you take this dish back to the kitchen?' Rather than: 'Oh, you stay right there. I'll take your dish for you.' "

Dr. Scolaro nodded emphatically. "Exactly! And when we

begin to reward *wellness* rather than *pained* behavior, we helpers must be able to take a lot of resistance, hostility, and anger from the people who come to us for help. Many of them have grown used to being cared for. Now they learn that, in order to regain control and reduce their suffering, they must first become responsible for themselves. This can be a pretty difficult adjustment for them to make.

"In most hospitals, a nurse brings breakfast and says, 'Here, dear, how are you this morning?' At the Pain School, our nurses say, 'You're late for breakfast. Hurry up!'

"We ask all our patients: 'What do you want to do when you graduate from the Pain School?' And we urge them to think about their future employment as productive individuals. Not all of them can get back to doing what they did before, because some patients have lost limbs or are paralyzed or badly maimed. But they are all asked to set goals for themselves and then they're encouraged to go after them.

"We intersperse exercise sessions throughout the day, and you'd be amazed at how physically active the handicapped can be. It's good for their bodies *and* spirits. We also have group sessions, called 'Stress Management,' where the patients talk about everything and anything. They help each other over various hurdles and discuss ways of handling their anxiety and pain.

"There are lectures on the body itself. We place a lot of concentration on giving our patients an understanding of the body: how it moves, what the nerves do, et cetera. The body seems more *manageable* when you can comprehend the mechanics of it.

"Each day, we hold 'pain management' sessions, which might include biofeedback, meditation, and muscle relaxation training.

"Through guided imagery or visualization, we teach them to relax each of the muscle groups. Patients report dramatic reductions of pain after these sessions. In addition to the regularly scheduled activities, medical treatment is also included during the day for those who need it.

"After seven to ten days, our students graduate from the in-hospital portion of the program and are thrust into a pattern of getting up at five-thirty A.M. on their own, traveling from their homes, and 'going to work,' as we refer to it."

I was curious about what happens at the close of the course and was interested to hear that treatment at the Pain School never comes to an abrupt end. After the three-month program, patients are given much-needed reinforcement. Amazing results have been achieved. Dr. Scolaro exclaimed, "Miracles *do* happen. We say to our patients: 'Accept the fact that you may never walk again, but let's work on those legs as hard as we possibly can. There are always new medical techniques in development. All kinds of breakthroughs regarding your condition may be just around the corner!'

"We've had patients with spinal cord injuries who were theoretically paralyzed for the rest of their lives. Some of them have learned to drive a car, live in their own apartments, and walk on their own two legs again!"

"Do people get depressed at the end of the course?" I asked Dr. Scolaro.

"Of course, absolutely," he replied. "There's a natural let-down feeling which patients in our program experience as they complete the main section of the course. But we don't really ever end; we say, 'You've graduated from the program.' But then we encourage them to attend open meetings once or twice a week at no charge. At these gatherings they meet new people who enter the program and they maintain contact with us for reinforcement.

"Over the years," continued Dr. Scolaro, "only five to ten percent have gone back to the original state of pain they were in before going through the program. Often, these are the patients who either didn't maintain some sort of connection to the school or didn't continue to practice aggressive pain management techniques on their own. It's easy to regress back to your old habits if you don't continue to practice new and better ones."

Dr. Scolaro added, "What the Pain Center does is to take disabled individuals who are nonfunctional and bring them to the point where they're sufficiently rehabilitated to say, 'Now, the doors are open. Life is starting again!' "

I asked Dr. Scolaro: "If a crime victim is in pain, at what point would you advise him to go to a Pain Clinic?"

"A crime victim," he responded, "should consider a comprehensive pain program such as ours when he has reached a state where his pain and his preoccupation with the assault are such that, over a prolonged period, the ability to function is severely impaired or entirely destroyed."

So, even for crime victims who feel there is no way out, that the pain they're experiencing is insurmountable, that their lives have been rendered utterly useless, there is definitely *hope:* At the Pain Rehabilitation Program in Los Angeles, and at various similar centers, *help is available.*

For the rest of us, many tools are at our disposal: psychotherapy, group therapy, exercise, meditation, visualization and relaxation techniques, biofeedback, and much, much more.

Pain hurts. And it can disrupt and alter our lives. But thankfully, there *are* safe, effective ways to find relief. Therapy can help us to work through our pain and return to enjoyment of life again.

FORWARD THINKING

One of the most unpleasant aspects of pain is its tendency to overwhelm the senses. It sticks to us like glue; it saturates us, permeates us, oppresses us, hounds us, and, when we're in its clutches, never seems to let us go. We will try just about anything to make it stop, or to get our minds away from it for a while.

After interviewing many pain-sufferers, I've come to see that the vast majority find at least some degree of relief by practicing their own personal versions of forward thinking.

It was a warm, sunny Saturday morning. Nick Otis, a lighting designer and engineer, was puttering around his lovely New England home. Nick is a tall, strong, distinguished-looking divorcé who appears far younger than his fifty years. He has always taken pride in his own resourcefulness and ability to handle most situations.

The doorbell rang and Nick went to open it. Two clean-cut men in their twenties stood on his front porch. They explained that they worked for a local newspaper, *The Daily Chronicle,* and were trying to locate a particular subscriber, a Mr. Carlson, who lived on that street.

Then, without warning, one of the men shoved Nick roughly away from the doorway. As he dropped back, a gun went off and a bullet cut through Nick's left arm and into his chest. Thinking quickly, Nick retreated into the next room and picked up an old .22 revolver. His only thought was to fight back, to preserve his own life. Moving into the doorway connecting the rooms, he shot at the assailants but they quickly returned fire. BLAM! BLAM!— their two shots rang out. One crashed through his right elbow. The other bored through his right upper arm. Nick felt the entire arm go dead. He pulled his own weapon out of his useless right hand and began firing with his left, at point-blank range. He still remembers the look of surprise on the faces of the gunmen. Hurriedly they fled, escaping in their car.

Nick managed to slam the door shut and drag himself to the telephone. It seemed to take forever to dial the paramedics, since his blood was flowing profusely, covering the numbers on the telephone. After completing the call, Nick leaned against the wall and slid slowly down. Numb and disoriented, he crouched there, staring ahead, until the police arrived. Then suddenly the numbness went away and pain set in—searing into his right arm. The paramedics rushed onto the scene and immediately directed their attention to the chest wound. But the most harrowing pain was coming from Nick's mangled, bullet-ridden right arm.

Nick cried out, begging the paramedics to splint or immobilize the limb. But at that moment, their only concern was to save Nick's life. Heedlessly, they continued to attend to his chest, their every movement jostling the wretched arm and sending him into spasms again.

Soon the paramedics were rushing him toward the waiting ambulance. Nick remembers screaming on the gurney as they ran with him, bouncing the right arm all the while; it was his first memory of ever screaming aloud from pain.

Minutes later the ambulance arrived at a nearby trauma center. The doctors worked frantically on Nick. One bullet had entered his chest under the arm, passed his spinal column, and missed his heart by only one-half inch. Another had

smashed in and out of his right elbow. The third had completely shattered the bone and destroyed most of the muscles
and nerves in Nick's upper right arm.

A top-notch surgeon, Dr. Brinkley, was called in. He
suggested amputating the right arm, since it was so badly
ripped apart. "I doubt that you'll get any use out of this arm,
Mr. Otis," Dr. Brinkley said.

But Nick refused. "No way," was his only response.

One bullet was now lodged in Nick's chest cavity and he
was bleeding internally. Dr. Brinkley decided to do thoracic
surgery in order to stabilize the situation. He also elected to
operate on the wounded arm, since Nick would not allow
him to amputate.

Many hours later, Nick awoke in ICU. His chest had been
surgically opened in order to repair the internal damage; he
now had a "zipper" scar. And his right arm was encased in a
huge cast from shoulder to wrist.

For three days Nick drifted in and out of consciousness in
ICU. Then he was moved to a regular recovery room for a
week. He was so heavily medicated that the physical pain
seemed distant, as though it belonged to someone else. But he
was haunted by terrible uncertainty about his arm: No one
knew how much, if any, movement would return. It was
possible that the nerves were dead and that it would never
move at all. There was no way to find out until after the cast
was removed, ninety days hence.

Ten days after the shooting, Nick Otis was released from
the hospital. He spent five days at his parents' home, sleeping
fitfully night and day before he felt strong enough to return to
his own house. The first thing Nick did at home was to clean
up his own blood, which seemed to be everywhere, a dark
reminder of the worst day of his life. There, in his own house,
the full impact of his ordeal finally hit. Nick braced himself for
the coming months, knowing he would be forced to do battle
with pain, fatigue, and depression.

The attack was not Nick's first brush with near-death and
trauma. In 1974, while he was working as a lighting technician
on the *Barnaby Jones* TV show, a scaffolding he was walking
across collapsed. Nick fell into a concrete pit and suffered a
severe spinal injury. Because of a herniated disc, doctors feared

that paralysis might result. In 1975 and again in 1976, Nick had spinal surgery.

The delicate operations took their toll: Following the second surgery, Nick developed chronic pain in his skull area and back; it was brutal, relentless, and constant. For two years Nick endured the agony, until he felt he could bear it no longer. Nick's surgeon referred him to a psychiatrist who worked with him for a year. Although Nick found the therapy helpful, the pain continued to plague him. Finally the psychiatrist referred Nick to Dr. Scolaro's Pain Rehabilitation Program at St. Vincent's Hospital.

Today, Nick says that he'd definitely suggest a comprehensive pain program for a victim of crime or anyone else who finds himself at the end of his rope. "Once you've tried to cope with it on your own for a good period of time and have realized that you are still in chronic, uncontrollable pain, despite your best efforts," says Nick, "then it's time to seek help from professionals."

After the shooting, once Nick was back in his own home, sensation returned to his body. Every part of him was sore, stiff, inflamed. He couldn't move at all without pain, so he kept himself immobilized.

"I basically knew that most of the pain in my body came from the stress and trauma it had gone through," Nick told me recently. "And some of it was a reaction to all the anesthesia and medication. But luckily, I realized that most of it was *transitory*.

"I knew that at the moment I was in a lousy, pain-filled reality. But thankfully, other than my arm and hand, my body was on its way to recovery. So I spent a lot of time looking forward to the time when much of my pain would be gone.

"I remembered the visualization techniques and the goal-setting we'd worked on at the Pain School, and I decided to put it to use again. And so I set a short-term goal for myself: to be up and about the neighborhood within fourteen days. I created a mental image of myself walking around and moving painlessly—and I affirmed that I could do it. In my mind's eye I saw myself out of bed, strolling outside, enjoying the fresh air, talking to my neighbors, shopping for groceries, et cetera.

"Within a week, just as I'd thought, a lot of the pain had

slacked off. And only nine days after I'd gone home, I went for my first walk. Sure, I still felt tender and a little shaky, but I wasn't suffering terribly. The mild exercise of walking about was therapeutic. And frankly, I was tired of being an invalid."

The aches and pains in most parts of Nick's body subsided fairly quickly, but the mental anguish about whether his arm would be functional gnawed at him.

Nick spent the next three months building up his strength both physically and mentally, projecting his thoughts ahead to the day when his arm would be free of the cast. He always imagined it *moving*. When depression or terror threatened to engulf him, Nick fought back and set his mind toward the future: His arm would work; it would function; it would eventually *heal*.

When ninety days had passed, Nick's cast was finally removed. The arm was totally dead; there was no movement at all. His elbow was wooden, fixed rigidly in the crooked position of the cast. Nick stared at the pale, flaccid limb as though it belonged to someone else.

For the next few weeks, Nick fought desperately to keep from sinking into a state of catatonic despair. Luckily, he trusted his doctor and kept up the hope that an operation would help.

One month later, exploratory surgery was performed. The surgeon opened the top of Nick's arm and dug the nerves out from within a calcium sleeve that had formed—nature's way of protecting the shattered bone. They also removed the bullet.

Though his wrist hung limply and his hand was completely paralyzed, Nick pushed himself to the limit in physical therapy and slowly regained a bit of movement in his elbow. Then, abruptly, all progress ceased.

But at the Pain School, Nick had learned that it often takes eighteen months or longer for nerves to regenerate. Knowing this helped him to continue his therapy.

Nick refused to accept defeat. The injured muscles and tendons caused his hand to curl up into what is commonly called "wrist drop." Yet he persisted in working the muscles and trying to get them to move. No matter what Nick was doing, if his hand was free, he tried to coax some motion into it. He imagined himself pounding a nail, swinging a bat, playing tennis, hanging lights, chopping wood: all the activities he'd done before and firmly believed he'd do again.

One evening, a year and a half after the attack, Nick was working his hand as he watched a television show, when up came that limp, hitherto lifeless wrist. He could hardly believe it. The arm had no strength, but at least there was a bit of movement. He began to work the hand and wrist harder still.

Nick went for further surgery. The doctors transplanted nerves from the bottom of his hand to help the ones on top.

After this operation, Nick developed an entirely *new* relationship with pain, one that few people experience. He actually *looked forward* to it, *hoping* to feel it—the more pain, the better.

Within a few weeks, a mild tingling developed in Nick's arm—clear proof that the nerve transplant had worked. Then, finally, the arm began to hurt—really hurt. As far as Nick was concerned, this was a lucky turn of events.

Recently, Nick had yet another operation. Now, when pain kicks up in that hand or arm, Nick *loves* it. Sometimes, he feels a prickly, burning feeling. It is a decidedly unpleasant and strange sensation, but to Nick Otis, it feels like heaven. This burning pain lets him know that his arm and hand are still alive. "It hurts so *good*," Nick says today.

"I'm lucky to have gone through the Pain School," Nick said. "The staff there taught me an invaluable lesson: If you dwell on pain and disability, your life will *be* pain and disability. One way I deal with the pain I feel now is to think of the situation as transitory. I know that if I work hard enough, I'll be out of all this someday."

Nick finds that it helps to concentrate on what he *can* do, despite the severely limited use of his arm.

"After many months of intense therapy, I am finally able to write with my right hand," Nick said recently. "It's a bit shaky, but I can *do* it."

"What's your secret? What do you think is helping you to become functional again?" I asked him, as a final question.

"Well," he responded, "I keep a mental image of my hand just as it used to be—strong, powerful, and active. And I envision a time when I'll be able to pound nails again, to use a handsaw, and do all those physical things I used to do. The image I keep in my head isn't of a shattered arm but a healthy one. I visualize myself doing all sorts of things with my hand again. Visualization is vital. So is imagining a healthier future."

FORWARD THINKING

Edith Varsay, a successful Miami attorney, is a vibrant, independent, self-made woman. At thirty-five, she is one of the most well-respected people in her field. Creative and articulate, with a keen wit and a strong sense of optimism, Edith has a genuine "take charge" personality.

Not long ago, Edith lived through a stabbing attack as painful as it was shocking. Edith had known Willy Orsini for most of his twenty-three years. The son of Edith's best friend, Yvonne, Willy was always a troubled boy. But he considered Edith his friend and mentor, often turning to her for advice and support.

As he grew up, Willy's problems became worse and his behavior grew progressively more violent and obsessive. He had been in and out of mental hospitals and, over the past few years, had been arrested for a variety of crimes, some of them involving violence.

In November 1984, Willy broke into Edith's house and stole a number of valuables. When she confronted him with what he'd done, he became enraged and threatened to kill her if she called the police. Judging from Willy's present threatening and irrational behavior, Edith felt he was fully capable of murder.

She called the police, who arrested Willy for the burglary. While incarcerated, the young man called Edith a number of times, again threatening to kill her. Edith knew he was dead serious.

She reported Willy's threats to the authorities. Yet, days later, despite his record of violence and mental illness and despite the ongoing telephone threats, Willy was released *on his own recognizance.*

On November 20, Edith left work and returned to the small, lovely home she'd bought for herself in a quiet beachfront community. She entered the house and went upstairs to her bedroom.

Willy, wielding a large butcher knife, rushed out at her. They wrestled and she fought him with all her might, pulling him to the floor and biting his arm deeply. Willy pulled his arm away and Edith raced down the stairs. He followed close on her heels and forcefully plunged the blade into Edith's side.

Agonized, she pulled the knife out of her body and ran out the front door, screaming, "Help me! Help me! I've been stabbed." Then she fainted in the driveway. Seconds later, Willy ran past her and escaped on foot.

Neighbors rushed out to try to help. Edith regained consciousness when the police and paramedics arrived. They bound her midsection with a wrenchingly tight tourniquet. She howled miserably. The pain, both from the wound and from the pressure of the tourniquet, was unbearable. Blood was gushing out. Edith felt as though she were trapped in a horrible nightmare.

The searing pain grew even more intense. During the ambulance ride, Edith kept nodding off. Each time, the attendants jostled her awake, calling out her name. Every return to full consciousness meant being confronted with still more pain. She asked repeatedly, "Am I going to die?", and they quickly, but unconvincingly, responded, "No."

In the emergency room, Edith was prepped for surgery. The enormous pressure of the tourniquet was driving her mad. She felt it was crushing her to death. Finally they brought her into the operating room and pumped her full of anesthetic. Gratefully she lapsed into unconsciousness.

When Edith woke up in ICU, she felt groggy and confused. Then there was a mighty onrush of pain in her side, reminding her of what had happened. Unable to speak because of the tubes down her throat, Edith moaned. A sweet young nurse came close to the bed, handed Edith a memo pad, and helped her to hold a pencil. Oddly enough, the first thing Edith did was to write a note about one of her clients.

The nurse looked down at the pad and called Edith a "miracle girl." She told Edith that her lung had been punctured and that part of her liver had been severed. "It's amazing!" the girl exclaimed. "They transfused you with fifty units of blood!"

Edith stared at the nurse, her mouth agape.

"But you're doing beautifully now, just beautifully," said the young nurse. "Don't worry about a thing. We're taking care of you now. You're just fine." Edith, comforted, drifted off into a restless, drugged sleep.

Minutes later, unbeknownst to Edith, the doctors told her close friends that she now had only a 2 percent chance of living. They were amazed she'd survived at all and had not lapsed into a coma. The doctors said the damage was so severe that the risk of complication was enormous.

But by the end of the first week after the attack, the doctors amended their prediction to 5 percent. After that, they realized that Edith had beaten the odds.

Her first few days were filled with pain, sleep, pain, and sleep. Visitors came in and out, but Edith had little real awareness of them. Her only thoughts were to get through to the next shot—and *to be safe.* For days after the attack, Edith was terrified that Willy, who'd not yet been apprehended, would find her there in the hospital and finish what he'd set out to do.

She had an added pressure: concern for Willy's mother, her best friend, Yvonne Orsini. Edith asked another close friend, Zoe, to call Yvonne and reassure her that the attack wasn't her fault, that Edith was still her friend.

Whenever Zoe visited, Edith asked, "Did they find Willy?" Each time she heard the words *not yet,* spasms of fear shot through Edith's entire body. Five days later they finally caught him. And Edith was able to feel more at peace. At least she was safe for a while. The authorities assured her that Willy would not get out on bail.

Now Edith could concentrate on getting well. A fiercely independent woman, she hated being hooked up to so many machines. And her lack of control over even the simplest personal task made her furious.

Recently Edith told me: "The physical agony I was going through was something I'd never experienced before. I felt like there was a phonograph record in my mind screeching 'I'm in pain, I'm in pain' all the time and the needle was stuck on that spot. I knew that somehow I had to get it *un*stuck or it would drive me nuts.

"When I was really hurting," she continued, "and that

pain recording in my head spun round and round, I tried to place my thoughts on the *good* things I had: a flourishing law career, wonderful friends, a house I loved, a fine social life. I didn't want this crazy incident and the sheer physical anguish which resulted from it to destroy everything I've worked so hard to build. I told myself countless times that I'd suffered through the worst part and that I was a winner, not a weak little defeatist.

"I know that the single most important thing I did for myself," Edith said emphatically, "was to project my thoughts as far from my current miserable reality as possible.

"The last place I wanted to be was *there* in that dreary hospital. And the last thing I wanted to feel was pain. So I kept thinking about the life I was *going* to have. The people I was *going* to see, and the sheer physical comfort I was *going* to feel. I've always known that I'm a strong lady and I knew I'd recover. I tried to think of myself in terms of the future.

"I imagined myself to be:

WELL — not sick

COMFORTABLE — not pained

STRONG — not weak

"I also trained myself to think in opposites, at least where my problems were concerned. If I felt rotten, I made myself think quietly: *Edith, soon you'll feel wonderful.* If my muscles were tense and cramped, I'd think: *Soon they'll feel relaxed and soothed.* I let myself experience the present pain, but I never allowed myself to think of it as permanent."

Edith reminded herself constantly that, as much as she hurt, the pain was transitory. Thankfully, the doctors told her she was making swift, steady progress.

She found that thinking about going home to the house she loved and the profession she excelled in took her mind off the pain and horror of the moment and refocused it upon her healthy, pain-free future.

"There's really not a whole lot you can *do* about pain, other than accept it, bear with it, and let them give you drugs to ease its hold on you," Edith explained. "But it really can help to put your mind someplace far removed from that monotonous boring hospital life.

"Sure," Edith said recently, "I could've lain there and thought over and over again: *I've been stabbed by my best friend's kid, whom I've always been good to. Part of my liver is gone. I'm scarred for life. I will probably need more surgery. My medical bills are astronomical. None of this is fair. I'm in agony. I feel like dying.* And that was all *true.* But where would these terrible thoughts have gotten me? I would've been more anguished, more depressed, and more hurt. So whenever I found my mind heading off in that dreary direction, I reminded myself to *keep looking ahead.* In the sorry state I was in, I could be pretty sure that things were bound to improve."

The most important thing Edith focused upon was going home. She spent hours picturing her beloved dog and her two cats, and imagining what it would be like to curl up on her warm velvet couch, near a roaring, comforting fire. She asked her friend Zoe to bring her favorite soft, heart-shaped pillow and her beautiful down comforter to the hospital and she was soothed by the presence of these familiar items. Even when she slept, she dreamed of being there in her cozy little house again. With typical wit, Edith says now, "I felt like Dorothy in *The Wizard of Oz*—all I could say, think, or even dream was: 'There's no place like home! There's no place like home!'

"I often projected my thoughts forward to a very specific point in time. For example, if I couldn't fall asleep in that narrow, cagelike hospital bed, I'd think to myself, *In ten days, I'll be in my own bed, with my dog and cats snuggled up beside me.* It helped me to relax and get a little rest because I saw an *end* in sight. When I thought about post-hospital events and situations, I was, at least in my own mind, beginning to return to my real life."

In addition to her other injuries, Edith had a pinched nerve. As a result, her neck and shoulders ached constantly. When the nurses weren't too busy, they gave her massages to ease the pain.

Edith's friend Zoe had a great idea: She went to a local health club and purchased a card which would be good for a series of four professional massages. One day when Edith was feeling especially stiff and sore, Zoe presented her with the card. Edith laughed and hugged her girlfriend. And during the following weeks, she thought so much about those deep, soothing massages she'd get that she could practically *feel* the masseur's hands expertly kneading and relaxing her aching back.

"I fantasized about those massages so much that *no* masseur could ever live up to my expectations," Edith confided. "When I was finally able to use the card, I discovered that some of the nurses who'd been rubbing me were more expert and sensitive than the pros turned out to be. But those thought-projections were delicious!"

Edith loved her law practice. And so she spent time imagining and planning for her return to professional life. She missed both her colleagues and her clients.

As soon as Edith felt up to it, she asked her partner to bring her some work from the office. She also worked on future ideas by telephone. She called and apprised certain long-term clients of her condition and actually gave them verbal consultations.

"I rarely felt much pain when I was *working* in the hospital— and a lot of my practice consists of telephone contacts anyway. Of course, occasionally I was a bit dopey and forgetful because of the medication. But the hours of work I was able to do did me a world of good."

In her mind's eye Edith pictured her law office. As she envisioned it, she came to a decision to change it. Not being the wait-and-see type, Edith summoned a local decorator to visit her in the hospital. He brought swatches of fabric and lots of ideas. She made a few selections and asked for more sketches and plans. By the time Edith returned to work, the decorator had nearly completed the office changeover.

Now she has a bright, beautiful, ultramodern office. "I'd wanted to redo the place for months, but simply didn't have the time," Edith said. "So, while I was lying there in the hospital, I put lots of energy into making color and fabric selections and looking at magazines for ideas. I wasn't just *thinking* about the future—I was actually *doing* something. And I didn't make any major mistakes, either. I really love the way the office looks now. When my clients comment on how much they like the decor, I sometimes tell them a bit of the story. They usually get a big kick out of it."

When the doctors performed painful or uncomfortable procedures on Edith, she tried her best to get her head out of the present. She loves handmade jewelry and would dream up beautiful, exotic pieces she could have an artisan friend make up.

"It was pretty bizarre," she says now. "At times, the doctor would be putting in or pulling out a chest drainage tube. And I'd be lying there, my head spinning with ideas for a snazzy jeweled belt or a great clunky bracelet. But anything was better than concentrating on the painful, oppressive *now*. These simple mind-images didn't stop the pain. But at least they were a diversion."

Edith managed to persuade her doctor to discharge her after only three weeks. It was a remarkably short hospital stay, considering the extent of her injuries.

"That attack and my recuperation were nightmarish," Edith told me. "The pain, the fear, and the frustration combined to make me feel as though I was in hell. But I also gained a much deeper appreciation for life because I came so close to death. I realized I'm quite a lucky girl. I enjoy career success, a comfortable financial situation, a pretty home, friends who love me. Not everyone gets an opportunity to stand back and examine their life. I was able to do that. And I saw that my own fantasies, which I clung to during that painful recovery period, were simply thoughts of the real, day-to-day life I've led all along. They sustained me through my suffering and now I'm actually living that dreamy, comfortable, mostly painless existence. I can honestly say I feel like a lucky lady just to *be here* today."

After talking to many crime victims, I've been convinced that most of them can find some relief from an odious, untenable, pain-racked present by concentrating and planning toward a better time to come. Simple? Yes. But very, very effective.

REACHING OUT TO OTHERS

Soon after my attack, I was faced with the grim realization that I would never be completely free of scars again. But I refused to live the rest of my life with the brutal-looking, haphazard, crescent-shaped reminders of that horrendous day.

And so, six months after the attack, I began my quest for a plastic surgeon who would replace the knife wounds with neat, slender, unobtrusive surgical incisions. Living in L.A. was a terrific bonus: Cosmetic surgeons abounded! I dragged my sister, Maria, all over the plastic-surgeon circuit: Beverly Hills, Encino, Sherman Oaks, Santa Monica, Hollywood, and beyond. I consulted more than a dozen of the most prominent specialists in the field. Eventually, I decided upon Dr. Harold Clavin, who'd been highly recommended by a trusted friend. Dr. Clavin was young but very respected, and I liked his attitude: He completely understood my psychological need to have *every single mark* on my body revised. He was straightforward and frank with me: There would be a marked improvement, but he was not a magician. The scars would not simply disappear.

Dr. Clavin recommended that because the wounds were spread out over so many areas of my body, I should have the procedures done over a period of time: first the legs, then the chest area, and so on. But I convinced him that I wanted it all done at once. I'd lived with those hateful scars long enough, and I wanted each one of them to be altered as soon as possible. Dr. Clavin warned me that such a massive undertaking could possibly involve the use of over a thousand stitches. But I was determined to do it.

During a checkup, I told Dr. Stein, my original surgeon, about the upcoming operation. He suggested that while I was in surgery, he could remove the steel in my chest that he'd used to wire my sternum together during the initial thoracic surgery. *More pain* was my first thought, but all I said was: "We might as well." In recent weeks the steel wires in my chest had begun to protrude. The little knotlike bumps they formed on my chest looked and felt very strange indeed.

On January 5, 1983, I once again checked into Cedars-

Sinai. My mom had flown out from New York to be with me; a cot was placed in my room so that she could sleep at the hospital. Although I felt nervous about the surgery, I was also excited. I'd been waiting a long time for this.

In the morning they gave me a strong pre-op sedative.

I was feeling pleasantly high and in a mischievous mood. As I was wheeled off to surgery, I appalled my mother by joking: "Mom, if I don't make it, please get me a pink coffin and pink roses, okay?"

Dr. Stein reopened my chest and removed the wire. Then Dr. Clavin went to work. For hours he painstakingly incised, corrected, and resutured each of the scars on my body.

His estimate had been accurate: More than one thousand internal and external stitches were required during the operation.

When I woke up, the first word that sprang into my mind was *pain*. My skin was on fire! Every one of the newly opened, freshly sewn wounds felt as though it had been set ablaze: my arm . . . my leg . . . my ribs . . . my torso . . . and, worst of all, my chest.

I heard my own wretched moans: "Oh, God, I can't take this again—I just can't take this." Tears rolled down my face. It had been a long time since I'd felt such unspeakable agony; the horror of the past and now the present pain swept over me and I wept on and on.

My mom, as usual, came to the rescue. She ran for help, and seconds later, a crisply efficient nurse gave me a shot of Demerol. I hadn't had such powerful medication in many months, and I was soon floating—in relative comfort—on a Demerol cloud.

Adrift on Demerol, I turned to another favorite pain-buffer: the telephone. Slowly I dialed the number of Iris Weithorn, who was then vice-president of Victims for Victims. The organization was barely two months old at the time, but through media exposure we had leaped into the consciousness of the L.A. public. Calls were pouring in from those who wanted to help—and from those who *needed* help. I had already worked as a peer counselor with more than a dozen victims; many more were on a waiting list. Ten volunteers were ready to be put through crisis intervention training.

We were a fledgling organization—but things were already jumping.

I lay there, cradling the phone in that all-too-familiar hospital setting, and I wanted *contact*. And so I was reaching out, via Pacific Bell. Iris's phone rang once, twice, three times, four. Just as I was about to hang up in frustration, Iris answered, huffing and out-of-breath. "Who is it?" she said.

"Me! Your favorite victim."

"Theresa? I thought you were in surgery."

"Yeah—I was. I just got out. What's new?" (Giggle, wince.)

"I can't believe you. I was just on my way over there."

"Well, come on over!"

"I'll see you, nut."

By the time Iris arrived, I was sound asleep. She sat and talked to my mom, who repeated what I'd told her just before nodding out: that I wanted to keep doing Victims for Victims business and seeing clients right there in my hospital room.

Iris and Mom were a bit worried. Being active was one thing, but being *crazy* was another. They both hoped I'd forget what I'd said by the time I woke up.

Iris and I had become a team immediately after the first public meeting of the organization. She had come with her husband, Howard, a psychologist who was interested in the group. Iris wasn't a victim but had recently undergone a bout with a prolonged, incapacitating illness. She knew what it was like to feel pain, alienation, and loneliness. The woman worked like a demon; I could never have gotten the organization off the ground so swiftly without her. By the time of my plastic surgery, we'd known each other only seven weeks but had already formed a strong, binding friendship.

When I next awoke, the pain was back again, but just at the level of a dull roar. And it wasn't yet "needle time"—I had another two hours to go. So I asked Iris to take out our appointment book and help me plan a schedule for the coming week. Iris said, "Theresa, you'll be in here at least a week. You're supposed to rest. Aren't you in pain?"

"Yes, I am," I answered. "In fact I'm going to go out of my mind with it if I lie here thinking about it all day."

Iris exchanged glances with my mother, who said, "I

guess Theresa knows best." Sighing, Iris agreed, and pulled out the calendar.

We pored over various requests for meetings and services. So much needed to be done! As Iris and I discussed which matters needed to take priority and began to set up our schedule, the pain grew steadily worse. Beads of perspiration dotted my brow. But I swallowed hard, sipped some tea, and went on with the work before us. Finally, all the pressing decisions were made, and we agreed to stop. My nightgown was drenched with sweat. Glancing at the clock, I saw that I still had an hour to go before my shot.

I looked down at the completed agenda, which included the following items:

1. Our five-person steering committee would meet in my room at Cedars the next evening.
2. Gerri Keller, an actress—and recent victim—would come in for a one-on-one session with me.
3. The leader of another local victims' group would meet with me at the hospital to share ideas and information.
4. A woman who'd been assaulted by her ex-husband would visit me for help in writing her Victim's Impact Statement.

Iris asked if I was sure I could handle so much activity. I looked at her and said, "I *need* to do it." And so she went home to make the necessary calls.

Razor-sharp, the pain jabbed at me again and again, burning and searing into my flesh. While Iris was there, I'd been immersed in our work and in our conversation. My mind had been focused on the schedule, the meetings, the people who needed help. Now that I had time to lie there and think about *myself*, I noticed a dramatic change: I could not take my thoughts off the pain; in fact, I could barely stand it.

I tried telling myself: *Theresa, you need to get your mind off things.* And so I asked my mom to bring me a magazine and I tried to lose myself—and my pain—in its glossy, colorful pages. But it just didn't seem to work. Sure, staring at the magazine was an activity, but it was basically just activity for activity's sake.

Simple diversion had helped me cope with pain in the days immediately after the attack. I was experiencing "systems overload" at the time; I had not yet integrated the horrible experience, my mind wasn't 100 percent ready to grasp it all, I wasn't able to concentrate well, and I surely wasn't yet capable of focusing on someone else's suffering. So, at that point, diversion was a good pain-buffer.

Now, however, many months had passed. My mind was always searching, always in need of activity. I'd developed a deep need to help others, to be instrumental in making changes, to be in a constant state of working toward some positive end, to put practically every minute I had to good use. Now, flipping through those advertisements and articles would serve no useful, positive purpose for me or for anyone else. It was merely a distraction. Because I'd switched from a meaning*ful* activity to one that was (at least for me) meaning*less*, my pain level had shot way up.

I tried to hold out for more than an hour after Iris left, but to no avail. Exactly fifty-five minutes after her departure, I had reached the end of my endurance. I rang for the nurse, and she gave me a beautifully numbing pain shot. Relief was swift. I sank into a long, exhausted sleep.

The next morning, I awoke with chest pains: That painfully familiar feeling of ripping apart was back again. I hadn't felt this frightening, upsetting sensation since the early days after my initial trauma. Wincing and moaning, I reached for the call button.

When the day nurse arrived, I requested a pill rather than a shot. It was only seven A.M. I knew this would be a long, dragged-out day. Ahead of me that evening was the third meeting of the Victims for Victims steering committee. Important decisions affecting the future of the group would be made. I had to be able to stay on top of all that transpired and to interact with the committee members. These people were the charter members of the organization; I had to help them get what they needed as leaders and as individuals—most of them were victims who had problems and needs of their own. In order to do all this I needed to be in control of my faculties. And so I chose a less-potent pain medication.

All during that morning and afternoon, I subsisted on mild oral doses. I felt pretty wretched, but it was endurable. Midmorning I had a real picker-upper when Adele Hesse, the head of a well-respected hospital crisis clinic, phoned. We had a long chat, and she agreed to train ten of our volunteers along with her own at no charge. Our members would then use their training to become counselors for Victims for Victims. This was a dream come true. My good spirits enabled me to get through the next few hours without Demerol.

By one o'clock I was white-knuckled, trembling, and sorely tempted to call for a shot. But I knew I had a meeting at two. I needed to be alert.

An hour later Libby Golding arrived. She ran a small local group for crime victims. We were getting together primarily to "network," to share our ideas, plans, and experiences. Crotchety as I was, I found it helpful. She talked about various clients with me and described some of her success stories. But Libby saw that I was drained and tense, and so she kept the meeting brief.

Soon after she left, Dr. Clavin came in, checked the incisions, and said I was coming along really well. But I was hurting too much to display more than token enthusiasm.

My mom explained what I was trying to do, and the young doctor chided me. "Look, I won't deny you these meetings, if they help," he said with concern. "But when you're in a lot of pain, that's what the shots are for." I nodded weakly and told him I'd think about it. He said, "I trust you, kid," and went off to complete his rounds.

Lying there, I began to feel I'd bitten off more than I could chew. Sure, it had been great to hold out until now—three P.M.—with only the relatively mild pain pills, but I'd had a thousand stitches just yesterday! I realized that I was being just a bit too hard on myself. So, feeling slightly guilty, I asked for a shot. Moments later I was blissfully happy that I'd given in. My mom was right: *Stoic* was one thing; *crazy* was another. I settled into my cushion of drug-induced comfort. "Mmm," I murmured with relief. I slept all afternoon.

Early that evening, I awoke as people began to arrive for the steering committee meeting. Almost as soon as I opened my eyes, the pain was rearing its ugly head. I felt totally rested and lucid, but my body *hurt*. Momentarily I was tempted to ask for an injection. But I knew that if I did so, I wouldn't be able to concentrate on the issues or on the other people. So I toughed it out, clenching my teeth and calling for a chocolate milkshake instead of Demerol. It tasted sinfully delicious (I had been trying to diet and lose a few pounds), but it certainly didn't possess the beguilingly palliative effects of a narcotic. Before the meeting was over I'd polished off *two* of those shakes.

I conducted our committee meeting from my hospital bed, referring to a slew of notes I'd made during the previous weeks. I'm sure I was a sight to behold: sitting there in my bed (cranked up to a half-sitting position), once again bandaged almost to the point of mummification, wearing pink baby-doll pajamas, and sipping away on those diet-destroying ice-cream shakes. At first some of my thoughts couldn't help but go to my throbbing wounds. Occasionally that old-standby chant of mine would pop into my head:

> Into all lives some rain must fall;
> Into all lives some pain must fall.

But I was able to concentrate *most* of my energies upon the matters at hand.

Like all fledgling organizations, we had before us a dizzying list of ideas, problems, and considerations to discuss and resolve. After a while I forgot the pain entirely as I threw myself heart and soul into the decision-making process. The meeting took on an air of excitement. We all felt it: This was truly the launching pad of an organization that could reach out to thousands of people across the country.

"Ladies and gentlemen, I think Theresa should get some rest." We all turned to see the night nurse, hands on hips in the doorway. I could hardly believe that three hours had passed!

The committee members gathered up their belongings. Most of them made plans to visit me again—this time, just for pleasure and company.

When my mom and I were once again alone in the room, I mulled over the events of that evening. There was really no question about it. When I focused my energies upon something important—particularly if it involved reaching out and helping people who were in need—I was either better able to handle pain or entirely unconscious of it.

Why? Because in looking outward I was taking my energies away from a preoccupation with pain. And, on a more spiritual level, I was sending out lots of good, positive, creative thoughts to others, and feeling in return a sense of deep satisfaction and well-being.

Why exactly did I try to concentrate on the problems of others? Was it because I am a saintly woman? Or was it for purely selfish reasons? Neither.

I reached out to others because of my need to know that the intense pain that plagued my body and soul was not a total waste. If I was able to use my trials and tribulations as a way of inspiring and helping others, then all my pain would have served some useful purpose. And yes, I desperately needed distraction and release from my own suffering; I *needed* to thwart my crushing, debilitating pain by funneling it into a plan for serious, positive, creative action.

And so, in the days after my plastic surgery, I followed a strict, self-directed course. When it was all just too much to bear, I requested and received pain medication, sometimes to the point where my mind was numb for entire afternoons or evenings. But whenever I knew I had an appointment, I was able to exercise enough control to refrain from taking shots of Demerol.

Victims for Victims business was conducted at least four hours daily from Cedars-Sinai room 824. There was a fairly regular flow of clients (victims who needed help) during that twelve-day period. And whenever I was in session with someone who needed my advice or help, I felt little or no pain. Either the pain itself abated, or my perception of it altered the extent of its effect upon me. If this had happened only once or twice, I might have chalked it up as a fluke. But as time went on, I noticed a distinct pattern: Step 1, I reached out to someone. Step 2, the person felt better. Step 3, I felt better. It was remarkably consistent.

I learned, during that hospital stay, that the *perception* of pain can be vastly altered, depending upon which direction you take. There is no way to deny the very real physical and emotional experience of pain. But you can greatly alter the impact it has upon you by consciously using your mind-energy to reach outside of yourself. All I can say is: IT WORKS!

*   *   *

For Rita Shyer, a commercial model who lives in Tennessee, religion and reaching out have always gone hand in hand. Raised on a farm in the Midwest by a close-knit, loving Lutheran family, Rita has always felt a strong relationship to God and a commitment to helping others. When the crops weren't good, the Shyer family motto was "The Lord will provide for us." And somehow, He always did.

A framed, hand-embroidered cloth hung in the Shyers' warm, cozy kitchen. The classic biblical quotation "Do unto others as you would have them do unto you" was stitched in brightly colored thread. Mr. and Mrs. Shyer taught their children to be of service to friends and neighbors, to share their material possessions and their good will, to give of themselves. The entire family was active in the church and often helped people who were poorer than they.

Two years ago, Rita's faith in God and her love for people were sorely tested. Rita had been dating a man named Tom Unger, for six months. Although she cared for Tom, Rita felt that their relationship had become stagnant. She explained to Tom that she thought it would be best for them to break up. Although he was sad about it, he seemed to understand and accept Rita's decision. The two remained close and continued to see each other often as platonic friends.

About five months after their romance broke up, Rita became worried about Tom. He was under tremendous financial pressure and was having serious problems at work. He was frequently moody and depressed; he didn't seem to be dealing well with the stress at all. Rita suggested that he visit a mental health clinic. Tom seemed grateful for the suggestion, and followed her advice.

But one night, soon after Tom went for help, he called Rita at about eleven P.M., sounding groggy and disoriented. He told Rita that he'd swallowed pills as well as some alcohol. At first he said he'd taken two pills, then he changed it to five, and finally, he said he'd taken seventeen pills.

Rita wasn't sure whether Tom was telling the truth, but she decided to call the paramedics anyway. They asked her to go to Tom's apartment, see what shape he was in, and then call them back if he needed medical attention.

Rita rushed over to Tom's place in a taxi. As soon as he answered the door, Rita noticed that he was acting rather strange and "high." But he behaved as though he'd taken only a few pills—certainly not a massive or dangerous amount. Seeing that there was no need to call the paramedics, Rita simply walked Tom all over the apartment, talking to him quietly for a few hours. He seemed grateful for the company and became more lucid and relaxed. After a while, Rita told Tom she was going home.

Without warning, he pounced upon his former girlfriend and began beating her savagely. Again and again he punched her in the face. Terrified, Rita managed to get out of Tom's apartment, darted across the hall, and knocked on a neighbor's door. But Tom pulled her back inside and continued the relentless beating.

When Tom knocked her to the floor for the third time, she tried to play dead, hoping he'd leave her alone. But the sight of Rita lying there motionless infuriated Tom all the more. He picked her up like a rag doll and punched her with even more ferocity.

For the second time, Rita managed to escape into the hall, screaming at the top of her lungs. But again Tom dragged her inside. This time he began to choke her. Rita couldn't breathe; everything began to go black; the life was draining out of her as she clung to the last vestiges of consciousness. "Help me, God, please help me," she prayed silently.

Just as Rita was about to black out, the neighbors knocked and yelled, "Stop! We've called the police." Their shouts distracted Tom. He loosened his grip on her throat and went to the door to tell them to go away. Rita, gasping for air, struggled dizzily to the door, which was now partly open. She could see five people standing outside. She desperately thrust her arm out to them through the opening and begged for help. Yet again, Tom yanked her back inside and resumed the beating.

Suddenly he stopped his vicious onslaught and picked up a heavy iron poker. Brandishing it near her face, he threatened, "If you press charges, I'll slash your face and breasts so you'll never model again!"

Rita's only thought was to keep Tom from killing her. Blood covered her face. She could hardly see as she said,

"'Tom, the police are on the way. They're bound to come in here. Why don't you help me wash my face so I won't look so bad when they get here?''

Tom, who was now pale and shaky, seemed to understand what Rita said. Hurriedly, he walked her into the bathroom and helped her to wash the blood off.

Minutes later the police knocked. Tom went to the door and called out, "Nothing wrong here, officers. We just had a little argument. Everything's okay now." The policemen replied that they needed to come in and check the situation out anyway.

As soon as Tom let the police officers in, Rita walked unsteadily out of the bathroom and stood there weaving in the doorway. When the policemen saw the condition she was in, they arrested Tom immediately.

Rita lost consciousness and was brought to the hospital in a police vehicle. The policemen carried her into the emergency room, where she regained consciousness. A nurse took one look at Rita's face and gasped, "Oh, my God." One doctor said to another, "I think underneath all this, she must've been a pretty girl."

Must've been, Rita echoed to herself.

There in the emergency room, Rita fought her pain and fear with a steady flow of earnest, silent prayers. "Help me to get through this, God," she prayed. "I know you wouldn't have let this happen to me if I wasn't strong enough to take it." And she remembers now that she made a conscious decision to place herself in God's hands. "I trust you, Lord," she prayed, "and I know you'll take care of me."

Everything hurt. Rita's face was in the worst shape, but bruises and lacerations covered her entire body. Not an inch of her skin had remained untouched by Tom's forceful blows. In addition to the pain, which permeated every part of her anatomy, Rita felt ice-cold, chilled to the bone. No matter how many blankets they put on her, she couldn't stop shaking; she felt she'd die of the cold.

A nurse told Rita that her nose had been broken in two places. The doctors stitched it up and placed ice packs all over her face. There were fracture lines on Rita's front teeth, and one back tooth was totally shattered. Some bones in her head were broken, and her entire jaw had been knocked completely out of alignment.

Rita's eyes were puffed and swollen like balloons. A doctor warned her that by morning they'd be completely shut. If she was lucky, a tiny crack might remain open so that she could see.

When she was released many hours later, John and Ellen, two close friends, drove out to the hospital. They picked Rita up and took her to their home. Tenderly, her friends placed her on the couch, where she tried to rest.

But Rita's body was covered with welts. There was no way to find a comfortable position. She slept fitfully until morning.

Rita woke to a blinding headache and pain all over her body. Her beautiful blond hair was matted with dried blood. She walked slowly to the bathroom, her entire body throbbing.

When she looked into the mirror, Rita said aloud: "That can't be me." Her eyes looked as if they belonged to a demented frog; the flesh surrounding them literally protruded more than an inch from her face. All the skin surrounding the eyes was a bright purplish red.

The whites of her eyes were completely red. Later she was told there were contusions inside the eye area. The entire left side of her face was bloated and misshapen beyond recognition. She couldn't see her nose at all. That area was so swollen that only the nostrils showed.

Rita saw Tom's fingerprints on her throat, vividly outlined by reddened bruises. And her entire chest was covered with angry-looking welts and cuts.

As Rita stared at her reflection, a comforting thought popped into her head: *Facial cuts and bruises look worse than they are.* She remembered that one of the cops had given her a list of plastic surgeons. Now, looking into the mirror, she understood why he had done so.

Rita's shocking physical appearance didn't drive her to despair. She eased herself down onto her friends' couch and reminded herself that little more than eight hours before, she had almost been choked to death. Despite the pain and horror of it all, Rita's mind was focused on the fact that she had made it through.

Rita told me, "I could never have made it through without my faith in the Lord. Night and day I prayed, asking Him for sustenance. I was in plenty of pain at first, and I looked to God to help me cope with it all. When the going was roughest, I asked Him to show me some way to make sense of the situation, to have it help me to become a better and stronger person, and to show me a way to use what happened to me for some positive purpose."

"Did you ever blame God for what happened to you?" I asked her.

"Never," she replied. "Although, since then, I've met many victims who initially railed against God for letting their tragedies happen—and I can understand that reaction—my own thoughts didn't go in that direction. From the very beginning I was *thankful* to God for letting me live. And luckily, I've continued to think that way ever since."

During the first days after the attack, when Rita was terribly achy and uncomfortable, she took a self-prescribed "rest-cure," forcing herself to sleep both day and night, for only when she was sleeping did the throbbing, aching, and itching of her wounds ease off. She slept and prayed, slept and prayed.

Rita took solace in the fact that once the healing process began, her face changed colors as she slept. She considered that a sign that she was on the mend. She would often wake up after hours of sleep to find that her face had become just a shade less red. Encouraged, she returned to her couch and slept still more.

The police informed her that Tom, who was a first-time offender, was now out on bail. Fearing that he might attempt to harm Rita again, they warned her not to return to her old apartment, which she had recently renovated. They also advised her not to resume her former job as a salesgirl, which had kept her going between modeling assignments. And so Rita stayed in the home of her good friends John and Ellen for five months. They all jokingly referred to it as Rita's hide-out.

Rita found that her emotional pain outweighed the physical. Even in her sleep, frightening dreams pursued her, never allowing her an escape from her deep psychological anguish. Time and again she turned to God in her pain and distress.

Rita felt as though she was in a time warp. Her extended sleeping pattern made her feel fuzzy and disoriented. For weeks, her head, face, and eyes remained swollen. And Rita's mind was never at rest. She couldn't help worrying about the medical bills, and about finding a new job and apartment.

Worst of all, Tom had been calling all her friends; he was looking for her. Rita was terrified that he would find her. This time, she believed, Tom would kill her.

When she felt she couldn't endure the pain and discomfort, she told herself: *Maybe an acting job will come along where I'll have to act out pain and suffering—I'll certainly be able to do a good job of it! And maybe I'll be able to use this experience to help someone else.*

In the painful weeks following her attack, Rita was plagued by blinding headaches. As time went on, they grew progressively more severe. Her head seemed to pulse and pound all day.

After a few weeks she could bear the pain no longer and sought the help of a number of physicians. Eventually, Rita was directed to an orthodontist, who found the answer.

She needed to restore the alignment in her head and jaw. Those bones had never gone back into place and were the cause of her severe headaches.

He told her that she'd need to wear a "bite splint" for about a year. She followed his orders. Despite the discomfort the splint caused, wearing it made Rita feel she was regaining control over her physical condition. Gradually the headaches began to subside. Months later, they completely disappeared.

Tom's trial was imminent, and after much consideration, Rita decided to play an active role in it, to appear as the key witness. Tom's attorney called, begging her to drop the charges, but Rita was adamant. So many people, including the police, had said, "Women always drop charges in battery cases." Rita wanted to be an example to other women like herself who'd been battered. She wanted to make a statement about the situation. And she wanted to make sure that Tom would never think he could get away with such violent abuse without suffering the consequences.

Rita went through with her plan. Tom was eventually tried, found guilty, and sentenced to 30 days, of which he served 20. Despite Tom's ludicrously light sentence, Rita was proud of having proven to herself—and to others—that she had the courage and determination to fight back and stand firm until her attacker was actually tried and convicted.

Rita's personality type made her recovery more difficult. All her friends had always considered her the "strong one." She was the quintessential leader and helper; others went to *her* for advice and support. Because of this, Rita felt uncomfortable about displaying vulnerability; she didn't feel free to express her pain and her fear to them. Everyone in her circle of friends seemed desperately to want Rita to "be okay," and she felt pressured to put up a front of courage for them. So the only "friend" she really confided in and leaned upon completely was God.

Rita felt reticent about letting others know she'd been battered. She told most people that a car accident had been the cause of her physical injuries. Only a very few knew the real story. Her parents, who still lived in the Midwest, had recently been through a very rough period with their health and finances, so when Rita talked to them she downplayed the entire event as well as her physical state.

As the weeks passed, the pain eased off and her wounds healed nicely. But the ache inside did not. She prayed and prayed, but the internal wounds just wouldn't heal.

Rita had always been a sociable girl but had felt more withdrawn lately because she was uncomfortable about burdening her friends with her problems. However, the need to share her experience became too pressing to ignore.

Unable to keep things inside any longer, Rita confided in Terri, a long-term but casual friend.

Rita poured her heart out to Terri. She described the mental anguish she'd been feeling, the isolation, the pressure of friends for her to be strong, the fear of Tom's trying to hurt her again, the fact that not even prayer was enough to stop the emotional pain anymore. She burst into tears and apologized to Terri for taking up so much of her time, admitting that she felt deeply humiliated about being a victim of battery.

Terri took Rita into her arms and, to Rita's amazement,

sobbed. "I know what you're going through. It happened to me too." The two women clung to each other and wept together.

After that evening, Rita and Terri's friendship deepened and they became bastions of strength for each other. Rita learned that Terri's attack had occurred only weeks before her own.

Two of Terri's ribs had been broken and she'd spent four days in the hospital recuperating. Terri, too, was a churchgoer who prided herself on being independent and resourceful. Her elderly parents could provide little emotional support and she had felt a lack of understanding from most of her peers. Terri, too, had been "going it alone."

Now the two women had each other to confide in, to lend support. Both of them felt their mental burdens and anxieties lifting as they shared their pain.

Once their self-imposed vows of silence had been broken, Rita and Terri found they were eager to learn more about battery. Why did it happen? To whom? How often? They decided to explore the subject together.

One day Terri read a notice in the paper, announcing a public meeting at a nearby women's shelter. A noted author and expert on the subject of battery was to be the speaker. Terri and Rita made arrangements to go to the meeting together.

That Thursday night, they arrived at the shelter, not knowing what to expect. At the registration table a glance at the sign-in sheet told Rita that some attendees were residents of the shelter, but most had come from the outside.

The speaker was introduced and opened the program with a slide presentation. Rita had seen a few pictures of battery victims in books and magazines, but had never been confronted with detailed blowups like the ones the speaker was showing. The slides depicted women who had been hurt— beaten . . . bloodied . . . damaged. So many sad eyes stared out hauntingly from bruised and swollen faces. Young girls, mature women, even elderly ladies—all victims of battery. All different. Yet, in a way, shockingly similar.

Rita felt as though she was staring again at her own mirror-image from the past. *Why? Why? Why does this happen?* she asked herself.

The lights came up. Sounds of sniffles, sighs, noses blowing filled the room. Only then did Rita notice the wetness of her own face. Sitting beside her, Terri, too, was damp-eyed.

After the slide presentation, the speaker discussed the battery syndrome and gave shockingly high statistics on the incidence of this violent crime. Facts. Figures. All grim. All terrible. All, unfortunately, true.

One of the saddest things the speaker told the group was that most battered women didn't press charges. Because of fear. Harassment. Low self-esteem. Rita was repelled by the thought of how many men were out there committing battery and abuse without ever paying the consequences. How could women be encouraged to follow through and see that the men who attacked them—even if they were their own husbands— were brought to justice?

An open discussion began. Nearly all participated. The air was charged with emotion—pain, anger, grief. But camaraderie, too, was present. And it helped.

People introduced themselves. Some shared their stories. Some wept. Some hugged one another, glad to be no longer alone. Rita and Terri spoke, too, giving brief synopses of their own attacks. Both were shocked at how many women continued to live with the men who battered them.

After that, Rita and Terri met two or three times a week. They read and shared books and articles on battery.

Rita decided to do her master's thesis (she was a communications major at State College) on battered women and how they are depicted in the media.

The more she learned, the more deeply she became involved in the issue. She began to explore not only battery but other types of violent crime as well.

About two months after Terri and Rita had begun to share their experiences, Terri's job forced her to relocate to South Carolina. The women would really miss each other's friendship and support, but they knew that both of them had grown tremendously.

After Terri's move, Rita continued to explore the subject on her own, reading everything she could find on the subject. And what she learned compelled her to take action. She realized that God was now answering her prayers of months before by pointing her in the direction of helping others. She *could* use her painful personal experience as well as her new book-knowledge by reaching out to other victims.

Rita called the local district attorney's office and asked how she could get involved with their Victim Witness Assistance program. The program representative invited Rita to come down for a meeting with their volunteer coordinator, Kathryn Devlin.

After hearing of Rita's personal experience and the extensive research she'd done on her own, Kathryn suggested that Rita could play an important role in the development of an outreach program. Victims needed court accompaniment, transportation to trials, hand-holding, information, and much more. The people at the D.A.'s office tried to fill the need, but there were just not enough staff members to handle the calls for services. In addition, Kathryn told Rita that National Victim's Rights Week was fast approaching. The office was often contacted by newspapers and TV and radio shows in search of an actual crime victim to interview. Rita was attractive, intelligent, and well-spoken. She also had both personal experience as a victim *and* further research to back her up.

"Would you be interested in interviews or speaking engagements?" Kathryn asked hopefully.

Without hesitation, Rita said yes. She prayed that night, and thanked God for heading her in the right direction.

And so Rita became a familiar face around the D.A.'s office. She went there two or three times a week and absorbed as much information as possible. Kathryn frequently called on her new volunteer for help.

An elderly woman, Claire DiLeo, had been brutally beaten by a youthful offender. Her social security check and what little cash she had were stolen. After three months the assailant had finally been apprehended. Kathryn asked Rita to escort Claire to the pretrial hearing.

Rita arrived at Claire's tiny apartment early in the morning. The little woman was trembling, terrified, and tempted not to go to court at all. Rita sat and talked with her for a while and told Claire a bit about her own experience. She assured the elderly lady that she'd be safe in the courtroom. Finally Claire agreed to go. Rita drove her to the courthouse, waited with her, and remained nearby when Claire testified.

After it was over and they were on the way home, Claire exclaimed to Rita: "Thank you for convincing me to do that. The boy who hurt me was sitting there *as bold as brass*, glaring at me hatefully. He deserves to be punished. Then maybe he won't try and do this to someone else."

Later, Claire followed through and testified at the boy's trial. Because of his youth, his sentence was relatively light. But the prosecutor told Claire he would have gone completely free and unpunished without her testimony.

Victim's Rights Week arrived, and Rita did her first press interview. She felt sufficiently well-versed and prepared and was able to handle the reporter's questions with ease. The next day an in-depth article appeared in a prominent local newspaper. It talked a bit about Rita's case, focusing on the issues of battery and violent crime—and upon Rita's opinions as a victim. At the end of the article, the paper printed a list of places where victims could find help.

People called Rita all day, impressed with the write-up and with her comments. When she dropped by the Victim Witness office after work, the staff gathered around her excitedly. They told Rita of the calls that had come in throughout the day in response to the article. People were asking for both help and information. Rita was thrilled at the role she'd played in helping other victims link up with services.

At first, speaking about her own attack was difficult. But each time she did it, the act of sharing her experience became less painful. Rita concentrated on the fact that she wasn't just rehashing her tale but was using her own painful ordeal to help others gain a better understanding of the issue and to encourage victims to seek assistance. She repeatedly urged battery victims and others to press charges, to follow through, to break their silence and have their assailants punished.

The minister of her church asked Rita to speak to the congregation, and she readily agreed. When she addressed the churchgoers, Rita stressed the role that God had played in her recovery from the ordeal. She encouraged members of the church to contribute to victims groups and to donate time and services to the cause. She asked them to open their ears and hearts to people among them who might have been attacked. And she let them know that silence was not the answer.

It had been a release to speak to her congregation. Their response was warm and open; Rita was sorry she hadn't looked to the churchgoing community during her crisis. But she was glad she was there *now*. A number of teenagers and women asked how they could contribute, and Rita filled them in. She hadn't felt so good in a long time.

One evening when Rita was relaxing in her apartment with her date, Ron, they heard someone screaming, "He's gonna kill me." She and Ron ran outside and saw a young woman holding a small baby in her arms. Her face was puffy and swollen.

Rita quickly brought her into the apartment. The terrified girl, who said her name was Denise, seemed both shaken and embarrassed. Rita held the baby and soothed the frightened girl, encouraging her to talk.

After a while, Denise explained that her husband, Hal, had been acting rougher and angrier in recent months. At first he had only abused her verbally. But now things were much worse. In the past week alone, Hal had struck her on three different occasions. Tonight he'd hit her so hard she'd been knocked to the floor—and worse, he'd threatened to hurt their infant son.

Rita commiserated with Denise and told her that this was a terrible but common problem. She explained that she, too, had been assaulted. Denise said she was deeply afraid her husband would kill her—or their baby—if she returned. Rita advised the girl to call the police and ask for help. Denise was nervous about doing this, but saw no alternative.

They called the local precinct, and two officers soon arrived. After taking the report, they checked Denise's house and couldn't find her husband. Because there were no visible injuries, the police advised Denise that she would have to leave her husband if she wanted the charges against him to stick. Grimly, the girl said, "I will, officer. He may have gotten away with hitting *me*, but I won't live with a man who threatens his own baby."

The police checked a few women's shelters and found they were all full. Rita offered to take Denise in, and the girl gratefully accepted. The next morning, however, Denise grew frightened that Hal would find her, since she was hiding literally next door. Denise called her aunt and uncle and explained the situation. Luckily, they asked their niece and her baby to stay with them for a while. Soon after, her uncle came by to pick them up.

Rita heard from Denise a number of times in the months that followed. At Rita's suggestion, Denise went for counseling and found great support there. Denise stuck to her plan and pressed charges, legally separating from Hal before the criminal proceedings had even begun. Hal had no police record, and so was sentenced only to probation. But he was legally restrained from being near Denise and could visit his small son only under close supervision.

Denise telephoned Rita often, sharing the pain of the crisis and the trial. Eventually she agreed to go to a marriage counselor with Hal after his probation was over. She said, "Rita, there may be hope for that man. But I won't go back to him unless I know in my heart he's been cured of what made him violent. If not, the baby and I will have to make it on our own."

Rita has continued to reach out to victims of battery and assault. She has become a popular speaker at church and community functions and feels deeply rewarded by this work.

Along the way, the terrible knot of pain in Rita's heart has lessened. Reaching out to others helped her to resolve her own personal anguish. She truly loves her work and the people she has been able to help.

Rita has learned a lot about the men who batter. She has seen that many of them can in fact be helped, through counseling. Some even go on to have normal, nonviolent relationships with women. But Rita still firmly believes that battered women *must* press charges and that they should be encouraged to leave the men who harm them—unless and until the men are capable of controlling themselves and refraining from violence.

Rita has been able to learn and accept the fact that though battery is shockingly widespread, not all men are violent. She is now able to trust men again and is involved in a supportive, promising relationship.

*   *   *

Whether the impetus to reach out comes from one's own pain and despair, out of a need to make sense of disaster, or, as in Rita's case, out of deep religious conviction, it is undeniably positive. The wounds in our bodies and in our minds heal so much faster when we share our experiences and our pain with others.

Imparting good wishes, good thoughts, good advice, and, hopefully, good examples to someone else can help you to feel fulfilled, rewarded, and far less *pained*.

CHAPTER 6

FAMILY AND FRIENDS

Doting mothers
  proud fathers
    loving spouses
      soulful lovers
        adoring sisters
          protective brothers
            best friends
              caring cousins
                favorite aunts
                  playful uncles
                    kindly grandmothers
                    devoted grandfathers

What happens when these special people become tortured, helpless onlookers after a violent attack is committed against someone they love? When they must witness the horror of either an attack itself or its terrible aftermath? When the person they love—and their relationship to that person—is suddenly, inexplicably, unjustly, and irrevocably altered by one brutal stroke of fate?

What happens to the friends and relatives of crime victims?

There is no simple answer. So much depends upon the people involved, the type of crime, the physical and emotional condition of the victim, and other individual circumstances.

But one fact remains constant for all friends and relatives of victims of crime: Their lives—as well as that of the "actual" victim—will never be the same again. They, too—at least on a psychological level—are victims.

Until March 15, 1982, my mother, Divina Saldana, was an irrepressible optimist, a person who basically believed that if you lead a good life, you will be rewarded. A devout Catholic, she was active in the church and attended Mass faithfully.

Before the attack, Mother led a simple and quite sheltered life. A woman who has never longed for or cared about wealth or prominence, she was always deeply content with the simple pleasures and joys of home and family.

My mom was that rare individual, a genuinely happy person, a woman at peace with herself and with the world. As far as she is concerned, it is only natural that people should try to care for one another's needs, particularly in troubled times.

It was beyond Mother's comprehension that people should hurt or oppress one another. Watching or reading the news—and seeing the pain people suffered, particularly as a result of physical violence of any sort—brought her to tears.

Whenever she was directly confronted with people in pain or crisis, she did everything in her power to soothe, console, or assist them. As for the others—the people she heard or read about but never actually met—she offered up prayers and good wishes for them, frustrated that there wasn't more that she could do.

She had taught my sister and me that if we tried to be kind and loving to others, God would watch over us and protect us. And she tried not to worry about us, relying on the faith she had in God's watchfulness and loving protection.

But on March 15, 1982, Mom's entire life—and all that she believed in—were shattered when she learned that a deranged man who claimed to be acting on a divine mission directed by Saint Michael the Archangel had stabbed and nearly murdered her firstborn daughter.

Mother was sickened by the thought that someone had actually done this to me with willful intent. Aware of my tenuous hold on life itself, she prayed as she had never prayed before. But she knew that all the prayers in the world could never change the ugly, unjust reality of what had happened.

Leaning on Dad for his quiet support, Mother made it through those first hours and days. She focused her every thought and hope upon my simply staying alive. Day and night, she whispered over and over: "You're gonna be okay, baby. You're gonna make it." It was many days before the doctors finally agreed with her.

For a while, Mother was overjoyed: she was so grateful I would *live* that there was no room in her heart for anything but thanks. But after that first onrush of relief had passed—and the shock of the situation had begun to wear off—terrible questions began to gnaw at her.

Where was the loving God she'd depended on faithfully to protect us? Why wasn't He watching? How could He let me suffer so? What did we—our entire family—do to deserve this swift, near-deadly punishment? How could so many have stood and watched until Jeff Fenn rescued me?

The questions that swept through her mind were too horrible and confusing to voice, so Mother kept these conflicts to herself.

As anxious as she was, Mom knew that in order to encourage my healing and to help the family—and herself—to overcome the crisis, it was important to retain both hope and optimism. She told herself there would be time later to deal with the questions and conflicts churning within her. And so, for the time being, she took hold of herself, summoning every ounce of courage, optimism, and energy she could muster.

Mother went to the hospital chapel daily. She prayed for my recovery, and for respite for our family. Though problems continued to assail us, she thanked God that my life had been spared.

Mother was eternally grateful that I had somehow survived. But it was nonetheless heart-wrenching for her to watch helplessly as I grappled with physical and emotional suffering so severe that it was almost beyond human endurance.

"It hurts, Mom. It hurts so much," I would cry out again

and again. And, holding me as she had when I was a tiny child, Mom wiped my tears away, frustrated that she couldn't make the pain disappear.

Wherever she looked, Mother saw her loved ones in torment: her daughter racked with pain, consumed by fear, plagued by bloody nightmarish visions; her son-in-law beside himself with anxiety and confusion, quavering on the verge of collapse; her younger daughter struggling valiantly, though not always successfully, to remain calm and to bolster the rest of us. And her husband, the man she'd loved since they were schoolmates, suddenly gray, aged overnight, his health declining, his heart broken. Desperately wanting to do something—anything—to stop his daughter's agony, he was reduced to pacing back and forth in the hospital room like a caged animal.

Mother watched this grim horror film our lives had become, and she tried to hold on to her faith in God and in mankind. But the cycle of pain and disillusionment just would not seem to end.

Fact after painful shocking fact unfolded. The assailant was caught, but showed no remorse. His only regret was that I hadn't died. This news dug into my mother's heart like still another thrust of the blade.

We were told that even if he was tried and found guilty, the maximum sentence he could be given was twelve years. With this, the knife seemed to twist still again.

When Mother tried to explain the heartache she felt, she was often met with remarks like "Just be thankful your daughter's alive." And so Mom felt isolated, cut off, misunderstood.

As for Mother's spiritual pain, a priest told her: "It was God's will."

God's will? Mother asked herself. *God's will? How can it be God's will for my child to endure a living butchery?* This time, the knife seemed to have pierced her soul.

Somehow, during those hospital-bound days, Mom managed to keep from plunging into despair. She directed her energies to helping me get well, to planning for the future, and to making the best of a terrible situation.

Thank God she's alive, she would tell herself many times each day. And that thought would help to keep her spirits up.

Each morning she would bustle into my room, usually

with a package for me in her arms. Bursting with energy, she'd fix my hair, read to me, plump the pillows, and tell me—always—how pretty and well I looked.

Mother peppered her conversation with phrases like *when you get well . . . when you're better . . . when you're out of here. . . .* Never for a moment did she let me believe she saw my future as anything but bright and healthy.

I could never have gotten through that tortured period without my mother's constant support, encouragement, and good cheer. She was absolutely amazing.

Like a little magpie, Mother chattered on and on to me about all the things we could look forward to: my hospital discharge, the birthday party she'd throw for me, the Christmas holiday we'd spend together, and all the joy that lay ahead for us once we'd surmounted the crisis.

Mom giggled over my puppy, Totsie, laughed at my jokes and antics, and made friends with the nurses and the families of other patients. I'd tease her and tell her to stop talking everyone's ears off. But in truth, the staff, patients, and families who populated both Cedars-Sinai and Motion Picture Hospital adored her. She was an inspiration to me and to everyone else around.

When she returned home to New York in June, however, her entire being underwent a radical change. With the immediate crisis over, Mother finally allowed the complete, grisly reality to sink in. Now, she felt unending pain, rage, and despair. The months of high spirits had been necessary to encourage me and to sustain herself during the ordeal. But now she gave in totally to an all-encompassing depression.

When I was released from the hospital and flew to New York, I was shocked at my mom's appearance. Her face was drawn and taut, drained of all signs of life or happiness.

Her soft brown eyes had always been clear, innocent, hopeful, brimming with joy and good will. Now they were clouded over, dazed and despondent—two deep, dark wells of unvoiced misery and despair.

On the night I arrived home, I had trouble sleeping. I went downstairs to make some tea and found my mother slumped over the kitchen table, weeping alone. We held each other and cried. Then, for a long while we simply sat together, keeping each other company during the sleepless night.

I worried over the changes in my mother. Her Brooklyn-accented voice had been chattery, bright, high-pitched, and varied, the voice of a much younger lady; now it was a hollow, wooden, parched monotone, more dead than alive—a voice that served only to communicate necessary instructions or requests.

When I asked if she was okay, Mother would say, "I'll be fine, Theresa, just fine." But her words were spoken without conviction.

Mother's gait and movements had become halting, unsteady, slowed by depression and a sense of overwhelming futility. Her mouth was pinched and tight, her brow furrowed with wrinkles, her skin gray and lifeless. She had suddenly become an old woman—tired, beaten down, and filled with unspoken misery.

Mother had always darted up and down the stairs of our home; now it seemed to take her forever to climb that single flight of steps. Once I came upon her sitting right in the middle of the staircase, a look of exhaustion and puzzlement on her face.

"I can't decide whether to go up or down," she said to me, her voice quavering.

Then, remaining motionless on the stairway, Mom asked, "What happiness can I ever feel after what this horrible man did to you, Theresa?"

"Mom, we *should* feel happy," I responded quietly. "I'm almost well, and things'll get better real soon." Then I coaxed her to come upstairs and watch television with me for a while.

Seeing my mother in this condition made me realize the extent to which my family had suffered. The painful truth was that the attacker's onslaught had left in its wake an entire family who'd been assaulted, tormented, and made to wade through a quagmire of undeserved depression and despair.

"Things are going to be great, Mom. I'll be completely better soon. The worst is over," I told her again and again. But my words had little effect. Mother needed time to admit to her pain, her anger, and her fear.

Days would pass when Mom would scarcely speak or

communicate. Silently and sadly she drifted about the house, doing her chores, reading, watching television—but with no enthusiasm.

Sometimes she acted spacey and forgetful. "Mom, you already dusted that table five minutes ago," I'd remind her.

"Oh, you're right," she'd say with a sigh and move on mechanically to another task.

Then, on other days, she seemed to brighten. Suddenly she'd exclaim, "Oh, Theresa, you're looking so much better!" and she'd give me a big hug. At times like those, I detected traces of that spark she'd always had. And it made me hopeful.

Fortunately, my presence in the house and the fact that I was now truly on the mend seemed to cheer my mother up. Mother showed real joy and excitement when she put together an enormous family party in my honor. At the celebration she seemed to glow from within, happy that I was really *alive* on this first birthday after the attack.

I saw Mom's eyes light up when I blew out the candles on the huge pink birthday cake. And for the first time in quite a while, she wore makeup and had her hair done at the beauty shop.

But when we cleaned up the house after the party, she stared at the half-melted candles in her hand. "At your last birthday, if someone had told me what would happen to you, I never would have believed them," she said, looking up at me mournfully.

"Neither would I, Mom. Neither would I," I replied. And we went on with our cleaning.

After a month in New York, I left for Los Angeles with my sister, Maria. Although Mom seemed much better than when I'd first arrived, I was still worried about her and hated to leave while she was still so depressed. But Mother begged me to go on with my life.

At the airport she promised me: "I'll be better by Christmas, Theresa." I hugged her tightly and said, "I know you will, Mom." Then my sister and I flew west.

Once we were gone, Mother had even more time on her hands. Frequently she found her mind turning to thoughts of the attack and its aftermath. Mom longed to share her feelings but found that most people were unable to listen to the disturbing things that preyed on her mind.

Although a few of the people closest to Mother reached out to help, many more shied away, refusing to deal with her pain. Often, people urged her simply: "Forget it all—put it behind you."

Though such pieces of advice were frustrating, Mother found it far more saddening to discover that during her worst period of suffering, some of those she'd counted upon as being closest of all simply disappeared from her life.

Concurrently with Mother's period of depression, our family underwent prolonged dealings with the criminal justice system. Virtually everything connected with the trial and the eventual sentencing of the attacker worsened my mother's despondency.

From Divina's point of view and that of the rest of our family, all the concern, all the safeguards, even justice itself seemed to be meted out to one person: the criminal.

With a mixture of surprise, anger, and confusion in her voice, Mother kept repeating, "There *is* no justice. There *is* no justice." And none of us could disagree. The American criminal justice system—with all its loopholes, postponements, ill regard for crime victims, and ludicrously light sentencing structure—seemed to be making a mockery of the suffering of our family.

Months after the sentencing, we learned that because the judge had omitted a jury instruction, my assailant's conviction had been reduced to second-degree attempted murder, rather than first-degree attempted murder.

"How can you stab a person ten times in the second degree?" my mother demanded to know. But, as usual, no answers were forthcoming.

Later we were told that the assailant would serve only half his sentence and would be released in 1988—without even a parole hearing.

Stunned, Mother wondered aloud if *we* would ever be free of the devastating effects of the brutal attack.

*   *   *

It took many months, but eventually my mother managed to climb out of her pit of depression. Although I suggested therapy to her many times, she preferred to heal on her own, clinging to her faith in God, her love for her husband and daughters, and her gratitude that I had, indeed, survived.

As time went on, Mother's state of mind came to be very much in sync with my own. Whenever I made a step forward, she, too, seemed to thrive.

In November, when I was finally hired for my first post-attack acting job, Mom's spirits began to soar. I think it was the first time she dared allow herself to believe that a totally normal and functional life was within my grasp. And, knowing this, she was able to let go of some of the pain and worry that had been plaguing her—and to reclaim some of her former faith and optimism.

"Can your dad and I come and visit the set?" she asked playfully when I called her from my shooting location.

"Sure, Mom, if you want to fly out to California to do it," I answered.

"Oh, well, I guess we'll take a raincheck . . . but get some autographs of the cast for your cousins," she replied. I was thrilled to hear her sounding cheerful again.

A few days later, Dad told Maria and me that Mom was running all over the neighborhood, pleased as punch, telling everyone that they could soon watch me on TV again.

By Christmas time, when Maria and I flew home for the holidays, Mom was doing much, much better. The crisp, cold air, the excitement of the Christmas season, and the passage of time which distanced us from the horror of that past spring seemed to have had a healing effect.

We had a beautiful, happy Christmas celebration. Under the blinking multicolored lights of the tree we'd trimmed together, I looked over at my mom. She was teasing Totsie with a long piece of ribbon, laughing as she watched the dog leap up at it again and again.

Years seemed to have fallen away from her face. The pallor was gone; her eyes were bright and shiny.

I saw that my sister and Dad were watching Mom, too, and the three of us shared a look of happiness and relief.

*　　*　　*

The attempted murder has had unending repercussions for my entire family—particularly my mother. It showed her that the innocent are not necessarily protected or rewarded. That danger lurks and may leap out at us at any time.

But the most painful lesson to learn was that good does not always triumph over evil. Mother believes that the outcome of our case—and many others like it—is a travesty of justice. Sentencing the attacker to twelve years—and having him serve only six—is, in my mother's opinion, like saying "Go out and hurt people—you'll hardly be punished at all."

More than four years have passed. My mother has tried to pick up the pieces and put her life back together again. But much has been lost.

Yes, Mom has learned to smile again. But it is now a wistful smile, not the broad, infectious grin that used to light up her entire face.

Mother has continued to attend Mass and to receive the sacraments, but she is plagued and discomforted by the anger and despair that still intermittently rage within her, and by spiritual questions which have never been adequately answered.

My mother no longer has the quiet peace of mind and unquestioning devotion she once possessed. She still finds solace in church and in God, but the questions and conflicts at times create a climate of inner turmoil.

One of the saddest and most long-lasting effects the crime has had upon my mother is a lingering sense of futility and hopelessness. Never before had my mother said words like *What's the use?* But for many months after the attack, she asked this question constantly, in response to many kinds of situations. Even after that Christmas when her mood made such a dramatic turnaround, Mother would occasionally regress.

In February 1983, I once again visited my family in New York. Mom's mood seemed relatively upbeat and stable. My dad, sister, and I decided to take her on a family outing and bought tickets to a matinee performance of a Broadway show, *Brighton Beach Memoirs.*

At the theater we were all tickled as we sneaked looks over at Mom and saw that she was *really* enjoying the play. That rare little smile kept turning up the corners of her mouth.

Afterward, still elated, we all went to Mamma Leone's restaurant.

After ordering, we cheerfully enjoyed an aria sung by an enormously fat soprano. Mom dug heartily into her appetizer, and seemed to be relishing both the food and the festive atmosphere of the restaurant.

But her good spirits evaporated when she heard someone at a nearby table say, "There's the girl who got stabbed."

Mom's eyes filled with tears, her mouth drooped downward, and she stared numbly at her plate. "What's the use?" she said. "I can never forget." She wouldn't eat another bite, and we all quickly headed home.

Because our parents loved my little Totsie so much, Maria and I bought them a playful white cockapoo puppy—Snowball—who is now my dad's best friend and companion. Though Mother protested about the work that having a dog would entail, she now adores and dotes upon her little "Snowy." Having a puppy to take care of gave my mother something outside of herself to focus her attention upon.

Slowly but surely she struggled through the pain and is, once again, a contented, cheerful woman who can enjoy life.

We share jokes, vacations, family outings—all the things we did together as a family before the attack, and in many ways we're closer because of what we've suffered through together. I thank God for that.

I despise the attacker for the agony he inflicted upon my mother. Thankfully, however, she has had the courage to conquer her despair and to continue her loving life with her husband and her two daughters.

My mother—like many other mothers of innocent victims—gave enormously of herself. I believe she suffered more than any of us. But she's here today. And, to me, the most beautiful sight on earth is my mother's face—*smiling*.

Here are quotes from victims of different types of crimes:

"What I hated most was the look of pain on my husband's face. It has never really gone away."

"My daughter still has nightmares. She's afraid even to take out the garbage. My sexual assault made her terrified of boys and men—even her own cousins. She is only nine years old."

"My dad took it hardest of all. He spoke to no one for three weeks. A month later, he had a massive heart attack."

"Bessie, my closest friend, visited me every day after my attack. She was my family's tower of strength. Then she almost had a breakdown and has been in therapy for over a year."

"I will never forgive what this assailant has done to my beloved family."

These quotations point out two facets of the problem: First, that families and friends indeed suffer greatly, sometimes to the point of physical collapse.

Second, that the actual victim—in addition to all the other problems—must cope with the fact that his or her victimization emotionally rips apart the people he or she cares about most.

THE INNER CIRCLE

A crime victim's inner circle consists of all the relatives, loved ones, and friends who play key roles in his life. These are the people he will deal with most frequently after an attack. And they are the ones who will shoulder the dual burden of caring for the victim and dealing with their *own* problems resulting from the attack. It is not easy to be an active member of a victim's inner circle. If, after a victimization, any relationship is to survive—and perhaps even deepen—much jointly suffered pain must be endured and coped with.

It is of utmost importance that the people within the victim's inner circle, particularly those who assume the most responsibility for the victim's day-to-day care, communicate well with one another. In the aftermath of a crime, there will be much confusion, anxiety, and pain over what has happened. The victim himself will be in a state of turmoil, and the members of his inner circle will be dealing with their own personal and complex reactions. There is not much time to ponder, plan, or consider the future. People are mainly functioning on "automatic pilot," doing what needs to be done by rote, to the best of their abilities, and trying somehow to come to grips with the horror of what has happened.

But, despite the chaos, it *is* possible to create a support system that will benefit not only the victim but all who surround him.

During the crisis period it is extremely important for family members and friends to pool their resources and work together so that the victim is made to feel as loved, secure, and comfortable as possible. The victim's mood and behavior may well be erratic and difficult to handle. And, at least initially, the best mode of behavior for those in the inner circle is to listen, to attend, and to accept all that is forthcoming.

For the first few days after an attack, relatives and friends should try to present an attitude of optimism. The last thing a crime victim needs immediately after the trauma is the added stress of seeing the pain and anxiety of those he loves. This could make him feel guilty, ashamed, and responsible for the suffering of the people he cares about most. And these feelings may lead him to repress or deny his own pain in an effort to protect his loved ones.

Sara Bosley, an attractive executive secretary in her mid-twenties, lived in a large apartment with two other young women. One night when both her roommates were out, Sara was awakened in her bed. Looking up, she saw a large, muscular man standing over her.

Sara tried to scream, but he gagged her with a scarf and warned her that if she made another sound he would kill her. He proceeded to rape her, all the while threatening to kill her when he was done.

Sara lay there, her mind a tangled mass of confusion, revulsion, and fear for her life. She heard her alarm clock ticking away and tried to focus on its steady, persistent beat, blocking out the horror of what was happening.

Finally, the man finished his relentless assault, and escaped through the same bedroom window he had used to enter the apartment.

Shaking and near hysteria, Sara called the police. They soon arrived and took her to the hospital for tests.

Sara's mind went completely numb. She allowed the doctors and nurses to perform their tests, feeling distanced from all of it.

Sara's boyfriend and closest girlfriend, who'd been contacted by the police, picked her up at the hospital and brought her back to the apartment. Still in a daze, she called her parents, who lived in a nearby town. They offered to come and take her home with them, but Sara refused, preferring to stay at her own place with her two friends.

The weekend after the rape, Sara, her parents, and her brother, James, had been scheduled to fly out of town together to a cousin's wedding. Because of what had happened, they all agreed to cancel these plans. None of them felt like attending a marriage celebration.

Sara's parents wanted to help their daughter. So, rather than staying home altogether, Mr. and Mrs. Bosley took their son and daughter away to a seaside resort for the weekend.

Sara remembers those three days as strained and miserable. "It was bizarre," she told me recently. "My family meant well, but I don't remember any of them asking me directly, 'How do you really feel?' Instead, there were a lot of lowered eyes and periods of silence. They seemed to be thinking, *Let's take Sara away and make her feel better somehow, but, God, let's not encourage her to dwell on it.* My parents seemed to feel that discussing it would provoke more pain, but the pain was *there*, hanging between us all anyway.

"I felt stifled. Frozen. I wanted to talk to them, but as much as they love me, I could tell they really didn't want to hear the details of what had happened. They were not emotionally prepared to listen to the facts of what I'd been through. And—though there'd be an occasional 'How are you, dear?'—I could see their eyes begging me not to respond in depth.

"So I clammed up. I took my feelings and jammed them down deep inside until they were numb. And I walked around like a robot.

"My dad took pictures of me during that weekend and they are hideous—my eyes were completely dull and vacant. I looked shell-shocked, stupefied, completely lifeless.

"Deep inside, I felt resentful that even here, out of town with my closest relatives, I could not open up and let them see the pain I felt. I saw how hurt they were already, and I couldn't bear the responsibility of making them feel even worse.

And at the same time, I felt guilty about my resentment toward them. So I was really a mess.

"I wanted to scream, 'Why take me away with you if you can't really face up to my problem?' But I didn't want to hurt them. So I said nothing at all.

"The life we'd led before my rape was picture-perfect. My brother and I were ideal kids. We were clean-cut, wholesome, obedient, good-natured. All in all, the Bosleys were the Happy Model Family. When this happened, it shattered my parents, bursting the bubble we'd all lived in.

"I know how hard this has been on them and they did the best they could with it. But I must admit that it would *really* have helped me so much if, soon after the rape, I hadn't felt pressured to repress and silence my pain whenever I was around my family. Eventually, they opened up and learned a lot about the subject of sexual assault. They became very supportive of me, and they've really grown through this experience."

WHO GETS THE ATTENTION—AND WHEN

While it is true that the friends and relatives of a victim suffer terribly, the person who has actually *experienced* the violent act—the victim himself—is, in the majority of cases, the one who suffers most of all. Therefore, particularly in the period immediately following the crime, much of the attention and concern of the inner circle should be concentrated upon the victim.

Nancy Kless, a therapist who works frequently with crime victims, described a situation encountered by one of her patients, a victim whose inner circle—in this case her mother and aunt—spent so much time immersed in their own hysteria that they ended up ignoring the victim's needs.

Lorna Perez, a shy young woman in her late twenties, moved to Houston, Texas, from her home in a small town in New Mexico. She'd just settled into her new apartment and had worked at her new job as a dietician only two weeks when she was mugged at a bus stop.

The two assailants took all her belongings and knocked

Lorna unconscious with a metal pipe. Moments after the attack, she was discovered by a patrol officer and taken to the hospital. Luckily, Lorna suffered only a mild concussion. She was admitted to the hospital for overnight observation and released the next day.

Lorna called her supervisor at work and explained what had happened. Concerned, he suggested that she take the rest of the week off. The young woman, who came from a protective Hispanic family, called home.

Knowing how worried her relatives would be, Lorna behaved calmly on the phone and insisted that she was just fine. But Mrs. Perez became hysterical. Despite her daughter's protests, she insisted upon flying to Houston with Lorna's aunt the next day.

Lorna had mixed feelings about her mother's and aunt's arrival. She had—at the age of twenty-seven—finally moved out of her parents' home and begun a life of her own. In a sense, she felt defeated at the thought of giving up her newfound independence. At the same time, Lorna was relieved that she wouldn't be alone in her sparsely furnished apartment. Her injured head throbbed, and she kept fighting off waves of panic and terror. No matter how hard Lorna tried, she could not forget the smirk on the face of the man who'd attacked her.

From the moment her relatives arrived, Lorna began to feel even worse. Both her mom and aunt were so distraught and hysterical that she could scarcely get a word in edgewise. Rather than listening to and soothing Lorna, the two women wept, moaned, and shouted about their distress.

Lorna felt utterly ignored. The only thing the two women really paid attention to was the enormous gash on her forehead. And each time they looked at it, it made them even more hysterical. Worst of all were their constant pleas for Lorna to pack up and move back home with them.

At times Lorna tried to confide in her relatives her own innermost thoughts and terrors about what happened. But they managed to use her expressions of pain as even more reason for her to leave the city. Because the two older women were so distraught, Lorna found herself taking care of *them* and trying to make *them* feel better.

"Everything will be fine, Mom," and "Don't worry, Auntie, I'm okay—just relax," she heard herself repeating again and again.

Inwardly, Lorna fumed: *I'm the one who got hurt. Why can't they pay attention to me?* But outwardly, she remained silent.

Lorna desperately needed to regain feelings of strength and autonomy—not to mention peace of mind. But when she suggested that they leave Houston earlier than they'd planned, the ladies were insulted.

Adamantly, they refused. Both women felt they were doing what was best for Lorna: cooking, cleaning, "fixing up" her apartment, telling stories about back home, and trying to entice her to return.

When the women finally left, Lorna, tense and unnerved, knew she needed help. She was thankful when a co-worker referred her to therapist Nancy Kless.

In her sessions with Ms. Kless, Lorna unleashed the pain she'd been keeping locked up inside. Eventually she learned to cope with both her post-traumatic stress reactions and her conflicting emotions regarding her relatives.

Generally speaking, it is a good idea to remain as calm and positive as possible while in direct contact with the victim. This is not meant to imply that members of a victim's inner circle should deny or repress their own feelings and torment. On the contrary, all concerned will fare better if they do indeed express their pain, their rage, and their confusion. The question is: *Where* should they turn for much-needed support of their own?

The people who may best understand their frightening and conflicting emotions are other members of the inner circle. Turning to *one another* can be an excellent idea. Two or more of the people involved can get together—at someone's home or elsewhere—in order to share their feelings and lean upon one another for support and consolation.

Recently, my best friend Patricia described the role-playing that she and others in my inner circle found helpful during the time I was still in critical condition.

Although Patricia had never met my mom before, her heart went out to her the moment they were introduced.

Patricia looked at the tiny gray-haired lady who looked so frightened and vulnerable, and vowed to help her through the ordeal.

Sensing my friend's kindness and sincerity, Mother allowed herself to confide in Patty and turned to her for solace. Often the two women sat huddled together in the corridor outside my room. Quietly, Patricia held Mom's hand, allowing her to weep and express the fear and anguish she so carefully hid from me.

For my mother, Patricia played the role of "compassionate listener," keeping her own pain and anxiety in check. Then, sometimes only moments later, Patty found herself needing to reverse roles completely.

Once Patricia felt that Mom was taken care of, she went off in search of my husband, who was holding up reasonably well during the initial crisis period. Finding Fred somewhere in the hospital—usually hunched over a cup of muddy cafeteria coffee—Patricia turned to him for support, weeping disconsolately in his arms and sharing her own pain with him.

Comforted by Fred's support, Patricia then felt strong enough to saunter into my room for a visit, once again composed and able to exude an attitude of hope and cheerfulness.

Although, before my attack, Patricia had never even met my mother and had not been particularly friendly with Fred, she was able to sustain herself—and help my mom—by alternately providing and seeking comfort.

AFTER THE CRISIS

Hopefully, within three or four days—unless there continues to be a threat of death—things will begin to settle down. At this point the victim still needs plenty of extra care and attention, but will probably begin to focus a bit more on those around him. Now is the time for members of the inner circle and the victim himself to be as open as possible about feelings and needs.

A good way to start this process is by asking the victim a few simple questions, such as:

"You're looking much more rested today—are you feeling a bit better?"

"Does it make you nervous when too many people visit all at once?"

"Are you up to talking to Aunt Helena this morning?"

"Would you like a little time by yourself?"

"Do those injections cause you a lot of pain?"

"Would you like Steve to come back tomorrow instead?"

Once members of the inner circle have ascertained some of the victim's basic opinions and desires, they can begin to share their own feelings with him. For example:

"I'm very tired, Kim. Would you mind if I left a little early tonight?"

"This has been very upsetting. I need to talk to our pastor this week about my feelings. Would you like him to visit you too?"

"Mother has been so distraught over everything. I think it's better to let her stay home for a few days. How do you feel about it?"

"We feel so terrible about what happened. Is there anything more we can do to help?"

The key is to proceed with caution. It is fine to admit to the victim that you're very upset over what happened and that you're having trouble sleeping. It is *not* fine to collapse in front of him and sob hysterically in his arms. He is just not ready for this.

It is important for members of the inner circle to begin to share their feelings with the victim *slowly*, being careful not to overwhelm the victim—and one another—with a massive, unrelenting flow of anguish and emotion.

After an attack, the victim often feels helpless, disoriented, frightened, depressed, and alienated. Somehow, nothing seems to be the same as it was before. One's relationship to friends, family, work, and home are all inexplicably altered. It is common for a victim to feel as though he is frozen or standing still while people and events spin madly all around him.

Although members of a victim's inner circle may be doing their best to handle the situation and meet the needs of the victim, the victim's perception of what they are doing and how they are behaving may be somewhat askew.

During this crisis period, the victim's emotional state—

and, often, his physical condition—are fragile. Having just had his psyche attacked and his entire being threatened, the victim often comes to see the world as an ugly and fearsome place. And, along with this altered perception of his environment comes an altered perception of the people in it.

For a while a victim's mind is occupied with the terrible event that has just occurred and with his own efforts to grapple with what has happened. Everyday realities of life—like eating properly, getting rest, paying bills, adhering to schedules—may seem extraneous or futile. It is hard to concentrate on anything not directly tied to the attack itself or its aftermath. And it may be difficult for the victim to understand that the needs and schedules of the people in his life are important to them and deserve consideration.

Members of the inner circle must function in society as well as help to care for the victim. But since, for the victim, "normal life" is far from being resumed, the people dearest to him may now seem—in his eyes—to be going around in circles.

On the other hand, members of the inner circle who are literally running themselves ragged trying to take care of the physical and emotional needs of the victim and who are met with apathy or perhaps even hostility can begin to think of the victim as "ungrateful," "spoiled," "thankless," "selfish," or worse.

One morning, only a few days after my attack, my fever had risen to 103 degrees, the pain jarred my nerves, and I was feeling panic-stricken. To make matters worse, a police officer had come to bring some of my clothing which had been found at the scene of the crime. While he was there, my mother tried to adjust my blanket and inadvertently jostled my IV pole.

I screeched in pain: "Mom! For God's sake, *tell* me when you're going to do something like that."

Mother flinched at the sharpness in my voice, and the police officer said to her: "Ma'am, if she were *my* daughter I'd kill her."

"No, you wouldn't, sir," Mother said quietly, and ushered him out of the room.

I felt terrible that I'd yelled at my mom. And the man's remark made me feel both hurt and guilty. So I lay there in bed, weeping miserably and apologizing to my mother.

"Theresa," she said, "I understand. The pain is getting to you—and I *should* tell you when I'm going to adjust something."

I felt a little better, knowing Mom wasn't angry, but the policeman's words still made me feel as though I'd been slapped.

Luckily, the people in my own inner circle were understanding and didn't make me feel guilty or terrible about my outbursts. But in many cases, family members make quick and unfair judgments, as the policeman had about me.

The best way—perhaps the only effective way for friends and family to preserve their long-term relationships with the victim—is for them to try to understand the rather perverse reactions of the victim as *normal* behavior under the terrible circumstances; and, above all, to realize that this early post-attack period of extreme stress, anger, and pain is temporary.

The person they love and cherish is still there—still capable of being the warm, loving, caring, considerate, thankful human being he was before the attack. But right now, the mechanisms of the victim's mind and body are not operating at 100 percent capacity. And it will take him a while to get back to his former level of functioning.

For anyone, a victimization is an enormous blow—a blow that is often unjust, unforeseen, and unutterably painful. The horror of the situation can cloud the mind with doubt, fear, and anxiety, awakening and exacerbating dormant negative feelings. And, temporarily, it can deaden the person's ability to feel hope, happiness, gratitude, and joy.

Unfortunately, a victimization can lead to radical personality changes, mood swings, and a despair so profound that it is bound to affect the way the victim relates to those around him. This dramatic and negative change in the victim is, thankfully, most often temporary.

While a victim's angry, hostile, depressed behavior may be hard on the members of the inner circle, it is even more painful, perplexing, and disturbing to *him*. Therefore he will often try to repress or change his own behavior. The result can be sudden and dramatic mood swings.

When confronted with unpleasant attack-related problems—like upsetting phone calls from the police, the arrival of staggering medical bills or the need for painful medical procedures—a victim may simply go off the deep end, flying into a rage, weeping nonstop, or withdrawing into a sullen, wordless sulk. This reaction may last for days, hours, or merely a few minutes, depending upon the victim's personality and the degree to which he has become upset.

Although the angry hostility of the victim is temporary, it is nonetheless painful for members of the inner circle to deal with. Therefore it is important for them to cope with their own resulting feelings, so that they don't come to resent or even abandon the victim.

A victim's inner circle is certainly not a fun club of which to be a member, but those who are in it can be a tremendous help to one another—as well as to the victim himself—by sharing the pain and trauma and, hopefully, the pride and satisfaction of triumphing over a horrific ordeal.

PROFESSIONAL HELP

Perhaps the most important question for members of the inner circle to deal with is: Should we seek professional help in getting through the early stages of this ordeal?

It is usually a relief for members of the inner circle to know that the victim is under the care of a mental health professional who can both guide him through the rough times ahead and give the loved ones advice about his needs. But the victim's psychological condition must be considered. Hopefully, he will request, agree to, or at least consider the idea of consulting a therapist. If, however, a victim refuses to see a therapist, it is best, at least initially, to acquiesce to his wishes, unless the victim's mood or behavior begins to seem severely disturbed, dangerous, or suicidal.

After the issue of psychological care for the victim has been dealt with, the members of his inner circle should consider whether some or all of them might benefit from therapy, either as a group or on an individual basis.

It is important that at least one friend or family member stress the value of seeking therapy as a positive and healthy step during a terrible ordeal, rather than as a last-ditch despairing act taken by a group of people too weak to cope with a crisis on their own.

SCHEDULING

As the days pass, it becomes more and more important—particularly if the victim is hospitalized—to develop a schedule that will coordinate and focus the group's efforts. This will help the victim while making sure that the needs of individual inner-circle members are dealt with.

Informal meetings of the people in the victim's inner circle are a good idea. Everything from the simplest to the most complex problems can be discussed. The time and place of such a meeting will be dictated by the needs, schedule, and geographic location of everyone involved. Private homes, hospital conference rooms, or other quiet areas are ideal.

Nina is a thirty-six-year-old housewife, shot and critically injured during a robbery. Here is an example of some of the problems faced by members of her inner circle:

MARY   (Nina's mother): is able to visit her daughter daily from nine to six but she needs a ride home from the hospital every evening.

JOHN   (Nina's husband): works all day and can be with his wife during evening visiting hours. But he needs someone to babysit for their eight-year-old daughter and infant son.

KAY   (a close family friend): has the flu and should not visit Nina. But she can make phone calls and inquiries about Nina's needs—future nursing care, a physical therapist, and help from the local Victim-Witness Assistance Program.

JOAN   (the victim's best friend and next-door neighbor): is having serious marital problems. Because of this, she can visit Nina only twice a week. But she promises to bring John and the children a home-cooked dinner every evening before he leaves for the hospital.

JULIE   (Nina and John's eight-year-old daughter): is having nightmares and doing poorly in school. Someone must have a conference with the teacher and discuss taking her to the school guidance counselor or to a child psychologist.

HEATHER   (the victim's sister): has three small children of her own. She offers to take five-month-old Billy into her home and care for him until Nina is out of the hospital and on the mend.

John, the husband, is already feeling burned out and overstressed. He cannot concentrate at work. Someone suggests that he take a leave of absence. But John feels that his family desperately needs the income his job provides. So he decides to take a week of his vacation time and try to catch up on his rest before going back to work.

Mary, the mother, feels guilty and frightened. She finds it increasingly difficult to relate to Nina. Her normally quiet, reserved daughter is now embittered, angry, and acting out her rage loudly and often. Mary wants to help, but these outpourings of anger are upsetting. She finds it hard not to weep in front of her daughter. Although she had never before considered the thought of seeing a therapist, Mary is grateful when her elder daughter, Heather, agrees to accompany her to a consultation with a psychologist.

Luckily, this victim's family and friends are able to communicate well with one another and to share in the responsibilities. And it is true that after a tragedy, groups of people who normally would be uninterested in each other—or even downright hostile—often "pull together" to help the victim and themselves.

But what do you do when those in the inner circle are unwilling—or unable—to deal with one another effectively? One solution might be to have a social worker or therapist lead one or two group sessions to clear the air and help delegate responsibilities, or at least to let the members hear one another out. If this is impossible, the next best thing would be for the inner circle to break into two or three smaller groups, separating those who are incompatible.

At least one person in each small group should be asked to communicate by phone with the other group or groups, so that people don't duplicate time-consuming errands and duties.

It is important, regardless of the dynamics and climate within a given inner circle, that no one or two members become overburdened. Naturally, the relatives or friends closest to the victim will accept a larger portion of the responsibility, but it is unfair to expect them to do virtually everything. Within the inner circle, everyone should be encouraged to take on as much as, but not more than, they can handle well.

Even those outside the inner circle can be invaluable to the victim and to his loved ones simply by filling in for the people who are doing the most. If a casual friend or neighbor genuinely offers to help—accept graciously. There are many tasks at hand which need not be done by a member of the inner circle.

Some examples: providing transportation to and from the hospital for an out-of-town relative, shopping for groceries for the victim's family, watering the victim's untended garden, or feeding his cat or dog. Little chores like this take time and energy—the two things which, for members of the victim's inner circle, will most likely be in short supply.

Despite the horror of the circumstances, it's wise to remember that all involved need an occasional break. Those friends or relatives who are helping part-time but are not overburdened might try to see that those who are truly exhausted take a morning off once or twice a week. Or they might offer to take the victim's spouse's place as a hospital visitor one day while he takes his children to the park.

When the victim is ready physically and emotionally, he may want to play an active role in the goings-on within his circle of friends and relatives. If this is the case, he will probably contribute a great deal simply by sharing his feelings, thoughts, and desires. In this way, the inner circle has immediate feedback and will not need to *guess* what the victim needs or wants.

It is crucial that members of the inner circle really *listen* to the victim. He may not always need what you think he needs. The victim may honestly be craving a morning or so alone. Or, rather than needing peace and quiet after an upcoming operation, he may actually want lots of visitors to distract him.

Every victim, of course, is different. One victim may want his friends and family to talk about their own feelings and problems in his presence, so that he will feel a part of all that is going on. Another victim—particularly someone who has been gravely injured or psychologically damaged by the attack—may need to concentrate solely upon his own healing and his own emotional condition. He may, at least initially, prefer to have others make decisions for him and keep their own problems and anxieties away from him for a while.

REACHING OUT TO OTHERS

Quotes from members of various victims' inner circles:

"Thank God for Megan's boyfriend Jake—without him, I'd have gone out of my mind."
—Mother of an assault and battery victim

"My wife was truly amazing. She spent nearly every moment at the hospital and held us all together. I was a nervous wreck, but Laura kept me going."
—Son of an elderly mugging victim

"Members of our family flew in from everywhere. We rented hotel rooms, prayed together, ate together, and became much closer through it all."
—Sister of a woman gravely injured in a shooting

"Most of Jim's family lives in Eastern Europe, so all of his friends here in the States banded together and created a 'family' of our own. We shared the responsibilities and basically leaned on each other through it all. And he's come through it beautifully."
—Friend of an assault victim

"I didn't even *know* my sister's husband and best girlfriend. We lived three thousand miles apart. But, during the crisis, it was just the three of us. Without those two, I don't know how I could have coped."
—Sister of a kidnap/sexual assault victim

"My sister-in-law and I have never had anything in common. In fact, we pretty much avoided each other most of the time. But when Blake was hurt, she and I pulled together, took care of everything. We made all decisions jointly, nursed Blake back to health, and we even shared an apartment for a while. That was over a year ago. I can't say she and I are best buddies now, but I'll never forget that lady and all she did to help."

—Wife of a stabbing victim

"Elsa's boss and co-workers were phenomenal. They knew we'd just moved here and had few friends and no family in this town. So they really pitched in and helped. The office raised funds for the wheelchair my wife needed, and they connected me to a bunch of vital services I never knew existed. Not only that, but they invited me to dinner at their homes and kept me company too. It was amazing."

—Husband of a shooting victim

After interviewing a great many people who have been close to victims of crime, I've come to see that, almost without exception, the friends and relatives of victims do indeed reach out to others.

Many who've been part of a victim's inner circle may later go on to use their experience in order to help others, but throughout the crisis period and during the time immediately following it, *reaching out to others* usually translates into reaching out to *each* other.

Vera Kiley is a loving mother of five. When she found out that her only daughter, Janet (whom I interviewed for the chapter on anger) was shot—and rendered paralyzed—because she'd refused to dance with a stranger in a discotheque, Mrs. Kiley could scarcely believe the news. Only after rushing to the hospital did she realize the grim reality of what had been done to her child.

Luckily, Janet's four older brothers rushed to their mother's side and, together with Vera Kiley, formed a network of care and support for Janet and for themselves.

"We've always been a close family," Vera confided to me recently, "and when my husband passed away eight years ago, all my children rallied around me. But this terrible ordeal we've gone through recently has made us even tighter. Before my husband died, he spoke to my son Daniel and said, 'You're the oldest. If anything happens to me, you're in charge of watching out for the family.' "

Daniel really took his father's wish to heart. When Vera Kiley was widowed, Daniel was attentive to her emotional needs and made himself available to help her whenever she needed him.

Then, after Janet was shot, Daniel assumed the role of father-protector. A forty-three-year-old bachelor, Daniel gave up his apartment and moved in with his mother and sister. Though Mrs. Kiley is able to take care of many of her daughter's needs, she doesn't drive and is physically unable to lift and carry Janet or her heavy wheelchair and braces. Daniel now does nearly all the heavy work, including transporting his sister to numerous appointments with doctors, therapists, and the like.

"He's a delight," Mrs. Kiley exclaimed. "He never complains and is always there for Janet and me. For the moment, helping us through this rough period is Daniel's lifework."

Recently I met Daniel Kiley and was impressed by his warm, easygoing manner. Slender and muscular, Daniel is very athletic—each day he runs about six miles.

Janet and her brother Daniel obviously have a mutual admiration society. I found it especially impressive that there is nothing in Daniel's attitude that implies he feels overburdened, put upon, or trapped in a role he doesn't want to play. What Daniel Kiley does for his family is clearly done out of love. He seems a man at peace with himself, satisfied that he's doing the best he can to cope with a painful situation.

Janet is very much at the center of the family circle. Basically uncomplaining and cheerful, she knows she is loved and cared for, realizes how much her family does for her, and tries to accomplish as much as possible on her own.

"David is another of my sons," Vera Kiley said. "He lives close by and is the pastor of our church. He and our congregation have been praying for Janet ever since she was shot, and it has been a great help to all of us. But David doesn't *only* pray for his sister. He does plenty of other things, too.

"For example, it's been pretty hot lately and we've felt very cooped up and kind of fidgety, so I told David about it.

That same evening, he and I participated in a prayer meeting together and asked God for a way to bring us all closer together and break up our routine for a while.

"On the way home, David spotted a motor home and said, 'Mom, that's it!'

"The very next morning, he went and rented a big old motor home. We're all going down to Utah together for a week. We surely can't afford a real vacation, with hotel rooms and restaurants and the like, so we're just going to buy some groceries, pile into that motor home, and drive on out there. And it was all David's doing.

"The family takes care of each other now. What happened to Janet has been painful for each one of us. Something like this is a terrible shock. But we turn to each other with our feelings—both the good and the bad. And we all share the work.

"This is my life now and I accept it. My daughter has been so brave through all this and I am happy to do my part: overseeing Janet's health care, washing diapers and catheters, helping with her physical therapy, and anything else I need to do. I'm her mother—her secretary and her friend too. I call Janet 'my roomie' and we get along just fine.

"And the beautiful thing is I know I can rely on my sons. Daniel lives right here, but my other boys are always helpful too. If I need anything, I can call any of them and they're here in a flash.

"My sons take me grocery shopping and to church, and they make sure that Janet gets out for some air and to all her appointments. Nobody feels resentful in this family—we just plain love each other and we are so *grateful* our Janet is alive. You can just imagine how proud we are of the hard work she's doing to build herself up again.

"We take Janet's injury—and all the needs it creates—as facts of life now. This is the way it is—for a while, anyway. And we just pitch in and get it all done. There's nothing formalized. We don't say, 'Hey, Dave, you're in charge of this and Mom will do that and Daniel has the other.' We just all do what we can and we appreciate each other for it.

"I'm lucky. When I talk, my children listen. They've always looked up to me since they were babies, and their dad and I did our best for them in every way. And now they are wonderful grown people.

"My other son Vincent was hit the hardest. He and Janet had been ballroom-dancing partners for years. He could not believe anyone could hurt his sister like this. I remember him weeping and weeping for hours on end.

"Vincent is a fashion model in Colorado, so of course we don't see him very often. But his calls are wonderful and he is a *big* spirit-booster for Janet. He telephones every weekend and they talk forever. I have to pry her away from the phone so his bills won't get too high. But he gives Janet his special pep talks and tells her how much faith he has in her and urges her to stick with it and keep working at getting her strength back. And of course Vincent perks me up too. He's darling. His work is out-of-state and we're all fine here now, but I know if he was needed, Vincent would be here too.

"*Thank God for my family* are the five words I say and think the most. We have always been able to be completely honest with each other. Though we might disagree at times, we are always supportive and back each other up.

"This trip to Utah will be the first vacation we've taken together since the kids were little. And we can hardly wait. I guess some families would say, 'Oh, yuck—seven days cooped up in a motor home with all of you—no way!' But this is just the kind of thing we love to do.

"I guess if a family doesn't get along, a tragedy like this could make things even worse. But for a family where there's a lot of love and concern for each other to begin with, the one *good* thing to get out of all this horror is that you find yourselves reaching out to each other and helping each other through it all. And you end up even closer and more loving because of it."

Many people would look at the situation the Kiley family is in and feel enormous pity and sorrow for them. But after speaking to Vera Kiley, I honestly believe that despite the tragedy they have had to contend with, the Kileys have—by reaching out to one another during the crisis—managed to get something positive out of it: the growth and strengthening of their family ties and of the love they have for one another.

*   *   *

Recently, I spoke with the people who made up the inner circle of Diane Craine. Diane, you'll recall from the chapter on fear, was beaten brutally with a board, kidnapped, and left for dead.

The two people who took on the responsibility for Diane right after her attack were her mother, Agnes Mahler, who flew out from Wyoming to be with her, and Tony Cruise, the man Diane had been living with for five years. In addition, both Mrs. Mahler and Tony were in constant telephone contact with Diane's eldest sister, Barbara, who became an important—albeit long distance—member of Diane's inner circle.

Tony received the first call from the hospital, which had just admitted Diane. They told him only a few sketchy details of what had happened, but stressed the critical nature of Diane's condition. After assuring the nurse that he'd leave at once for the hospital (which was over two hours away), he hurriedly dialed Diane's mother in Wyoming.

"I'll be there soon, Tony," Agnes said, swallowing hard. Less than an hour later, she and her husband boarded a 727 to Chicago.

"It was the longest three hours I've ever lived through," said Mrs. Mahler recently. "All that time, I had no idea of what was happening to Diane, or whether she was even still alive. I can't find words to describe how I felt except that I had a completely sick feeling in the pit of my stomach. This was the kind of thing that happened to people on TV—not in the quiet suburbs of Chicago."

Finally the flight was over. The Mahlers took a taxi to the hospital, where Tony met them in the corridor.

"She doesn't look good, but don't let her know it," he said quietly. Then they went in to see Diane.

"She looked awful," said Mrs. Mahler. "She was bruised and bandaged and ghostly white. And her eyes looked absolutely terrified. But I was utterly relieved just to see her lying there alive.

"The moment I saw her, I felt so many emotions beginning to rush to the surface. *Keep calm*, I told myself. *Be strong for Diane.*

"So I made a conscious effort to keep my emotions under control and not show anything. This has always been my pattern anyway—I tend to do well during a crisis and then fall apart later.

"That is how I responded to my first husband's death. And I did the same kind of thing after Diane's attack. I was there one hundred percent for my daughter and remained strong throughout the ordeal.

"Later, once I returned home to Wyoming, I paid for it with a lengthy period of depression and anxiety. But at least I was able to hold up and help my daughter as well as I could. That was the most important thing of all.

"As Diane's mother, I immediately assumed much of the responsibility for her care. But I was supported by Tony, who was wonderful.

"Tony and I had met briefly a few times before, but we were really only casual acquaintances. During this time, I came to see what a fine young man he is.

"It was a relief to have someone else there whom Diane loved and trusted. He was, above all, steady, supportive, and caring.

"I wasn't thinking of needing support for myself at that time, but I must admit I appreciated that he, above all, seemed to understand my feelings. Just talking to Tony was helpful to me. In our family we don't cry easily or break down. Instead, we express our feelings verbally. My husband was wonderful in his own way, but didn't know Diane intimately. But her boyfriend, Tony, was more than willing to listen and to talk, as well as to help in any way.

"Here was a fellow who truly loved my daughter and was kind and respectful to me. A helping hand goes such a long way in a crisis like ours.

"Tony and I soon fell into a fairly steady pattern of caring for and visiting Diane.

"Generally, I spent the entire day with her, from about eight in the morning until six-thirty or so. Then, after work, Tony arrived and stayed until very late. Therefore, Diane had someone with her during every waking hour. And at the same time, I was able to rest at night and Tony was worry-free at work during the day, knowing that I was attending to Diane.

"During the first few weeks, Diane's needs were especially great. Sick with worry, we tried our best to be positive for her. The biggest concern was how severely impaired she might be. Head injuries are so hard to predict. Basically, what the doctors said was: 'Wait and see.'

"Well, it was very hard to just 'wait and see,' because it was evident from her behavior that my daughter's personality had undergone a radical change. I was fearful that, because of brain damage, she'd never again be the Diane I'd always known. She was acting so difficult, unreasonable, and irrational.

"One day a nurse came in and said, 'Hi, my name's Amy,' and Diane, coldly and quietly, started repeating: 'Get her out of here, get her out of here, I don't want anything to do with her, get her out.'

"I tried to calm Diane down but she wouldn't listen. Finally the nurse agreed to leave and I asked my daughter: 'Why, Diane?'

"She said to me: 'That was the name of the "woman" who called to buy my car. That was the alias he used to get me there.'

"Although I now understood why Diane was so upset, I was still shocked. I had never heard such cold, calculated anger. Her voice had been icy, detached. She was so hard, so odd—so unlike herself.

"And there were other changes. She was terribly demanding and agitated all the time and always complaining about something. My daughter had *never* been a complainer before, and many of her gripes were petty and trivial. She wouldn't wash her hair. Wouldn't shower. And she's such a fastidious girl.

"We asked her doctors: 'Will she remain so unreasonable?' And they said there was no way to tell. The combination of the traumatic and violent assault plus the massive head injuries could actually cause a permanent personality change. Time would tell. This news was a great blow.

"Because Diane's behavior and condition were so erratic, I felt like I was on a big seesaw—whichever way the seesaw swung would depend on Diane's behavior.

"Some days she seemed much like her former cheerful and quick-witted self. Other days she'd be dull-eyed, listless, and unresponsive. After a day like that I'd sink to the depths, convinced that the brain damage was, after all, very severe. Those nights, I found it hard to sleep. I'd call Tony and we'd compare notes about Diane's behavior. Sometimes he'd found her much the same as she'd been with me all day. Other times he'd tell me that she'd become noticeably brighter and more responsive. In either case, it helped to talk to Tony, who knew exactly where I was coming from.

"The two of us were in much the same position. We both loved Diane, were worried terribly about her condition, and were committed to helping her in any way possible. We shared many of the same emotions, including the need to present an image of strength and calm.

"As a mother, I felt sickened and horrified by what my daughter had been through. And the worst part was the sense of powerlessness. I couldn't just kiss her bruises away and send her off for ice cream. I couldn't promise her a new dress. And I couldn't even say, 'This won't ever happen again,' because these awful, shameful things are happening every day. I am her mother, but I couldn't give her a solution and make her well again. And I couldn't take her pain away either.

"I don't know if I could have coped with everything quite as well if it hadn't been for Tony. In a sense, he knows the grownup Diane better than I do, because he's been living with her for five years of her adult life. So, sometimes he even advised me on how best to deal with a particular situation and how to respond in a way my daughter would accept. Of course, there's nothing *quite* like a mother's love and I don't downplay my role in her recovery.

"But Tony did many things for us and for her. He called their friends and even our family members and filled them in on Diane's condition. He was always there for me if I needed him. He was strong, uncomplaining, and willing to shoulder much of the responsibility. And he was always glad to talk to me about Diane or about my own concerns. I can't praise Tony enough for his help.

"My husband, Jordan, was wonderful in his own way. He

came with me many times to visit Diane and he was completely sympathetic to both of us. The way he expressed his feelings was to focus all his anger upon the assailant. I'd never seen Jordan so angry and hostile in my life. In a way, it was frightening. But I knew it helped him to blow off steam by railing against the attacker, so I felt it was basically a healthy reaction. At least he had a target for his rage.

"We were also in telephone contact with Diane's sisters and brother, all of whom live in different states. Barbara, who has multiple sclerosis, was the most emotional. We talked just about every day.

"This helped a great deal too. It was good to hear how much my daughters cared for each other, and how important Diane was to her older sister.

"Barbara called constantly and offered to help in any way. She desperately wanted to fly out, but her condition prevented that. It was encouraging to feel that my children rallied around Diane and me, and even though she couldn't be there, I felt my contact with Barbara provided me with solace."

Barbara Morris lives in Vermont, and when her mother said she'd agreed to an interview, I called her at her home. The wife of a college professor, Barbara enjoys a fulfilling life in the beautiful New England countryside. Talking to Barbara Morris pointed up the fact that even those key people in a victim's life who cannot be physically present throughout the ordeal are altered by what has happened. They suffer not only the pain of knowing what their loved one is going through but the added distress of not being able to *be* there.

"I've always felt a special affinity for Diane," Barbara Morris confided recently. "Although I'm the oldest of five—and Diane is nine years my junior, there has always been a tie linking us together.

"When I first heard what happened to my sister, I absolutely flipped out. I was shocked at the degree of emotional anguish and grief which Diane's attack put me through. I felt violated, angry, terrified, helpless. And it was horrible to be thousands of miles away, knowing how badly hurt my sister was.

"I immediately wanted to fly out and be there with Diane. But, having M.S., I can't travel easily. And after speaking to my mom and to Tony, I realized that there was no real need for me to be there. Diane was being completely taken care of. And in a sense I felt I would be more of a burden to everyone because of my own physical limitations. But if I'd felt that Diane really needed me there, I would have gone anyhow and helped in every possible way.

"During the first days and weeks, Tony helped to hold me together. Because he spent so many hours with me on the phone and filled me in on virtually every minute detail, in spite of the distance I felt a part of Diane's 'inner circle,' as you call it.

"The many miles between us felt unbearable at times. I wanted to see her with my own eyes—touch her, kiss her. I felt so isolated and helpless. When I told Tony this, he reached out to me and was wonderful on the phone. He was so patient and painstaking. Because he filled me in on all the details, I felt that I knew exactly how Diane was doing from day to day. This eased my anxiety somewhat.

"In the beginning, Diane was incoherent. She wasn't herself at all. She seemed so different and so distracted—not like the bubbly, extremely sharp-minded sister I've always known. When I was upset by the way my sister sounded, Tony would say, 'It'll take time but I know Diane's gonna be okay.' Now that I think of it, I realize how distraught he himself must have been. But he managed to act wonderfully supportive and uplifting for both my mother and myself—and, especially, for Diane.

"So I'm grateful for the kindness he showed to *us*—and even more grateful for the love, concern, and support he gave to Diane. Not all men would be able to stand by a woman throughout such a horrendous ordeal.

"Even talking about the attack right now, *I* start feeling angry all over again. I feel shaky—like I want to cry. There was so much pain my sister had to go through. And all of us who love her felt it too.

"Luckily, I was in therapy at the time, so I could talk about my own anxiety with my psychiatrist, as well as with Tony. People who heard about what happened to Diane often made remarks which suggested that she'd somehow asked for it, or that the attack could have been avoided. This freaked me out.

It absolutely enraged me. But I eventually realized that people—when confronted by a horrible situation—like to rationalize things so that they can believe it couldn't possibly happen to them.

"I have M.S., so I know what it's like to cope with something people consider frightening and unusual. And because I'm no stranger to health problems, I could empathize with Diane's physical ordeal even more.

"After my sister's attack, I found myself crying all the time. My husband was understanding and kind, but he didn't know Diane very well so it didn't hit him so hard. I went through a lot of changes over this. I became much more wary and fearful. In the past, I'd always generally trusted people, but since the attack I've grown tougher and more cautious.

"Although I love Diane deeply, in our family we rarely discuss these feelings out loud. So Tony became the go-between. I hadn't known him very well before, and in a way that made it easier for me to talk to him more freely on the phone. I didn't feel I could act overtly upset on the phone with other members of the family—and I certainly didn't want to burden or upset Diane.

"But Tony never discouraged me from being emotional. He just listened and responded whenever I needed him. It's amazing, really, that in a crisis you can sometimes get the most intense degree of support from someone you hardly knew before."

After my interviews with Diane's mother and sister, I was eager to speak with Tony.

"The role I definitely saw myself in," Tony told me, "was that of helper, supporter, provider of strength. I believed it was the most helpful thing I could offer throughout the crisis.

"My number one concern was about Diane. She needed to vent her anguish, as well as have her questions answered about all that had happened to her. She kept forgetting things all the time and found this frustrating. So I would fill her in on what she needed to know. We talked for hour upon hour.

"I made myself responsible for dispersing information. So many people were calling—particularly Barbara, who phoned all the time—and they needed *facts*. They needed to know how Diane was, both physically and emotionally.

"Barbara, especially, was torn up and hated being so far away. I found it touching to know how much she loved her sister. And I could hear the genuine pain Barbara felt. So I made myself available to talk whenever possible.

"As I think back," Tony continued, "Diane's mom was the biggest help of all. If it hadn't been for that lady I'm sure I might've been much more emotionally distraught and not much good to anyone else. The woman has a built-in calming effect on people. She works with the mentally retarded, so I'm sure that over the years she has developed a way of dealing with people that is soothing and level—even in a crisis.

"I found it comforting to share my feelings about Diane and the attack with Mrs. Mahler because she truly understood—from the inside. No one else even began to fathom the depth of my distress or the darkest reality of what had happened. It's still difficult to explain to others. They just aren't able to listen and comprehend it fully. But Mrs. Mahler and I—even without words—shared the total knowledge of the full, terrible truth of what Diane and we were going through.

"I tried to emulate Diane's mom by staying as calm as possible, no matter how bad things got. Diane, at any rate, was expressing enough upsetment and anguish for all three of us—as she had a perfect right to do!

"There's an instinct in most males—whether you're a macho type or not—to protect and provide. When something like this happens, even though you know it's not really your fault, you get an underlying feeling that you let someone down. Of course I wish I'd been there to protect Diane and prevent her from being hurt. But I wasn't. And I have to live with that. I knew I couldn't go back to the past and change what happened. So I felt the best thing I could do was take care of her in the present. Knowing I was doing right by Diane and by her family made me feel better about myself. I knew I was doing as much as possible to help.

"I felt badly enough about what happened. But the attitudes that other people expressed compounded my pain. When people don't understand something, they tend to say things which are hurtful and infuriating.

"I heard remarks like 'Why weren't you there? I'd never let

something like that happen to my girlfriend.' Or else they'd boast: 'If that happened to *my* wife, I'd kill that little bastard.'

"Some people implied that I had not only not done enough to protect Diane initially, but that I *still* wasn't doing enough. But Diane's mom didn't make me feel guilty about anything. She never pointed a finger at me and was always supportive about all I did in the past and present.

"Thoughts of vengeance and vigilantism go through anyone's mind after a thing like this. But that is a knee-jerk reaction. It's easy to fantasize about it, but when you consider the realities, you see how unfeasible violent retribution is.

"I am not a murderer. And if I ever tried to hurt anyone, I'm the one who'd end up in prison. Neither Diane nor her family ever suggested that I should run out and hurt or kill that guy. But we are all, nevertheless, absolutely enraged about what he did to Diane.

"To tell you the truth, after going through the trial with Diane, I can see how some people would feel that they *had* to take the law into their own hands. The man who attacked Diane got off so lightly that it is a complete insult to all of us. He was *not* adequately punished, yet Diane will be suffering forever because of what he did to her. And in terms of our pain and memories, so will her family and I.

"It makes me feel good to hear that Mrs. Mahler felt I was of value to her. All I can say is: I think *she's* the one who deserves most of the credit for creating a calm and supportive environment for us all."

Once the initial trauma of a victimization is over, some members of a victim's inner circle may wish to help others by sharing their experience. Those who do so often realize a dual benefit: first, of helping people in need, and second, of helping themselves by creating something positive out of a negative experience.

Claire Bosley—whose daughter, Sara, was sexually assaulted—has done exactly that. After her daughter's psychological recovery, Claire became involved in educating people about rape and related issues. Claire doesn't remember making a conscious decision to help others. Rather, opportunities came to her and she accepted—warily at first, but then gradually with a sense that what she was doing was truly helpful to others.

Claire is one of nine women who hold national executive authority over her college sorority. As one of her responsibilities, she attends a conference of twenty-six national sororities. Therefore she can help others, not only in her own group but also on a much wider scale.

At the conferences, resolutions are passed and action begun on matters relevant to college women. One recent project was a major campaign against drug and alcohol abuse. Another was a program concerned with eating disorders—anorexia nervosa and bulimia.

At one conference, the issue of sexual harassment and abuse came up, and as the women discussed the issue, Claire was amazed at the ignorance of most members. Many of them found it hard to comprehend the degree to which acquaintance rape, stranger rape, and sexual harassment occur on college campuses across the country. Some expressed a strong sense of disbelief.

Claire took a deep breath and said, "I know about this. My daughter was raped." Someone gasped audibly. Then the room fell silent. Briefly, Claire shared some of what had happened with the group and was surprised at the degree of discomfort and squeamishness they expressed about the subject. But as others joined in the discussion, most came to support the idea of a program to educate college women about the issue. A resolution regarding sexual harassment, assault, and abuse was passed.

Claire, now suddenly considered an expert of sorts, was asked to be involved in the exploration of the topic. "We don't have any resources on this," someone blurted.

"We'll *find* resources," Claire responded.

"The idea behind it," Claire explained, "is to educate young sorority women to heed warning signals regarding a potential instance of sexual harassment. To teach them prevention techniques and to tell them what to do if it happens to them or to a friend. When the program goes into effect, thousands of college women will benefit from it."

Recently, Claire's pastor asked her to speak about rape before a women's group in the congregation. The pastor's idea was to educate the ladies—most of them elderly—about this difficult issue which was unfortunately beginning to touch the lives of even these seemingly sheltered women.

For many of them, the very idea of an innocent woman being sexually assaulted provoked deep spiritual problems. The pastor asked Claire to discuss the rape of her own daughter, how it affected the family, and how, in fact, people can endure such a horrendous and traumatic event and still go on with their lives.

In a sense, Claire found it sad and almost cruel to crack the little shells of invulnerability that protected most of the church ladies, but she found that they were genuinely interested in hearing about sexual assault in this very personal way. They were truly able to grasp the inherent emotional and spiritual problems by hearing of them from the mother of a girl who had actually experienced rape.

Toward the end of the meeting, two of the women spoke up and said it had happened in their own families—to their granddaughters. Both had been afraid to broach the subject to the victims, fearing it would cause the girls too much pain. After talking about it to Claire, they both decided to be open with their granddaughters, to ask them if they wanted to talk about it, and even to suggest that they seek help at a rape treatment center, if needed.

When the group broke for the evening, a few of the women looked shocked and pale, but all of them thanked Claire and the pastor many times over for the presentation.

Claire Bosley also reaches out to others in her day-to-day life, simply by talking about the topic and sharing her in-depth knowledge.

"I've gotten to the point where, if the subject arises, I can speak out and say, 'It happened to my family,' " Claire told me.

"So many people have terrible misconceptions, and many still believe it is somehow the fault of the victim—or that it doesn't happen to 'nice' people. After people talk to *me* about it, they feel quite differently. And that is rewarding—just clearing up some of the sheer lack of understanding.

"My daughter, Sara, has gotten very involved in helping others and she often addresses large groups on the subject of sexual assault. At first it was hard for me to accept her doing that. I worried that it would prolong her pain. But I talked about it with Sara and came to see that reaching out to others is, in fact, helping her to heal. And I feel that, if she can do it, so can I.

"Sometimes I find it upsetting to be asked certain questions which bring up the pain of the past. But I take a deep breath and get on with it.

"Even though it's hard at times, I'm glad to be helpful— and Sara says she's proud of me for doing it.

"I definitely feel a sense of responsibility—that I need to at least attempt to make others aware of what's happening out there, so that some people may take steps to *avoid* being sexually assaulted, and others may come to a better understanding of it."

For Claire Bosley, reaching out to others with her newfound understanding of rape is far from easy. But it creates a positive way of using the pain of the past to help others—and herself—in the present.

HUMOR

While life in the aftermath of a crime is painful, confusing, and frustrating for all concerned, eventually the victim and his inner circle will discover that even the worst of situations has its moments of levity.

Recently I spoke again with Vera Kiley, mother of Janet Kiley, who was shot and paralyzed. The most remarkable— and utterly charming—thing about Mrs. Kiley is the loud, infectious chortle that peppers her conversation. As she herself puts it, Vera Kiley laughs "from way deep down inside."

When I asked how she held on to her sense of humor throughout the ordeal, Vera replied, "Well, if all our family and friends did these days was to get down and sad about the terrible things we've been through, how on earth could Janet feel good enough to continue her therapy and work toward getting well again? And how could *we* go on with our lives?

"Basically, we just won't let ourselves get too low and depressed. We look at the good things: the fact that Janet is alive and here with us, the fact that we're so close as a family, and the fact that there's still a lot of joy in our lives somehow.

"There's no way to deny the pain we all feel about what happened," she continued. "Janet's the youngest child in the family, and all four of her brothers worship her. When their baby sister was shot, those boys took it very hard. But in time, we all came to see that—both for Janet and for ourselves—we needed to keep our spirits high. So we tried to perk up her spirits—telling lots of jokes and getting her to laugh at even the dumbest, silliest things. And she responded to it.

"Luckily, Janet has always been a very 'up' girl. Sure, she gets depressed a lot—as she has a right to—but my daughter is not only brave and stoic, she's also an extremely fun-loving person.

"Some people, I suppose, are shocked when they hear my daughter making jokes about her own injury or about physical handicaps in general. But Janet's a very frank and straightforward girl, and these jokes of hers help her to cope with it all.

"One day Janet was having her therapy in the swimming pool at the Gibbs Institute and she said, 'Mom, what's a good name for a guy with no arms and legs in a swimming pool?' I told her I had no idea and she shouted, 'Bob!' and started whooping with laughter.

"I tried to shush her, wondering what the other patients would think. But I looked around me and saw that they were all laughing too!

"I'll tell you, Janet really learned to laugh again at Gibbs. The whole atmosphere there is like a big party. The patients tell jokes—about their handicaps and everything else under the sun. They work incredibly hard, but they have a good time too. And the staff encourages this, which makes all the difference in the world in terms of the patients' progress and attitude.

"In the other hospitals Janet had been in, all they ever did was discourage us and bring us down. The attitude was: 'This injury is terrible, serious, crippling. It's no laughing matter.' The outlook in those institutions was bleak. They never laughed, and—most of the time—they never even *smiled*.

"As a result, most of the patients and their families became more and more depressed and miserable. The patients and visitors felt *guilty* about laughing or cracking a smile.

"But then, when we finally found Gibbs, we saw that their approach was entirely different. Yes, they were serious about the hard work involved, but they *encouraged* humor and sparks of personality. They treated the patients and families like individuals. With their upbeat and positive attitude they made therapy a *happy* thing—something to look forward to, rather than to dread. And the staff is very friendly and cheerful—not that *fake* kind of cheeriness that's condescending, but a really bright and supportive attitude. The staff calls the patients by nicknames; they tease each other; they tell jokes—and all the patients there end up feeling good about themselves. Because of this, they do better in their therapy and make faster and better progress.

"It's so hard for these patients to do all the painful work required in order to get even a *minimal* response from their bodies. And it can be tough on the families and friends who accompany them each day, giving them physical and emotional support. It hurts to watch their struggle. So we—the families and friends—appreciate it so much when people allow us to let down our hair, to smile and relax awhile and to enjoy ourselves in spite of it all.

"Weeping and feeling depressed at times is natural, but it *drains* you. On the other hand, laughing and being happy makes you feel energized."

"I agree," offered Janet's older brother Daniel. "Laughter can be incredibly healing. And Janet," he said, "just like our mom, has always had an incredible sense of humor. Fortunately her spirit wasn't dampened at all by the attack. If anything, she came to rely upon humor even more in her life.

"I remember Janet laughing when she was still in ICU. It wasn't a shrill, hysterical kind of laughter, but an ability to see the whole situation from a different, and brighter, perspective. She just refused to be kept down, no matter what had happened. And we all followed her example.

"I often transport Janet to different appointments, and it can take her quite a while to perform certain tasks. When she's especially slow and I have to stand there and wait, I'm sometimes tempted to become exasperated—or to feel sorrow and pity for Janet because she can't get around the way she used to. But instead, I'll joke with her, call her 'slowpoke,' and in general take a lighter attitude about the whole thing. In this way I don't contribute to any frustration or annoyance Janet might be feeling herself.

"A lot of times it is inevitable for Janet—and the rest of us—to compare and contrast how she functioned 'before,' and how she functions now. The differences are striking. Janet was always so sprightly and nimble, independent in mind and body—never holding back on anything but pouncing upon life with incredible physical energy.

"Of course, for now, her abilities are altered. We can't avoid comparisons. But what we do is poke gentle fun at the changes and perhaps use a touch of sarcasm, rather than hanging our heads and seeing the changes as terrible, pathetic, or dismal. I always encourage Janet to look *up*, and to see this as a growth experience. It's not always easy. But being lighthearted is a big help.

"She showed us from the very beginning that she was able and willing to laugh in the face of her suffering. We've taken our cues from her, and that has allowed us *all* to retain our joy and our senses of humor."

Mrs. Kiley had a special story to tell: "Just the other day we were at the church where my middle son David is pastor. After the service ended, the organist was playing some lively music. Janet was wearing her leg braces and started rocking back and forth. Then she locked her legs tight and raised her hands over her head and started clapping. Obviously, she can't move from the waist down—*yet* that is—but she began to do this silly little wiggle with her upper body, twisting around like crazy.

"Well, she looked pretty funny gyrating around on those braces in the middle of a church, but it just tickled me that she was 'dancing' away and I burst out laughing. Then Janet and her brother began to giggle, and it sort of caught on. Practically the whole congregation started laughing and doing 'Janet's dance'—wiggling their upper bodies, clapping, and having a grand time.

"It was *fun*—and it was beautiful to see Janet moving and enjoying herself so much. In a way, that experience was like a great big prayer. Maybe it wasn't a traditional way to praise

God, but it's surely just as important to offer up our laughter and joy to Him as it is to go to God with our troubles."

After I concluded the interview, I continued to think about the Kileys. And I realized that their example had shown me that you could look at exactly the same situation in two ways. You could think of a paralyzed girl trapped in her braces and wheelchair, moving in a stilted way, as unbearably sad. You could remember the dancer she once was and feel blind rage and despair at the loss. You could see her movements as jerky, pathetic reminders of the horror she'd been through.

Or you could do just what the Kiley family did: see the humor, the comedy, and the joy in the moment, allowing the laughter to come ringing out loud and clear, and celebrating the fact that Janet still has the impulse, the verve, and the humor to triumph over her handicap and still rejoice in the movement of her own body.

Wanting a professional view on the subject of humor in relation to victims of crime and their families, I called my former psychiatrist, Dr. Peter Weingold, who is an assistant clinical professor of psychiatry at UCLA.

"Finding humor in a tragic situation is an extremely healthy step," he began. "It is a way of looking toward the future and of saying that this suffering can be put behind us. For the victim and his inner circle, sharing moments of humor is a way of shifting perspective, of saying that there's more to this person, to this relationship, to this friendship, or to this family than the tragedy itself.

"Humor, especially dark humor," continued Dr. Weingold, "is an effective way of fighting back. There is a lot of anger, a lot of life, a lot of energy behind this kind of humor.

"When the victim and his family allow themselves to laugh again after an attack, they are, in effect, saying to the assailant and to fate: 'You didn't destroy us! We are still here. We are still laughing. And therefore we have life and hope.'

"When a victim and his loved ones reclaim their right to laughter after a tragedy, they are thumbing their noses at the assailant and at fate.

"Obviously, humor cannot be the *only* way in which a

victim and his family deal with their problems. But it may be a very important coping mechanism for all concerned.

"Eventually it is crucial for people who have been struck by tragedy to learn how to laugh again. If all a victim and his loved ones did was to cry endlessly and sink into complete despair, they would all become seriously depressed. Prolonged upset and anxiety without release could just drive everyone crazy. Laughter is a way for people to let go of pain for a little while, or at least to deal with it in a different way—one which leads to laughter rather than to tears."

Dr. Weingold continued: "In terms of humor, it's wise for the family to take their cues from the victim. Everyone should first get a sense that the victim is ready and wants to start having fun and putting his sense of humor to work again. Timing is very important: Some victims regain their sense of humor soon after the attack, and others take longer to learn to laugh again. Joking about the assailant, the attack itself, the injuries, the trial—the dire situation—is all fine, provided it happens at an appropriate time and that the victim can deal with it.

"Clearly there is nothing inherently funny about a person being mutilated or hurt by an attacker. But laughter helps everyone to fight off chronic despair and depression. So it has a valuable function in and of itself, and as such, it is certainly desirable.

"And, of course, let me stress that none of us should be laughing *at* the victim or at the situation in a way that would imply cruelty or insensitivity. Rather, we can hopefully laugh *about* things in a way that is constructive and positive.

"For a victim and his loved ones, humor is something to strive for and to embrace. It is a step forward, a way of saying, 'The tragedy has *happened* to us, but it does not *define* us. Despite what we've been through, we are going ahead with our lives. And laughter, in fact, is a proof that we are still here—and still, in fact, capable of experiencing joy.' "

When my sister, Maria, was a little girl, I remember that she laughed hysterically whenever something went wrong. One day, for example, our next-door neighbor Mrs. Johansen slipped and fell down a flight of stairs. Luckily the woman was unharmed. But everyone who'd seen her fall was very concerned. Maria, however, stood there, shoulders shaking, trying in vain to repress an uncontrollable fit of giggles. She stared down at Mrs. Johansen as though she'd just seen the funniest thing on earth.

On another occasion, I accidentally bumped into a precious family heirloom—a beautiful crystal vase given to my mother by her father before his death. Our entire family was aghast as we watched the vase smash into thousands of tiny pieces. Everyone knew it had been an accident. But it was still painful.

Mom stood frozen, balefully staring at the shattered crystal. My dad sighed and buried his head in his newspaper. I burst into tears. And Maria laughed—great big heaving gusts shaking her entire body.

All of us were perplexed by Maria's rather odd behavior. We teased her about it and sometimes even got angry with her for it. But my sister just couldn't seem to change what was, for her, a spontaneous reaction. Even if she herself took a bad fall and was actually hurt, she would sit there on the floor rubbing at her swollen knee or ankle—and laughing all the while.

Mom, worried that her behavior would hurt someone's feelings, scolded Maria again and again for her odd response. But now I feel that, in part, Maria's tendency to laugh in the face of trouble got her through the extremely painful and turbulent six-month period she spent with me after the attack.

Maria constantly refers to these months as "the worst time in my life." Yet I remember that in spite of the depression she felt, Maria still kept her sense of humor.

I was in such a sorry state, both physically and emotionally, that Maria had to assume most of the responsibility. When bad news came our way, she was the first to hear it. I remember that when the phone rang and Maria started laughing, it meant trouble. But after a while, I joined in with her.

We were astounded by the problems that beset us: the bill collectors, the medical needs, the trial-date postponements, my frail health, the stares and rudeness of strangers, the perennial visits to doctors. But, Maria said recently, "We'd have killed ourselves—or each other—if we hadn't laughed together loud and often."

I was terrified to walk in public, so Maria was always at my side in the streets. Still in the throes of post-traumatic stress, I was hypervigilant: constantly on the lookout for potentially scary characters. Maria and I developed a code. All I had to do was murmur the words *weirdo alert*, and my sister would steer me quickly into the nearest shop, restaurant, or other place where we could get off the street. Then, once out of harm's way, Maria would give in to one of her typical laughter spells.

We'd peer out of the shop window and usually see the hapless, bleary-eyed, grimy fellow shuffling by and perhaps reacting to the fact that we'd just run from him as if from the devil himself. Moments later, my sister, usually still laughing, would take my arm and we'd continue on to our destination.

Maria still laughs when she remembers one of my "crazy" pieces of behavior. Whenever confronted suddenly on the street with someone scary—for example, if an odd-looking character came close to me before I had a chance to say "weirdo alert"—I would dart mindlessly and sightlessly into the middle of the street. My rationale was that I felt no one could attack me in the middle of a street full of traffic. Of course I was usually putting myself in danger of being run over. But I felt that I'd rather be struck by a car than ever be harmed again by another person.

Maria says I flew out into the street so quickly that I was unstoppable. I looked like a speeding bullet heading for its target. Of course she would quickly retrieve me, putting her arms into the air and trying to hold the cars at bay. Then, as always, when I was safe she doubled over, calling me "The Human Dart." At night, on the telephone, she'd recount my latest traffic-dive to my parents. Of course they were appalled. But my sister thought it was hilarious. And, after the fact, so did I. Even now, as I write this, the image of myself seeking *safety* in the midst of an onrush of cars on a crowded boulevard makes me laugh.

Our days were usually fiascos, filled with doctors' appointments, physical therapy, fittings for braces, long drives, and eternal waits. But the nights were different. Maria called the evening "playtime," and we operated on the unspoken agreement that, regardless of what had happened during the day, we would do something for fun at night.

Maria loves Mexican food and discovered a kooky local place called Guadalajara. From five to seven P.M. was "happy hour," and whenever possible, Maria made sure we were there. Actually the place was a godsend. Both of us were broke, and at happy hour the little tacos, chips, sauces, cheeses, and other munchies were free. Often this was our dinner, and a delicious one at that. Most of all, Maria loved the frozen margaritas. She sat there sipping away, and for her it really was a much-needed happy hour.

We would chat for hours at times, nibbling the spicy food and giggling together amid the festive Mexican decor. Maria flirted with the waiters, played her favorite tunes on the jukebox, and simply unwound. Sometimes we invited friends to join us and made a little party of it.

Often, during the day, Maria was quiet and moody. But in the evening the pressure eased and she just had a good time, cracking jokes about the day's activities. Sometimes, I felt she was another person at night. And it wasn't the alcohol—Maria rarely sipped more than one or two margaritas, and never once did I see her drunk. It was just her time to have fun.

My sister and I frequently visited my friend Patricia, who'd been so kind to our mom while I was hospitalized. Patty became a good friend to Maria as well. I would listen in amazement as Maria, in her own style, described to Patty the events of the day. Maria acted as though she were trying out a stand-up comedy routine. She somehow managed to make our basic day-to-day schedule sound like a laugh riot.

Because I often forgot when or if I'd taken my medication, Maria carried the pills and dispensed them to me. And so she called herself "the pusher" and reminded me whenever it was time for my "fix."

Occasionally Maria amused herself by playing little tricks on people. For example, if someone was annoying us, she'd strike a stance, fold her arms across her chest, stare coldly into the person's face, and say, "I'm Sergeant Gray, Ms. Saldana's personal bodyguard. Please remove yourself from this location or I'll be forced to call my superior." The person would usually slink quickly away, and Maria would grin contentedly.

For Maria, laughter became a way out of the misery—a momentary respite from responsibility—and a special bond to me. Laughing together helped to preserve our relationship and smooth over many of the rough spots and resentments that were only natural during that stressful period. Humor provided my sister with a healthy escape.

Recently I spoke to my mother and asked how humor might have helped her to cope with the ordeal our family went through. At first she was taken aback by the question, and said, "Oh, Theresa, that time was such a nightmare. There really wasn't anything funny about it."

"Think, Mom," I insisted, remembering how, during the hospital days, Mother tried to keep her spirits up for my sake.

After mulling it over, Mom said, "Well, I guess I did allow myself to laugh now and then. In fact, during the early weeks and months, I was so grateful that you were alive at all, that I *did* feel a sense of triumph and real joy.

"Sometimes I'd walk into your room and you'd be propped up with all your bandages and tubes and IVs, the phone stuck to your ear as usual, and you'd be telling Selma: 'Now I'm *sure* I could be doing a guest shot in a couple of weeks. Absolutely!' And I would grin from ear to ear at the amazing pluck you had. That fighting spirit of yours definitely cheered me up.

"I've always obeyed all kinds of rules—that's just my nature—and helping to smuggle little Totsie in and out of the hospital made me feel like a little girl playing a prank on the grown-ups. That puppy really brought all of us together and made us laugh in spite of everything.

"One day, when we had Totsie in your room at Cedars-Sinai, a big hospital executive decided to come and meet you. Somehow, your sister flung Totsie into my arms and whispered, 'The bathroom! The bathroom!' as she opened the door. The man came in and visited for a while. Meanwhile I was trapped in that tiny room only a few feet away. Totsie started whining and whimpering and I just couldn't seem to get her to quiet down.

"The man wondered what the whimpers and whines were all about. Then I heard you say, 'Oh, that's my mom in there. She's really broken up about all this.'

" 'Oh, I guess I'd better be running along then and give you some privacy,' the executive said. He left in a hurry and I came out of that bathroom giggling like a schoolgirl.

"Moments like that helped us a lot back then. God knows we were always being confronted with one problem after the next. But on occasion, we all had to throw off our troubles and enjoy a chuckle or two.

"I remember that, when you were well enough to go out on passes and eat in a restaurant, you would insist that I call you Alicia rather than Theresa whenever we were in public. You were still so afraid someone would try to hurt you again. But now and then I'd get nervous and I'd forget your alias, so I'd say, 'What's your name again?'

" 'Mom!' you would say, shaking your head at me. Sometimes people at other tables would hear you calling me Mom, and me asking what your name was, and that would tickle me.

"I also used to get a kick out of the kooky things you did. Without telling me about it, you managed to convince one of your friends to buy you a bottle of wine. One night you said, 'Oh, Mom, I need a drink,' and I said, 'Okay, I'll go and ask the nurse for some milk.'

" 'No, don't bother,' you said, and pulled out a bottle of Chablis from under your pillow. Although I don't think it was a good idea for you to be drinking, I couldn't help but laugh at the sight of you in your lacy pink pajamas sitting there in the hospital taking a big swig of wine straight out of the bottle.

"People might think I should've scolded you and had the nurse take the wine away. But it was such a relief for me to see you being mischievous and lively again—like your old self. I guess I needed to grasp anything that was encouraging or upbeat in those days. And seeing your spirits coming back made me feel there was a reason to smile and appreciate your antics, even when I disagreed with them.

"In Motion Picture, you didn't want people to know who you were. One day I was wheeling you outside as you dozed in your wheelchair. An elderly couple stopped me and asked who you were. As usual, I responded, 'This is my daughter, Alicia Michaels. Her dad's a director.'

"At this point you were wearing a low-cut robe to give the wounds some air.

" 'What happened to her?' they inquired with concern.

" 'Heart attack,' I said, crossing my fingers.

" 'But what are these other cuts—and that big cast on her arm?' they persisted.

"You'd been sitting there quietly in your wheelchair, eyes closed. Suddenly you snapped to attention and quickly said, 'I was on the second floor of a high-rise building when I had my heart attack. I crashed forward through a plate-glass sliding door and fell to the ground, breaking my arm.'

"These words rushed out of your mouth so fast I couldn't believe it.

" 'Oh, my goodness—you poor girl!' the couple gasped. Wishing you luck and health, they hurried back to their cottage.

"I wheeled you to your room and we laughed about it like two mischievous kids.

"Now that I think about it, I do remember so many moments when having a sense of humor came in handy. There just would have been no way to go through every day in a bleak, despairing state. What allowed me to have a laugh or two now and then was the fact that I knew—for your sake and my own—I needed to remain positive. No human being can feel optimistic if they don't allow themselves to be a little lighthearted now and then."

The victims, their loved ones, and the experts all agree: Humor can help to ease the pain. Suffering through an ordeal can, in fact, bring people closer together. And laughter in the midst of despair can also help to make the bonds of love and friendship stronger still.

FORWARD THINKING

Just as the victim himself needs to set his sights on a future point that will be happier, less painful, and more peaceful, so, too, do members of his inner circle.

After someone they are close to is victimized, friends, relatives, and loved ones find themselves trapped in a web of seemingly endless problems, burdens, responsibilities, and hardships. Sometimes, no end to the horror seems to be in sight.

Forward thinking can give them the comfort of realizing that, in time, they will no longer be suffering through the trials and tribulations of the present.

Envisioning the victim as healthy and recovered reassures family members and friends that their loved one *will* have a brighter future and that there will be an end to the current suffering for everyone concerned.

Recently my mother told me, "From the first day on, I constantly imagined you healthy again. Over and over I used to say, 'You're going to do it, Theresa. You're going to be fine again. I'm going to see you in shows again. You'll dance again, sing again, act again.'

"Even when you were sleeping, I'd whisper these things in your ear. I truly believed it all myself and I willed you to believe it too.

"When you were down I'd say, 'You're going to be walking around really soon, Theresa.' And sometimes you'd look up at me all teary-eyed and shake your head *No*. I would want to break down and cry then and there, because I hurt so much for you. But I knew that if I wanted *you* to believe in the future, I had to stay strong and convince you, even when you felt the weakest and sickest and most hurt.

"It was hard to see you so emotionally distraught, so frightened, so confused and angry. But despite it all, you were still an optimist and a fighter. So I kept thinking you could use all that energy of yours to get better.

"The day you first sat up, I envisioned you walking. Then, when you walked hunched over, I imagined you upright. Once you walked straight and unsupported, I believed you'd walk *faster*—and dance, and run. These steps didn't happen all at once. But I knew in my heart that they would eventually happen.

"We'd had this terrible disaster. But it was springtime—the season of hope, of rebirth, of newness. I realized there would be a long recovery process, considering the degree of all your injuries, but I looked ahead in my mind and heart and knew the future would be better.

"I had no choice, really. Things were so painful, so nearly

unbearable—so full of despair and grimness and awful pieces
of news. If I'd believed for a moment that things would
remain like that, I could not have taken it. If I'd felt you would
be terrified, downcast, and bitter all your life, my heart would
have been broken.

"During the hospital days, the biggest beacon of all to me
was Christmas. That was always your favorite holiday—and
mine too. We've always had the happiest and most beautiful
Christmases together, all of us. And when you were so sick
and weak there in Cedars-Sinai, I looked forward to December
and thought, *Next Christmas, we'll be together, just as always.*
Theresa will set up the Nativity set; Maria will trim the tree. Tony
will string the lights, I will cook and decorate the house—and all of
this will be like a terrible nightmare out of the past. Theresa will be
truly recovered and we'll all be even closer. I know it, I just know
it!

"Christmas was nine months away, but I knew you'd really
be fine by then. I felt amazingly confident about it. I knew
your love for the Christmas season—the festivities, the pag-
eantry, the giving of gifts. And I prayed and believed it would
really happen.

"Magically, thankfully, it did. When you and your father
and sister and I went to midnight Mass together, it was like a
dream come true. I was so happy to have you there—alive,
pink-cheeked again, standing upright and singing a hymn.
And we were all together. We'd survived it all. Your father
was beaming. Maria was happy—finally home in New York
again and ready to start school. It was my hope for the future
coming true.

"When you two girls were little, we'd ring little jingle bells
after midnight Mass and let you each unwrap one small gift
before going to sleep. We did it again that Christmas. And I
gave you and Maria each a little porcelain doll. I felt so much
in my heart. But I just hugged you and we all went to sleep.

"Then, the next morning, I was again really amazed at how
much happiness I could feel. I looked around at all of us under
the tree, lights blinking, really all there together—and truly, at
least for that Christmas morning, the attack and the hospital
and the torment really did all seem like a bad dream!

"When you and your sister were in L.A. and Dad and I

were back in New York—during those autumn months especially—I was horribly depressed. Life was bleak; I couldn't seem
to feel any joy whatsoever. I had too much time on my hands—
time to think about the attack, the pain, the trial, the injustice
of it all. My days were empty and drawn out. I couldn't smile.
Couldn't laugh. I felt like I was in a dark hole and couldn't get
out. I was so grateful you were alive and healing, but now that
I didn't have to be 'up' for you, I sank down very low. Yet,
underneath it all, I still held on to a quiet little germ of hope. I
even knew about *myself* that, as depressed as I was, I would lift
out of it at some point. I knew I *needed* the time to feel grief,
bitterness, sadness, anger.

"When you and Maria finally arrived for the holidays, it
was as though someone had pumped me full of life again.

"It took quite a few months after that Christmas for
me to bring myself completely out of that depressed state.
But having those past dreams of health and togetherness
come true went a long way for me. It proved that, no matter
how grim things were, we could manage to get through
it.

"I took strength from your progress. You were getting acting jobs again; your spirits were high; you'd started the organization. And I thought to myself: *I raised that girl. Just look how
strong she is.*

"And I slowly began to feel better. I looked ahead and
thought, *Divina, give yourself credit.*

"It takes a long time for a mother to get over a tragedy like
this. You ache so much for your child. But now, things are
good again. It still hurts terribly to think about what happened
but it's not on my mind night and day anymore.

"I went through the trauma with you. I helped as much as
I could; I stayed optimistic for you. I tried to encourage you
and I kept up my hopes for the future.

"During the worst times, I forced myself to look forward—
beyond the pain, beyond my misery. And now, for the most
part, I feel the horror is behind us. We are here—the future is
now—and our family is healthy, happy, loving, and functioning. My dreams and prayers have been fulfilled. All I can say
to other mothers is: Never give up—never! No matter what

happens, or how ugly things seem, just keep moving on. Keep encouraging your child. Keep telling yourself the pain will end."

Daniel Kiley—the brother of Janet Kiley, who was shot after refusing to dance with a stranger—is a tautly muscled, intense man with a passion for sports and physical activities.

Although the attack on his sister was a severe shock, Daniel does not let himself see the event as completely negative, or believe that her condition is entirely permanent. He practices his own special brand of forward thinking.

Daniel told me recently: "I believe that events which happened prior to Janet's attack paved the way for my being able and available to spend a great deal of time with her.

"I'd been working downtown for years as a supervisor in a collecting firm. The job was difficult and demanding, and for quite some time I'd been feeling underpaid and overworked. I was trapped and stifled by the environment and generally would have preferred a job including outdoor activity and a looser time schedule. But I kept the position and did my best at it for a number of years.

"Eventually, about four months before Janet's attack, I asked for a raise and was rejected. Finally convinced that it was time for me to leave and knowing I had a lump sum of money coming to me as a result of a profit-sharing arrangement, I made the decision to take some time off. I knew I could live on my savings, the profit-sharing money, and some occasional part-time work when necessary.

"I've always been extremely athletic, and decided that it would be a good period for me to get serious about my training. So I joined a running club to get some very long runs in each day. In addition, I began to bicycle and swim in earnest, aiming at doing some competition runs and triathlon events.

"Although I spent many hours working out, my time was my own and my schedule was adaptable. So, after Janet was shot, I was able to be there for her much of the time.

"When I first learned what happened and went to see Janet, my mind was consumed by thoughts of the assailant. I lay there in bed for hours at a time, shaking with anger and hatred toward him. But much more important was my need to find how to help Janet.

"I'm very much into holism and have taken courses in healing and related topics. So when this happened, I tried to channel healing energy in Janet's direction. But despite my efforts, I couldn't seem to connect with anything powerful enough.

"The thought came into my mind: *You can't help Janet until you forgive the assailant.* And so I consciously forced myself to put him out of my mind and release him. Then I was able to concentrate on thoughts of my sister.

"When Janet was lying there in ICU, as horrible as the situation appeared to be, I knew there was no room for despair. The concentration had to be placed upon healing and wholeness. I knew that if anyone had the strength and courage to survive and go forth after something like this, it was Janet.

"The doctors' depiction of my sister's condition was grim. But I never for a moment allowed myself to believe in their dire predictions. From the very beginning I refused to accept Janet's paralysis as permanent. And I employed certain techniques to help me continue seeing her on the road to healing.

"I visualized the bullet hole in Janet's back and envisioned the extent of her injury. Then I mentally surrounded those areas with healing colors, healing thoughts, healing imagery. I spoke to other friends who practiced healing and told them of the doctors' prognosis. We all agreed that we inwardly felt that, despite what we were hearing at the hospital, Janet would walk again."

"Do you really think these 'healing energies' helped?" I asked curiously.

"Well, put it this way," he answered. "I don't consider myself to be a great healer. But banding together with friends and sending positive thoughts to my sister was certainly better than doing nothing at all.

"At the very least, it made me feel I was trying to help. And it took my concentration away from all that was negative.

"I kept searching my mind for suggestions to give to my sister and asked myself: *How can Janet get better? How can she do it?*

"Inwardly, I felt that Janet, too, needed to place the assailant out of her mind in order to totally concentrate on getting better. But I saw she wasn't ready to do that, and I accepted it, knowing she needed to find her own path and deal with what had happened on her own terms. But I, nonetheless, continued to view the situation and focus energy upon it in my *own* way. I wished I could magically do all the healing for Janet, but all I could do was keep my own thoughts for her future positive, and encourage Janet's innate strength and power of will in a healing direction.

"I honestly believed—and continue to believe—that Janet will walk again," stressed Daniel.

"I certainly can't predict whether she'll walk as a result of her own hard work and constant efforts, or if some brilliant new surgical technique will come along that will enable doctors to go in and repair the damage. But I do envision my sister as walking. When I think of her, I think of her walking. In my dreams, my sister is walking. I am utterly convinced that this will happen.

"I feel that, on a certain level, this is a learning experience for Janet. She has been called upon to struggle with something few of us have to contend with. But to help her get through it, I believe it's important for all of us around her to encourage Janet to look forward to a future which includes health, activity, and truly walking again. She cannot be allowed to give up that belief—that spark, that ray of hope.

"There are other 'miracle stories' to back up this way of thinking. People who've had broken backs and spinal injuries, who've been told they'll never walk again but who somehow hold on to the dream and manage to beat the odds and actually get back on their feet again.

"Life's pretty short, but it's long enough to achieve many things. I feel all activity is good for Janet and will eventually add up to a healthier future. She's working on an aerobics tape for the handicapped now and it's great to see her on her mat working out, pushing herself to the limit, thinking of ways to help others do the same thing.

"The key is to take your concentration away from the disability and direct it toward the healing. My mind thinks of Janet as moving. Yes, rationally, I can see her legs aren't taking her any place right at this moment, but between her power of both mind and spirit, and medical advances which are being perfected all the time, I believe the end result will be a mobile person.

"Janet will walk again, sooner or later—but my belief is it'll be sooner. Put it this way: On our van, we keep Janet's disability card so we can park conveniently in the handicapped zones. But although she's entitled to a permanent license—which she wouldn't have to go through the hassle of renewing each year—she only has a temporary one. Just a few days ago she asked me if I thought she should get a permanent license and I said, 'No. One of these days you're not going to need a card at all.' "

As I said earlier, my sister, Maria, depended a great deal on forward thinking to get her over the rough times during my early post-hospital days, when she was living with me in Los Angeles as my constant companion.

Maria was resigned to standing by me and helping me through this difficult period, but that didn't make the situation any less difficult for her. My sister was often depressed, confused, anxious, and—most of all—deeply, inexorably homesick for New York and the people there she loved. In order to deal with homesickness or loss, many people try to put the image of the person or place they long for out of their minds. Maria, however, did just the opposite. She trained her eyes and heart ahead to the time when she'd be back at home and free of the worries of the present.

Nothing delighted Maria more than buying *The New York Times*, sporting a Mets T-shirt, eating a slice of "New York style" pizza, looking at pictures from our family album, reading letters from or chatting on the phone with friends from Brooklyn, or surrounding herself with other reminders of her life back east. She wasn't, however, looking *back* toward home, but looking *forward* to a time when she'd be there again and able to resume her own life.

Maria constantly said things like "I need a new coat for New York," or "I have so much to tell my best friend when I see her," or "I'm going to raid Mom's refrigerator night and day," or "Only two more months till I start school," or "My bed's going to feel so good," or "I think I'll redecorate my room" or—simply, and most frequently of all—"I can't *wait* to get home again!"

"All right! All right, Maria!" I'd snap at times, irked by what I considered her constant carping about getting home. From my point of view, I wished she'd try to enjoy herself *now* instead of always talking about what she was *going to do.*

But, for Maria, the future meant comfort, freedom, friends, and relief.

Early one Sunday, I was writing in the living room and Maria was watching TV in the bedroom. Both of us were relieved to have a morning of relaxation after a long and tiring week. All of a sudden I heard: "Look! Look! Look!" and Maria started laughing excitedly. I ran into the room and saw that she was watching the New York Marathon. Then I realized why she was so excited—the runners were passing right by the Brooklyn street where we live!

One of the things Maria looked forward to—short of going to New York—was the day when I would finally get my first post-attack acting job. For Maria, this milestone would symbolize two very important things: First, a return to work would undoubtedly give me confidence, security, and happiness. It would help me to feel stronger and more independent, and it would therefore help me to heal both physically and emotionally. Second, my return to work would give Maria assurance that I was on the mend and able to support myself. Therefore she would feel freer to make plans for her own future.

And so Maria practiced forward thinking not only for herself, but for me as well.

During the months we were together, as I went on countless auditions and interviews, Maria was my staunchest advocate and supporter. "You'll get a job soon. I can feel it," she told me again and again. "And not only *that*, but after you get *one* job it'll have a pyramid effect and you'll get a whole bunch of other bookings too."

Maria often consulted with my manager, Selma Rubin, who also knew that work would be the fastest route to my total recovery. Selma steadfastly tried to persuade agents and casting people to hire me, explaining that I was healthy enough to work and desperately needed a job. But initially, everyone seemed afraid to hire me. I was still quite thin, and people imagined that I might be emotionally disturbed or unbalanced.

My sister, however, never wavered in her belief that if I were given the chance to act again, I'd come through with flying colors.

She fervently willed someone to give me a break—and in the near future, at that.

"You'll be working before Christmas," she said in September. "Just mark my words!" Maria, as usual, kept her mind trained ahead—but not so far ahead that the future seemed out of reach.

Whenever I had an audition, Maria practiced the scenes with me over and over again, and she shopped with me for appropriate outfits. For weeks and weeks I continued to audition for one project after another.

"Why isn't she booking anything, Selma?" Maria would ask. And Selma would repeat to my sister some of the remarks she'd heard: "She's too thin, Selma," "too pale," "too hurt-looking," "too delicate"—"Is she still in pain?" Most of all, however, people said, "It's just too soon, Selma. We're worried she won't be able to handle it."

"Handle it?" Maria would snort angrily. "Don't these people know how much she *has* handled? What's a little acting role compared to everything she's already gone through?" But, moments later, Maria would turn to me and say, "It won't be long. A job is going to come through for you. And it's going to make you feel one hundred percent better about everything."

On Halloween, as I listlessly picked at some French fries at a local McDonald's, my sister said, "Theresa, I'll bet you dinner at the Brown Derby you'll get a job in the next month."

I skeptically raised my eyebrows and said, "It's a deal—at least I'll have a good meal to look forward to."

Maria was blunt at times. More than once she said to me point-blank: "Look, Theresa, I can't babysit forever. I know once you're working, you won't be needing me for long. So just believe in it: You're going to get a job *soon*—for my sake, okay?" I laughed and said I hoped she was right.

In mid-November, I had a reading for a guest-star role on *Seven Brides for Seven Brothers*. The episode would be shot on location out in Murphys, California a tiny rustic town way up north. The role I was up for was highly physical. This character would go through plenty: She would be widowed, kidnapped, harassed, and threatened. She would give birth in a ditch and would run through the woods to escape her pursuers. In other words, whoever played this role would require plenty of energy and stamina.

Maria drove me to the MGM studio, where the audition was to take place. "I know this is the one, Theresa," she said on the way. "We'll be on a plane tomorrow."

"Sure, Maria," I replied. But her words gave me confidence. I wanted to do it for Maria as much as for me. And I could tell she *really* thought I was going to get this job.

Minutes later I walked into the meeting room and saw Barbara Claman, a casting woman I've known since my days as a teenage actress in New York. Barbara had recommended me for many a job over the years. I knew that if any casting director in Hollywood was in my corner, it was Barbara Claman.

She greeted me warmly and walked me into the casting office, where she introduced me to the producers and directors.

The reading was terrific—one of those magical auditions where everything seems to go just right. I walked out feeling wonderful and drove home with my sister. But I tried not to hope too much. I'd done many other good readings which had not led to job offers.

Maria, however, was jubilant. "This is the one. Just wait and see, Theresa," she said as she drove. Twenty minutes later we arrived home, where we nervously watched TV, wrote letters, and waited for the phone to ring. When it did, I was almost afraid to answer it, but on the fourth ring I picked it up. Selma's voice was loud and clear: "You got it! You got it! You and Maria leave tomorrow!"

Stunned, I hung up and told my sister the news. Maria jumped up and down. "I knew it! Didn't I tell you?" she squealed.

We called our parents. "She got a job, Mom, a job!" Maria shouted over the phone. Our parents were ecstatic. That evening, Maria and I packed our bags. We were both so excited we could hardly sleep.

The next morning, we flew to Murphys, California.

Maria had been right all along. From the moment I arrived on the set of *Seven Brides for Seven Brothers*, I felt like another person. Suddenly the professional took over. I wore my arm brace and chest protector between shots, but took them off when the cameras rolled. The part was wonderful. The cast and crew were terrific: They all knew it was my first job since the attack and they couldn't have been kinder or more helpful. I was renewed, invigorated—not at all weak or frail.

I felt completely safe and at home with the show's cast and crew. And, since I was working twelve or fourteen hours a day, Maria had plenty of time to herself.

She went off on her own and did some sightseeing. She browsed in local antique stores, treated herself to sundaes in an old-fashioned ice-cream parlor, got to know some of the local townspeople, and reveled in the fact that, for a change, she didn't have to drive me anywhere or consult with any doctors.

Maria sensed after only a few days that I was already feeling more independent and didn't need to lean on her so much. I was even ready to talk openly with her about what I would do when she returned to New York. I told her that I could stay with friends and get along fine with a companion supplied by the Actors Fund of America. I felt strong again. Maria was ecstatic; she made plans to return to graduate school and begin her career as a teacher.

After the *Seven Brides* episode finished shooting, my sister and I returned to L.A. Just as Maria had predicted months before, now that I'd actually returned to work—and proven that I could handle the rigors of a heavy shooting schedule—others were eager to hire me. From that point on, I worked steadily, going from one job to the next. My confidence, stamina, and self-reliance continued to grow.

To this day, Maria says she could never have made it through all those months without a firm belief in a better, happier, more secure future for *both* of us.

*   *   *

For the victim himself and for those who—along with the victim—have had their lives and destinies altered by crime, forward thinking can make all the difference in the world.

THERAPY

Under the stress and strain of a victimization and the myriad problems that follow, it is quite common for marriages, romantic relationships, family ties, and friendships to become shaky or to crumble completely. Even relationships that, before the attack, were virtually trouble-free can weaken or disintegrate when rocked by attack-related problems such as post-traumatic stress disorders, surgery, hospitalizations, dealings with the police, and the trial of the assailant. These highly stressful situations faced by the victim and his inner circle are far from easy to cope with.

But relationships *can* be preserved or even strengthened by these ordeals. Some spouses, families, and friends of victims find they can somehow cope with and solve their problems on their own. For many others, professional intervention may prove beneficial, or even essential.

Recently I spoke with Nancy Kless, executive director of the Crime Victims Center, a nonprofit organization that offers comprehensive professional services for victims of violent crime and their families. Kless tries, whenever possible, to include in therapy the spouse, relatives, or others to play key roles in a victim's life.

Ms. Kless offered this: "People in general tend to go about their lives wearing blinders in order to feel safe in an unsafe world. But when someone you love is assaulted, you are suddenly faced with a very frightening reality. Some people react by becoming terrified themselves. Others struggle to make sense out of what is an irrational—i.e., random—attack.

"They may say to themselves: *If [their loved one] had taken precautions, this would not have happened. Therefore, if I take precautions, it won't happen to me.* This kind of logic may lead a person to ask the victim: 'Why did you leave that door un-locked?' or 'How could you be out so late at night?' Exclamations like 'If you'd closed that window, this never would have happened!' are common.

"Such insensitive questions and remarks are hurtful to the victim. They can lead to resentment, self-blame, and confusion. Therefore, when I work with the significant others in a victim's life, I try to educate them, sensitize them, and make them aware that it's possible to come to recognize and accept the potential dangers of the world without becoming obsessively fearful. And I help them to see that blaming the victim—or even themselves—for what's happened is both unnecessary and destructive to the relationship.

"The therapeutic environment can help to clear up a lot of misunderstanding that may be building up between the victim and his loved ones. The victim's behavior and angry lashing out may be hard to handle—and extremely confusing—for the people who are trying to help him. It is often easier for them to understand the wrath and rage of the victim—and to see it as temporary—if it is explained by a caring, knowledgeable outsider.

"Even though the people close to a victim may genuinely want to help, they are often in a crisis of their own. The attack arouses feelings of fear, pain, and anger. It is hard for them to detach themselves from their own troubled thoughts and simply *be there* for the victim who is crying out to them for help.

"For example, most victims have a need to ventilate by repeating the stories of their attack over and over again. A spouse, friend, or parent may genuinely believe it would be better for the victim *not* to rehash the saga repeatedly and dwell upon it all the time. The family member may comment, 'Forget it. That's all behind us now. Let's not talk about it anymore.' This, of course, is unrealistic. And if the advice is followed, the victim will often bottle up his story and be much the worse for it. He will also resent his loved one for not hearing him out. And, ultimately, both the victim *and* the relationship will suffer.

"The truth of the matter is that it *hurts* the loved ones to listen to the details of the victim's painful ordeal. It is hard to hear about the hurt which was suffered. And it may make them feel guilty or responsible. Because of these feelings, they may deny the victim the chance to tell his story again and again. A therapist can help the loved ones see the value of ventilation. Knowing that this process is a *positive* thing may enable the inner-circle member to listen more, or at least to recognize that it is helping the victim.

"Once in therapy, members of a victim's circle will learn *two* things: how to help the victim and how to help *themselves*. If they can express and learn methods of coping with their own pain and anguish resulting from the attack, they will certainly be better able to assist and relate to the victim.

"Some family members find solace and direction in just one or two in-person or telephone consultations with the victim's therapist. It's amazing how helpful a few direct answers to pressing questions can be. And having the therapist talk openly with him may lead the family member to feel more a part of the victim's healing process.

"Depending on the degree to which the attack affects the victim's loved one, the individual may opt for therapy of his own, or in a group situation with other families of victims, or with other members of his own inner circle. There are a variety of ways to go.

"One of the good things about seeking counsel from a professional is that it explains and validates the pain and fear the inner-circle members are feeling. They may well be thinking: *Why am I so scared, angry, bitter, confused? It didn't happen to me! I shouldn't be falling apart like this.* It can help so much to know how common it is for those close to a victim to go through plenty of emotional trauma of their own.

"The friend or family member may—for the victim—be playing the role of strong, stoic supporter. But internally, he himself may feel weak and terrified. If he turns to a therapist for support, he will have a place where he can vent his *own* emotions. Where he needn't play the stoic role. Where he can obtain solace, support, and sympathy for himself. This help and concern may nurture and sustain him so that he, in turn, will feel replenished and therefore better able to tend to the victim's needs without feeling resentful or overburdened.

"Whether or not a member of a victim's inner circle chooses to seek therapy for himself, it is important that he at least has a way of openly communicating with the therapist who is treating the victim. Although the spouse, parent, or loved one may be coping well on his own, he should be able to seek advice from the therapist at least informally. For example, before the trial, it would be good for members of the inner circle to ask the victim's therapist how the court proceedings might affect the victim and/or themselves—what behavior to expect at the trial, et cetera.

"A therapist can function very well in an advisory position. And it may be easier for a family member to consider going to a counselor for *advice* rather than for therapy. There are many straightforward facts a therapist can impart which will help make life easier and more bearable for members of a victim's inner circle.

"A therapist can also help members of an inner circle to avoid going to extremes. Those who care for the victim may, in fact, be doing too much. A therapist can let them know how important it is for a crime victim to begin to regain a sense of control. While care and support are necessary, at a certain point the victim also needs to conquer his helplessness.

"A therapist can guide members of the inner circle to strike a balance between helping and still allowing the victim to heal and become independent again. A therapist can give advice on how to be supportive without being oppressive. For members of a victim's inner circle, therapy will often prove useful as a way of educating themselves in how to care best for their own needs while still being there to support the victim."

Ms. Kless pointed out that "after a victimization, many marriages break up—regardless of whether the husband or wife was victimized. It is extremely difficult for any couple to deal with the confusion, the anger, the fears, the pain, and the unavoidable changes which the attack is bound to provoke in each of them.

"In most cases, it is ideal for the husband and wife (or—in cases of unmarried but deeply involved romantic relationships—both partners) to attend therapy sessions, some together and some individually. In this way, under the guidance of an objective third person, they can learn to be open about their feelings and to express them in the presence of their mate. And when they meet with the therapist separately, they will have the time—and the privacy—in which to reveal their innermost thoughts without regard to how their words, emotions, or behavior may hurt or affect their partner. Often, in the case of the mate of a victim, there is a tremendous—and usually unmet—need for a focus of attention on their *own* problems. Speaking to a therapist is an excellent way to unleash all sorts of doubts, worries, or even hysteria.

"It is hard enough for a relatively stable and trouble-free couple to cope with the sudden and radical trauma of a victimization. But when there were serious pre-existing problems, a violent crime can be the straw that breaks the camel's back. A couple in this situation must address and attend to their troubles soon after the attack occurs.

"If, for example, a husband has always been antagonistic toward his wife for taking college courses at night, and she is attacked on the way home from class, these old resentments will complicate and increase their post-attack problems.

"People who had serious marital or relationship troubles or major disagreements and differences prior to an attack are most vulnerable to a complete breakup afterwards. If I sense such a situation exists at home when I counsel a crime victim, I put particular emphasis upon meeting with the victim's partner and helping both of them to address and, hopefully, resolve their problems.

"One of the difficulties which the spouse or partner of a victim must deal with is the change of personality and behavior in his loved one. There is often a tendency on the spouse's part to want the victim to go back to being exactly what they were like before the attack. In therapy, a spouse will learn that this desire is unrealistic. Although the victim will surely not become, forever, an *entirely* different person, his life-shattering experience will naturally create some changes. And, if a relationship is to be preserved, the victim's mate must come to grips with this reality.

"Frequently, partners of victims ask me: 'When will this end?' Many actually want a *date*, a tangible time frame for when their loved one—and their own life—will return to normal. At this point, they must be told the truth: that, while the altered and uncharacteristic behavior of the victim will decrease in time, a person who is violently attacked will *never* be exactly the same as before it happened. While the victim, in most cases, will be able to return to a functional life-style and a way of communicating with his spouse which is comparable to their pre-attack dealings, there are unavoidable long-term adjustments which *both* of them will have to make.

"None of this is easy for a victim's spouse to hear. But even this painful truth will usually seem more acceptable if it comes from an expert—someone other than the victim himself. Usually, the victim and the therapist will be saying the same thing: 'The attack has made a difference. It can't be the way it was before. We must go on from here and rebuild our lives.'

"The victim's mate must come to grips with the fact that the assailant has altered not only the *victim* but his own relationship to the victim as well.

"The victim's partner may, at first, be resistant to the new situation, but if their love is strong, they can both get to the point of accepting and dealing with it. Both partners must learn new ways of relating and coping. While many couples find that they can accomplish this on their own, it is generally easier—and the process smoother—with professional guidance."

At my request, Ms. Kless put me in touch with a couple whom she'd counseled after a victimization, Sheila and Martin Kobell. They invited me to have brunch with them, followed by separate interviews with each.

On the morning of our appointment, I headed off to their exquisite house in a lovely, secluded area in Beverly Hills, California. Sheila came out to greet me. A tall, elegant woman, Sheila Kobell exudes an air of charm and grace while at the same time projecting a sense of genuine warmth. Although her voice and manner are soft in tone, I sensed immediately that Sheila is a woman of strength and determination. She ushered me inside and introduced me to her husband, Martin. Over a lovely home-cooked meal, the couple filled me in about themselves.

Sheila was born and raised on a farm and, in her teens, left home to become an actress. For many years she has divided her time between stage and screen engagements and raising her daughter, who is now grown. She and Martin were both married previously and have been husband and wife for twelve years.

Martin, a playwright and screenwriter, is a wry, intelligent man. One gets the impression that while he enjoys a good conversation and is quite extroverted when in the company of others, he would just as soon be left alone to think, reflect, and, most of all, write.

Both Sheila and Martin have strong personalities and opinions—which are not always in agreement—but they obviously love and admire each other greatly.

After brunch Martin went off to his study, and I followed Sheila into her own spacious and sunny sitting room. We chatted for a while, and then Sheila told me the details of her attack.

About fourteen months ago, Sheila decided to burglar-proof her chocolate-brown Mercedes. When she went to have the alarm put in, she also installed a "panic button" under the steering wheel. This way, if she ever got into trouble while in her vehicle, she could set off the alarm manually.

When Sheila's friends heard what she'd done, they teased her about it. Most of them felt she was being absurdly cautious. But Sheila, who was in the habit of being out and about on her own, often at odd hours, felt it to be a wise investment.

One cool January evening, Sheila drove off to a screening of a classic film at a nearby college campus where she'd been taking a writing course.

When the movie ended, Sheila had one of the friendly campus security guards walk her to the car. While driving along the tree-lined campus road, Sheila noticed that her trunk was open. She stopped the car for a moment and went to lock the trunk.

As Sheila walked around the car, a young man appeared from behind some bushes and headed straight toward her. An intense feeling of dread came over Sheila. She froze for a second, then tried to get back into the car. But it was too late. The man shoved Sheila violently into the car. Then he pounced upon her like a crazed animal and snarled, "I'm going to kill you!"

Bubbles of pain exploded in Sheila's head as the man pounded his fists again and again into her face.

"I'm going to kill you—kill you—kill you," he repeated.

Sheila screamed, fought, kicked, struggled as the crashing blows continued to slam into her.

"Oh, God, not like this," Sheila heard herself whisper when she saw the murderous gleam in the man's eyes. Then she began to scream at the top of her lungs, her shrieks piercing the still night air.

Two security guards, hearing her cries, began to run across the grassy campus, desperately trying to find the source of the screams. The deathly wailing seemed to grow fainter. Neither man could tell exactly where the cries were coming from.

Inside the car, Sheila was losing strength. Then, one tiny glimmer of hope forced its way into her rapidly waning consciousness.

The button . . . the button, she thought to herself. Summoning one last burst of strength, Sheila wrested her arm free and managed to push the panic-alarm under the steering wheel.

The alarm whooped its shrill and piercing mechanical noise. Both guards followed the siren blasts toward the Mercedes.

When he heard footsteps approaching, the assailant released Sheila and tumbled out of the car. One guard rushed to Sheila. The other tackled the blood-covered man, wrestled him to the ground, and put a gun to his head. The attacker knocked the gun aside, bounded out of the guard's grasp, and, shrieking with laughter, raced away.

The guard fired twice at the retreating man, but both shots missed their mark. The assailant escaped on foot, never to be apprehended.

With the guard's help, Sheila climbed out of the car. She could scarcely see out of her hideously swollen eyes. Blood poured from her broken nose, and her entire face was bruised and lacerated.

Moments later, an ambulance arrived and raced her to a nearby emergency room. The following days were a blur of doctors, tests, and operations. Bones were reset and her face operated upon by painstaking experts.

In spite of the physical anguish, Sheila felt positively high, her spirits flying on some comforting cloud of euphoria. She felt thrilled, exhilarated to have survived the deadly assault.

Sheila knew that her own strength and will to live had

kept her alive and battling the assailant. She had fought and won. And the alarm her friends had snickered at had truly helped to save her life. Without it, the guards might not have found her until too late. Sheila knew how lucky she was.

Martin, meanwhile, was at Sheila's side, supporting her totally. Sheila sensed how deeply grateful her husband was that she'd survived.

In the weeks following the attack, Sheila continued to feel like a true survivor. The cuts, bruises, and stitches in her face were, to her, badges of courage. And she knew that the marks would heal.

Sheila found herself repeating her story again and again, not as a litany of anguish but as a story of triumph. Although she felt strong and confident, Sheila interpreted the effectiveness of her car alarm as a sign and began to invest in a variety of other security devices, particularly those to be used in and around the house.

Three months passed uneventfully. Although she had a markedly increased awareness of the new security measures and devices, Sheila's personality, behavior, and life-style seemed relatively unchanged. Her face was healing nicely, and she and Martin soon settled back into much the same pattern of living they'd been accustomed to before the attack.

Sheila, convinced that the incident was completely random, did not feel frightened because the assailant was still at large. She believed that the man who'd tried to kill her was either drugged, insane, or both. She never thought for a moment that the man would try to retaliate or track her down.

Then, about twelve weeks after the attack, Sheila received an upsetting phone call on her private line. At first the male caller spewed a lengthy stream of obscenities and sexual boasts. Then, ending his monologue with angry name-calling, he quickly hung up.

Sheila, unnerved, reported the call to the police. They calmed her down somewhat, telling the frightened woman how common these obscene calls were. Sheila felt rattled, but put the caller out of her mind. Again, life went on as usual.

A few days later Sheila took her car in to have the security devices checked. The mechanic told her that someone had been inside her car and had dewired and disconnected all the alarms. Shaken, Sheila went home and told Martin what had happened. He, too, was concerned. The news was puzzling. But there didn't seem to be much that could be done about it.

Then came the telephone call that would send Sheila into a complete panic and alter both their lives.

Early one afternoon, Sheila picked up the telephone and listened in horror.

"I'm going to kill you, you disgusting bitch," a male voice growled. "Just wait and see. I know exactly where you are and how I'm going to get you. You won't get away from me. You're a dead woman." With that, he let out a grisly, perverse little laugh and hung up.

Sheila stood, receiver in hand, shaking uncontrollably. Every shred of security and confidence she possessed had been taken from her with that one hideous phone call.

She had coped with the brutal assault, had even felt strengthened by her own survival. But she could not deal with a murderous voice calling from God-knew-where and threatening to kill her.

Was it the same man who'd been thwarted in his bare-fisted murder attempt? Would he, in fact, find her and finish his deadly job? Could she ever feel safe again?

Sheila changed her private number instantly. But the damage had already been done. For Sheila, peace of mind was a thing of the past. And that is when the marital problems began between Sheila and Martin Kobell.

Sheila's terror led her to become obsessed about her safety. Whereas, before the attack, Sheila had been *cautious* and, after the attack, *extremely* cautious, with the death-threatening telephone call, Sheila became what most people would term excessively security-conscious.

Locks, bolts, and car alarms were no longer enough. Now, despite the relative safety and serenity of their exclusive and secluded residence, Sheila felt they needed to have a security gate put in. Martin objected. He felt things were going too far and accused Sheila of becoming paranoid. Furthermore, Martin resented the changes in his wife and in their life-style. Before, Sheila had gone everywhere by herself and had been a fearless and independent soul. Now, she was a shadow of the woman she'd been. She rarely left the house and was terrified to go out at night, even *with* her husband.

When Martin balked at the expense entailed by many of the security measures Sheila demanded, his wife became furious. She labeled her husband "unfeeling" and accused him of being naïve about the very real dangers of modern society.

Sheila saved her own money and used it to put iron security gates in the bedroom. She took a gun course and badgered her husband to do the same. She read countless books about survival and bombarded Martin with endless descriptions of the shocking ordeals others had been through—often in their own homes.

Sheila's obsessiveness and the anxiety it caused him were making Martin miserable. The trappings of his wife's terror were everywhere: alarm systems, buzzers, gates, intercoms, escape plans. These so-called "precautions" seemed to be taking over their lives.

They quarreled bitterly, Martin feeling that Sheila was being extremist and paranoid and she feeling he was insensitively trying to bury his head in the sand.

For the first time in their twelve years together, Martin said, "This marriage is not working. You are making my life impossible."

With her world crashing down around her, Sheila sought professional help. Through a casual friend, she was referred to Nancy Kless and began individual therapy with her at the Crime Victims Center. During their sessions Sheila talked about her fears, her needs for security—and her anger at Martin for not understanding. She wanted him to take charge, to protect her, or—at the very least—to be supportive about her security needs. But none of this was happening. Her husband was angry and seemed to hate her. And she felt even more victimized by his lack of understanding.

Nancy Kless, realizing that the relationship was now in severe jeopardy, asked if Martin would consider coming for therapy too.

Martin was receptive to the idea. He loved his wife deeply and, despite their recent difficulties, longed for a resolution to their dilemma. He began seeing Nancy Kless individually and also participating in joint sessions with his wife. Both Sheila and Martin found it helpful to discuss their feelings and differences in the presence of a therapist. Having a third person there put things into a much more objective framework.

Although he continued to feel resentment over having so much of his energy focused on Sheila's security needs, Martin at least developed a better understanding of where Sheila's need came from as Nancy Kless explained what victims go through during and after their attacks.

Because of his increased intellectual understanding of victimization, Martin learned to tolerate his wife's security needs. The Kobells' marriage reverted from a no-win situation to a stable, workable relationship. Sheila feels that through therapy Martin was able to open his eyes and his ears to the realities of a world in which attacks do occur, and can even happen a second time.

Although he continued to stress the statistical fact that danger doesn't lurk *everywhere*, Martin began to admit that in light of the phone calls and the tampering with the alarm system, there *did* seem to be more of a danger than he'd previously admitted to. And so, in Martin's eyes, Sheila's fears came to seem somewhat more based on fact and less paranoid.

Nancy Kless managed to make the Kobells feel she understood the needs and feelings of both—even when they differed radically. And each came to agree that the opinions and feelings of the other party had validity.

An exercise that Sheila found helpful in therapy was one in which the couple sat and took turns *truly* being the listener: being 100 percent attentive to whatever the partner wanted to express.

If Martin wanted to talk about sports, writing, his boredom with security-oriented topics, moving to Europe, a new art film—Sheila sat and listened. Even if there was something pressing on Sheila's mind, she practiced focusing all her attention and concern upon being there for Martin. Then they would reverse roles.

Martin sat attentively while Sheila spoke about a trip to the country, a new and better home alarm system, her fear of being alone, or her anxiety about Martin's refusal to buy an alarm for his own car. The exercise helped them learn to *really* listen to each other.

Sheila continued to see Nancy Kless individually while she and her husband were in joint therapy. She found the individual and joint sessions helpful in different ways. In private sessions Sheila could dig deep down inside herself and attend to her own innermost needs, fears, and problems. Having this time to take care of herself freed Sheila and enabled her to devote her energies in the joint sessions to the troubles that plagued their marriage and to learn how to communicate better with Martin.

Sheila noticed that, in time, Martin grew more receptive to her needs and even became more personally security-conscious and aware of his environment. Though he was far from pleased about it, Martin finally accepted the changes in Sheila and let go of some of his anger. They argued less and were able to discuss their differences without blowing up. After two months in therapy, the couple realized that while they still had some ongoing attack-related problems, they were no longer in marital jeopardy.

After Sheila and I had spoken at length, she led me into her husband's spacious and comfortable study. Books were everywhere. Martin continued typing until I'd seated myself on a cushiony sofa. Then he peered at me from across his enormous desk.

I began our talk with a question: "What did therapy do for you?"

"Well," Martin answered, "I feel therapy helped me to become much more attuned to Sheila's constant sense of danger. I realize that while my wife's attitude is extremely cautious—most people would say *overly* cautious—some of it has basis in reason: Danger *does*, in fact, lurk out there. I really hadn't been very conscious of that before. Also, while I still get annoyed with my wife over security issues, since therapy I feel markedly less resentful of all the changes Sheila's gone through and of the steps she has to take now in order to feel safe.

"My anger," Martin went on, "was and is very complex. First of all, I thought to myself: *How could this bastard mess up my life like this?* I was immediately hostile toward the uncaught and unidentified attacker and even had fantasies about doing a vigilante number—tracking the criminal down à la Charles

Bronson in *Death Wish*. But of course, you come to the conclusion that actually *doing* that kind of thing is unrealistic.

"Then, in addition to my rage about the nut who did this, I had come to feel a lot of resentment toward my wife. I felt as if the extremely heightened anxiety on her part was somewhat irrational. Nancy Kless made it clear that I'd have to learn to live with Sheila's anxiety and come to see that, while some of it was irrational, some of it actually was *rational*, in light of her experience and of the very real danger that exists in the world.

"In a way, the typical role a husband is supposed to play according to society is one I'm unsuited for. I came to resent Sheila's sudden need for me to take charge and be a protector and be so concerned about danger and violence. I grew tired of all these needs of hers and of the fact that all this focus on danger and fear and caution was taking away some of the sense of invulnerability I'd had before the attack.

"In therapy I learned that in a sense I'd been truly *ignorant* of what's really happening in society. Until this kind of thing happens to you or to someone you love, people tend to think these crimes only happen on TV. And I felt the same way.

"The therapy we had was very reality-oriented. I looked at Sheila and at our situation and was able to assess things. I took a really deep look at my wife and saw her as the incredibly special person she has always been for me. And I didn't want to lose her.

"So I worked at it. I tried to become more sensitive to her needs and see things from her point of view, which had naturally been changed by this terrible incident.

"I had to learn to adjust to the changes in my wife. And seeing these changes as a natural result of her experience helped me in doing this. But it wasn't easy.

"Sheila used to be one of the bravest people I knew. She'd go into *any* crazy neighborhood for her work or pleasure and often came home alone at one or two A.M., right up until the time of the attack. She went absolutely anywhere fearlessly.

"Now all that is different. She rarely goes out and prefers people to come here. She's like a totally different person at night—absolutely terrified. It's a terrible, terrible shame. What that man did to Sheila was bad enough. But the freedom and mobility he has taken away from her, in some ways, is almost worse.

"My main resentment about the change in Sheila is that it has radicalized our life-style. Locks and bars and gates and alarms are everywhere. And she's afraid to go out even when I'm with her. Sheila insists we go practically everywhere in groups or with another couple.

"We used to take these terrific trips together. Now we have to go in parties of four. It has completely destroyed the spontaneity we used to enjoy so much.

"Sheila and I bought this house because it was so private and isolated and secure. Now those very same attributes signify something entirely different to Sheila. She is afraid that, because of the extreme privacy here, we might be cornered and attacked. So we'll probably end up selling the place.

"Originally, I resented and opposed putting in the electronic gate. I felt like *we* were becoming the prisoners. But now I'm glad I listened to her. Intruders used to wander up here and I'd always thought it odd. I'm sure nearly all of them really were lost or confused. But I'm willing to admit that some might have been checking this place out for a robbery or something. Now I don't have to worry. This place is secure, Sheila feels better, and there's total privacy. So I never have to deal with uninvited strangers or wonder whether, in fact, they're up to no good.

"After the attack, I wanted to retain my own feelings of security. After all, if you wish to live normally, at some point you must say to yourself: *Okay, there are things out there, but statistically speaking, not everyone wants to get you.*

"Well, that way of thinking is fine for me, but in therapy I realized that Sheila's just not ready or able to think that way, after what's happened, and that it's fruitless for me to resent her or to badger her about it. I simply cannot expect her to do what she cannot do. Hopefully, in time, she won't be so terrified.

"I admire my wife greatly; the woman has guts. If she hadn't screamed and fought that attacker off long enough, she wouldn't be here today. She's been through a rough deal. And she is the woman I love.

"Recently, Sheila and I pretty much decided to move out of

the city and that's okay with me. As a writer, I don't need to be around people all the time and Sheila feels safer away from city life. So it's something we agree upon and can handle comfortably."

When Martin and I had finished our private discussion, Sheila joined us and we all talked together for a while. I was, by then, not only convinced that therapy had played a tremendous role in preserving the Kobells' marriage but I was also *happy* about it. Despite Sheila's attack, the telephone threats, the security needs, the other problems that still exist between them as a result of the attack, this couple is still strong, loving, and a pleasure to know.

"Well, thank God for therapy!" I said as I said goodbye to the couple.

"Exactly," Sheila said. Her husband, too, nodded in agreement.

I climbed into my car and eased slowly down the steep driveway. I waited inside the Kobells' property for a moment or two. Then the massive iron gate opened with a whirr and I drove away.

Visiting the Kobells and listening to their success story made me think back upon my own marriage. I often wonder if, with the help of joint therapy immediately after the attack, our marriage might have survived.

I believe the primary reason for our breakup was the fact that the attack changed me so much. Fred desperately wanted me to be the Theresa he'd always known and loved. But *that* Theresa—the girl who radiated good health, who trusted everyone, who walked about fearlessly, who believed that good always triumphed over evil—had ceased to exist. And in her place was a different person—damaged, disillusioned, crippled in mind and body, and devoid of trust in mankind.

Fred simply wanted his wife back. And this confused me and made me resentful.

I am not *the same anymore—and it is* not *my fault*, I would think to myself bitterly.

My body was so utterly devastated that all my attention needed to be directed at healing. And this left me little time or energy to focus on Fred and his problems.

When I noticed him becoming progressively more tense, anxious, and depressed, I suggested that he see a therapist. But Fred insisted that he preferred to handle things on his own.

In retrospect, I wish I had thought of having joint therapy sessions with Fred—perhaps even insisted on it. There were many things he and I were keeping to ourselves in order not to hurt each other.

Fred, for example, felt that his pain and trauma were being ignored—but he was afraid I'd get upset if he told me this.

I was trying to hide my deep resentment of what I considered his idealistic desire that I go back to being as I was before the attack. So we kept these thoughts and resentments to ourselves.

Had we worked together with a therapist, perhaps Fred and I could have aired our feelings, discussed them, and worked toward solutions. But, left to our own devices, we continued to keep our feelings and grievances hidden. This became habit, and soon there were more and more secrets to keep. We began to speak in generalities and to function around each other almost by rote.

What Fred and I needed, then and there, was intervention. Instead, we tried to muddle through on our own. But each day, we seemed to grow farther and farther apart. We learned to lick our wounds in solitude rather than together. And soon we could scarcely relate to each other at all.

After my release from the hospital, Fred and I continued to see each other. But we never again lived together as man and wife. By the time we sought the help of a marriage counselor, it was just too late. The gap that had grown between us had already widened to the point of no return.

We tried, in therapy, to reopen our problems and to work on them. But in a matter of weeks I began to feel that it was fruitless. I could no longer relate to Fred as my husband. I loved him—in fact, I adored him—but I no longer felt the closeness of a wife and partner. Sadly, I acknowledged—first to myself, then to Fred—that the damage to our relationship had been irreparable.

Because Fred and I had so much trouble communicating

with each other when I was ill, I'd grown used to relying on myself, my parents, and others for support, companionship, and love. The bonds of marriage had slowly but surely been stretched to their limit. Strangely enough, long before we made it official, I'd already begun to feel like an ex-wife.

There's no turning back now for Fred and me. But I feel that if we'd sought help early on, it is possible we would still be married to this day.

For this reason—and because I have seen so many relationships wither after a victimization—I strongly urge that all couples who experience problems in their relationship seek help in therapy. It is tempting to wait until things "settle down." But at that point, as it was for Fred and me, it may simply be too late.

I asked Nancy Kless exactly how openly the members of an inner circle should behave around the victim.

She said, "Victims need some protection at first. Being open does *not* mean overwhelming the victim. If you must scream or do any real acting out, it's better to do it elsewhere. The victim himself is too sensitive and emotional and may feel responsible, confused, or angry at this display from his loved one.

"But, while it's good to hide torrents of heavy emotion from the victim, it is fine to honestly share your feelings with him. It's okay to tell the victim that you hurt for him, that you're angry about what happened, that you love him and wish him well. It's even okay to cry with the victim. But screaming, yelling, and breast-beating should not be done in the victim's presence.

"Also, people must be aware that children who are close to victims of crime pick up the hurt, the pain, the fear. And it's wise to include them at times and not assume that you can hide everything from them. It's better to present children with some clear and simple information about what is going on and give them a chance to talk about how they're feeling. With very small children, you can use dolls, puppets, and picture-drawing just as professionals do. There's often a tremendous amount of anger, confusion, and hurt inside of a child who hears or senses the pain that someone he loves is going through. So it's up to the grown-ups to encourage him to open up.

"If you're worried about a child in the inner circle, it's important to watch his behavior carefully. Although he will often deny feeling troubled, you may notice sleep disturbances, poor appetite, problems in school, bed-wetting, or untoward aggression.

"Any of these may be warning signals that all is not well with the child. If just talking to him and being open doesn't work, it might help to see a therapist who works with children.

"One of my clients is a thirty-seven-year-old who was raped and beaten in her own home. Soon after the attack, while the police were still on the scene, her fourteen-year-old daughter returned home from school. It was terribly traumatic for the girl to see her mother bruised, bloodied, and hysterical and to hear the police questioning her mother about the rape.

"Now both of them are coming for therapy. The teenager is doing well and doesn't appear to have any serious psychological problems. But she has said that it's been really good for her to have a place where she can talk about it freely and know she'll be understood and taken seriously.

"At the Crime Victims Center we counsel people with many different relationships to the victim who are providing support to the actual victim. We've had female roommates of female victims, male lovers of homosexual victims, female lovers of lesbian victims, gay roommates (though *not* lovers) of both straight and gay victims, grandparents, best friends, cousins; we've even had ex-husbands and ex-wives of victims who are still close to their former mates and want to help. The important thing is that, whenever possible, whoever is closest to the victim should at least turn to a therapist for advice on how to deal best with the victim himself and with their own resultant problems.

"Sometimes, family members or intimates of a victim not only refuse to come in for treatment themselves, but actively discourage the victim from seeking help. I'm seeing a lady now who, during the first month she was in treatment, had to argue with her husband before and after every therapy session. Yet, she needed the outlet of therapy and was willing to fight for it.

"After four weeks, her husband stopped berating her and even admitted that the sessions seemed to be helping. Although she asked him many times, he has thus far refused to speak to a therapist, either on his own or with his mate. His wife is still hoping that one day he'll change his mind. But in the meantime, at least she is taking care of *her* emotional problems.

"There are, of course, many ways for those in a victim's inner circle to seek help. They may join support groups where all the members share a similar problem. Or, if they have a close personal relationship with their own M.D., they may be able to seek advice and consultation from him.

"Sometimes there are friends to turn to who are wonderful listeners. And, lately, there is some excellent written material on the subject.

"If members of the inner circle feel that the victim is in need of therapy, it's wise to pose the suggestion gently. If the response is negative, perhaps the victim does need to deal with his problems in his own way. It may be best to allow him to make his own decision.

"However, if a victim begins to exhibit signs of agoraphobia, alcoholism, drug dependency, psychosis, or—in particular—if he seems to be suicidal, then members of the inner circle must become assertive and see that the victim receives treatment.

"Traditionally, male victims and male family members are less willing than females to seek help after an attack. Perhaps there's a bit more of an underlying feeling that men should be able to handle things on their own. But recently we are seeing male clients with more frequency.

"Luckily, with increasing public awareness about victimization, people are more open to the idea of seeking psychological help after a crime occurs. And this is extending to the spouses and others in the inner circle: Victims and their loved ones are now more frequently referred for therapy by hospital staff, courtroom personnel, and even law-enforcement officers. So the stigma is loosening. Now people know that there is help available as long as they are willing to seek it."

¶   ¶   ¶

Sara Bosley, the executive secretary who was raped by a bedroom intruder, feels that therapy was a godsend to her and—in a different way—to her mother. Mrs. Bosley, you may recall, became involved in educating college women about sexual assault after her daughter was raped.

When I spoke with Mrs. Bosley, she told me she agrees with her daughter's belief in the importance of therapy, and credits the therapists at the Rape Crisis Center with contributing enormously to her and her husband's eventual understanding of their daughter's emotions and their own.

The Bosleys, who live about an hour away from their daughter's apartment, received a call from Sara only five or six hours after the rape occurred. Sounding relatively calm, and without going into specific detail, Sara explained that she had been raped. Sensing her parents' shock and anxiety, Sara insisted that she was surrounded by close and supportive friends and that there was really nothing her parents could do.

During the week, Sara went back to work. But her mother could hear, over the telephone, that her daughter was deeply disturbed and depressed. After canceling their prior plans to attend a cousin's wedding, Mrs. Bosley came up with the idea of going off to a resort. Sara agreed to join them, but was unenthusiastic.

Having already heard Sara's point of view about this trip, it was interesting to listen to what her mother had to say about that same weekend.

According to Mrs. Bosley, neither she, her husband, nor their twenty-six-year-old son, James, had any idea of what to say or how to approach Sara. The girl seemed numb, withdrawn, altered. Mrs. Bosley longed to support and help her child but was at a loss for the proper words or gestures.

Should I encourage her to talk about it—or would that make her feel worse? she asked herself. Claire Bosley had no frame of reference for anything of this nature. And she herself was feeling conflict: On the one hand, she desperately wanted to know exactly what her daughter had been through. But on the other hand, she was terrified of actually hearing the details.

Claire Bosley remembers: "The look of unbearable hurt and sorrow on Sara's face was so hard for me to deal with. I had a feeling of complete helplessness, frustration, and pain at being unable to help my daughter and ease her torment. When she was little, I could give her a cookie and make her feel better. Then, when she was grown, I could usually brighten her spirits by taking her shopping. But there was nothing—nothing at all—I could possibly do to ease her pain after the rape."

For that entire weekend, and for weeks to follow, the Bosley family tried their best to distract Sara and make her feel better. None of them had a clue as to how to handle Sara's pain or their own.

Claire Bosley's mind was clouded by grief, anxiety, helplessness, shock. Their family had never dealt with a tragedy like this before.

Sara, as we know, was resentful of her parents' helpless silence. Secretly she wondered why they didn't just ask her directly to tell them how she really felt.

Mrs. Bosley believed that it was best to say little and let Sara talk only if she volunteered to do so. Consequently, the woman said nothing to her daughter directly concerning the sexual assault, fearing that it might provoke painful memories. And so, mother and daughter remained silent about what hurt them most.

After they'd returned home from the weekend trip, Mrs. Bosley thought about herself and her family. Life had always been good to them. Mr. Bosley, chairman of the board of a major corporation, was a healthy, energetic, and intelligent man—a good provider, loving husband, and wonderful father.

Claire herself was an active, creative woman who held an Ivy League college degree and enjoyed her comfortable lifestyle. After raising her two children, Claire had become increasingly active in various organizations and philanthropic endeavors. Both Sara and her brother, James, had been model children—happy, healthy, attractive, well-liked. Both had graduated from college with honors. Both went on to successful careers.

The Bosley family had never been touched by a major

trauma. Now, their beautiful daughter had been sexually assaulted and emotionally damaged by a stranger. Claire Bosley felt as though someone had tied her up in knots. She had always shown her love for Sara by actions rather than words. Now she had no idea what to do or what to say.

To make matters worse, Claire found her own thoughts preoccupied by the rape. There was hardly a moment when it wasn't on her mind, gnawing at her conscience. She was plagued by sleeplessness and nightmares. But as sad and confused as she felt, she would not allow herself to seem outwardly teary and depressed. She wanted to present an image of calm and composure to her daughter. The most important thing, she felt, was to be strong and unshaken, so that Sara could lean upon her.

Mrs. Bosley was shocked by people's reactions to her daughter's rape. She felt insulted by remarks like "Don't worry—we won't say anything about it." It seemed as though people felt Sara had done something her family should be ashamed of.

Mr. Bosley's reaction was one of solid stoicism. At first he expressed venom and rage at the attacker, threatening to "have his legs broken." Then he settled into a strong, silent pattern of behavior. He was there for his wife to rely upon but avoided any open discussion about the rape. Basically, after the initial trauma, Mr. Bosley wanted things to calm down as quickly as possible. He just couldn't seem to understand why his wife and daughter continued to focus upon what had happened. But he was willing to pitch in and do whatever tasks needed to be done.

For the Bosleys, there was no quick, easy return to normalcy. Their son was going about his business as usual, but he was deeply disturbed by what had happened to Sara and by the changes it had provoked in all of them. Their daughter was troubled, miserable, anguished. Mrs. Bosley was inwardly depressed and filled with turmoil. Her husband acted disgruntled and pensive. All the harmony and smoothness of their lives had been stripped away.

Then, two weeks after the sexual assault, Sara told her parents that she was going for help at the Rape Treatment Center near her home.

Mrs. Bosley had mixed feelings about this. She'd always felt that people should be able to handle their problems on their own. "Won't going to therapy and concentrating on the pain and problems prolong the misery even more?" she wondered. But when her daughter explained that she felt deeply in need of outside help, both Claire Bosley and her husband immediately became supportive.

Now, Mrs. Bosley believes that going to the Rape Treatment Center was without question a vital, positive step for Sara—and, therefore, for the entire family. First, it was a relief for them to know that Sara was under the guidance of professionals. Now the *entire* responsibility for helping Sara was no longer upon Claire's shoulders.

"Before this happened," Mrs. Bosley said recently, "I never knew those rape centers existed. But once Sara told us how supportive and helpful she found it to talk to people who knew all about this subject, it made perfect sense to us. *We* surely had no expertise in the matter and it was good to learn that *someone* knew what they were doing."

Sara was in treatment for months and found herself coping better with all that had happened. She was no longer as silent or resentful when with her family, since she now had the center as an outlet for her darkest feelings. Things progressed smoothly until the time the trial of the rapist began.

On the day Sara was to testify, a therapist from the center accompanied her to the courtroom. Sara's parents were also there to support her. Both were nervous and concerned about Sara; they had no idea of what the courtroom procedures would be like, or of how Sara would react to testifying in the presence of the rapist.

For the first time, the Bosleys met Grace Morella, who had been counseling Sara at the Rape Treatment Center. The therapist's presence had a calming effect not only on Sara but on her mother as well. Mrs. Bosley sensed that the therapist had deep insight into her daughter's needs and problems.

During the course of their conversation, Grace handed Claire her business card and suggested that she call to talk not only about Sara but also about her own feelings and problems related to the assault. Grace also said she'd be glad to meet with Claire in person.

For many hours the Bosley family awaited Sara's turn to testify. At noon they were told to come back the next day. Frustrated and exhausted, Sara and her family left the courthouse. It was an anxious, sleepless night for all. At eight-thirty A.M. the Bosleys returned to the courtroom, all of them far more anxious than they'd been the day before. Claire Bosley glanced over at her daughter, who sat clutching Grace's hand. Finally the bailiff called out, "Sara Bosley," and the young woman approached the witness stand.

Watching Sara and listening to her testimony was a horrific ordeal for Mr. and Mrs. Bosley. Suddenly, she and her husband were confronted with the grim reality—down to minute, specific details—about their daughter's rape. They had heard the story in broad strokes before, but Sara had never filled them in on the moment-to-moment truth of what had happened to her body and her mind during the sexual assault.

Sara endured the ordeal of her testimony and cross-examination. Later, the prosecutor called her a "perfect witness." Mrs. Bosley agreed. She also told me that, when the public defender's questions were less than sensitive, Sara's responses were "downright sassy."

Eventually the rapist was convicted and sentenced to a fairly stiff jail term.

But Mrs. Bosley could not shake from her mind the ghastly images Sara's testimony had conjured up—could not rid herself of the grief and pain that raged within her. A few days after the trial, she called Grace Morella and made an appointment to meet with the therapist.

For the first time since Sara's rape, Claire was able to unveil her own emotions without considering the feelings of Sara and of everyone else in their family. She could cry, rail against what had happened, and express her fears. For Claire Bosley, the few sessions she had with Grace provided an exquisite release.

In addition to talking about her personal feelings, Claire turned to Grace for advice on how best to deal with Sara. She listened intently as Grace suggested that the couple allow their daughter to regain feelings of control by not overwhelming her with too much advice or keeping her from making decisions on her own. Grace informed Claire that many parents of victims felt the same urge to re-embrace their grown children and entice them once more into the protective custody of their hearts and homes. But in Sara's case, Grace felt that the Bosleys at times encouraged their daughter to become overly dependent upon them. They were constantly inviting her to do things with them—to attend church functions, go on trips, go to concerts, go on all-day shopping sprees, and the like. Obviously, they wanted Sara to know they were there for her.

But in reality, Sara now needed some time and space. It was important for her to move on. She wasn't a little girl anymore, and she needed to regain the feelings of independence and control that had been temporarily shattered by the rape. Claire listened—and followed Grace's advice.

From that point on, Mrs. Bosley allowed Sara to be more independent. She offered to be there when needed, but didn't suggest or insist upon a more than usual amount of familial contact. She also tried to be less assertive with her advice to Sara and to allow her daughter to resume the decision-making for herself.

After a few sessions with Grace, Claire felt noticeably better about the situation in general and discontinued their meetings. But she often telephoned Grace for advice and support when specific problems or concerns arose.

About a year after the rape Sara asked her parents if they would come to a benefit at the Rape Treatment Center. They readily agreed. Then, shortly before the scheduled event, Claire was invited by the center to share her feelings in an interview to be held in front of the benefit crowd of six hundred people. Sara urged her mother to be part of the interview, and Claire, for her daughter's sake, somewhat reluctantly agreed. That June night, in front of hundreds of people, Claire and Sara aired their experience of the sexual assault and how it had affected their family. In a sense this interview was a further extension of therapy, as mother and daughter admitted to the pain, the fears, and the anguish they had both suffered.

Mr. and Mrs. Bosley continued to support and attend functions at the center. Because of their involvement, they both came to a greater awareness of the realities of rape: the number of lives and families it affects, the trauma it causes for the victim and her loved ones, and the shockingly high incidence of such attacks.

One evening Claire and her husband went to the center and attended a panel discussion in which five rape victims discussed the sexual assaults against them. Hearing those women—who were of many different ages and backgrounds—pierced Mr. Bosley's consciousness and made for a 180-degree change in the way he thought about and spoke about Sara's rape. Before, although he'd tried his best to help his daughter in any way possible after her ordeal, Mr. Bosley had simply not understood the phenomena of rape and its aftermath. While he felt for his daughter, it was hard for him to accept what he considered a "preoccupation" with the sexual assault. "My God," he would sometimes say in frustration, "when will we ever be able to forget all this?"

After hearing the points of view of all five rape victims on the panel, Mr. Bosley finally understood the long-lasting residual problems most women who've been raped must grapple with. By witnessing this candid, painful discussion, Mr. Bosley came to accept the fact that it was entirely normal for Sara's post-rape trauma to take a long time to dissipate. And, even then, that Sara would never completely *forget* the nightmare she'd been through.

Although Mr. Bosley didn't actually attend any therapy sessions, he certainly benefited from the programs held at the center, where the entire Bosley family received education, counseling, and sympathy. And with the other families of rape victims, they shared a certain empathy and understanding.

Today, after surviving this horrendous ordeal, the Bosleys are a much closer family.

Perhaps therapy is not for absolutely everyone, but in light of my repeated interviews with victims and the members of their inner circles who have suffered through virtually every kind of crime, I must say that therapy appears to be an effective, reliable way in which all members of the victim's inner circle can come to a fuller understanding of what has happened, a greater awareness of how to cope most effectively with the victim, and a deeper understanding of their own emotions and feelings—as well as how best to help themselves.

Not a single day passes that I am not grateful to be alive today.

The life I lead now is certainly different from the life I led before the attack. It is an altered life. A complicated life. A life filled with some rather unusual problems, and a great many more responsibilities. But in many ways it is a richer and more fulfilling life.

Struggling through the hellish, brutal, oftentimes horribly painful ordeal has been far from easy. There were many times when I asked myself in despair: *Is it worth it?*

But, always, the answer was—and is—*yes!*

Victims who survive their attacks are actually living witnesses to the power and indomitability of the human spirit. They have been forced to confront human brutality, physical and emotional anguish, and overwhelming despair.

In the face of it all, they have said, "I am going on." And they have not only continued, but flourished.

This is why I consider the painful stories in this book, including my own, as proof that people can live through virtually anything—and come out at the end of the nightmare happy and whole.

Victims of crime have, thankfully, been treated with somewhat more sensitivity in recent years. Some of the taboos surrounding the very word *victim* are lifting. People have finally started to realize that most victims do *not* "ask for it," and that *all* victims are in need of concern and support. At least this awareness is a beginning. And I'm hopeful that the general understanding of what it's like to be a victim of a violent crime will increase in years to come.

Services for victims are increasing, and there are now many private and government support groups in cities across the country.

The most important message I want to convey is that hope, happiness, and health can exist even after the most brutal victimization. It may take weeks, months, even years to get there, but a person who's been victimized can achieve full recovery. It's simply a matter of hanging in there long enough, and fighting hard enough.

There's no way to avoid a certain degree of pain if you are victimized, but there are enough concerned individuals, victims and nonvictims alike, who are ready and willing to offer assistance.

Victims of crime seldom get through their ordeals completely unscathed, but we no longer have to suffer in shame or in silence.

"Are you over the attack?" is a question I am asked time and again.

In all honesty, my answer is usually: "Yes . . . and no."

I am not completely over the attack, because the memory of it will remain in my mind for as long as I live. And the horrendous images this memory conjures up are more than enough to sadden and depress me on occasion.

But in a sense, I *am* over the attack, because it no longer plagues me, no longer threatens to destroy me, and no longer lessens the quality of my life. It is basically a bad memory, a distant dream, a dark shadow I prefer not to dwell upon.

Just as my mother predicted four years ago when I lay in my hospital bed, I *do* act—and dance—and sing—and run. And each time I do so, I feel both grateful and amazed.

The braces are gone. The cast is gone. The haunted, hunted

gaze is gone. And now—like many others who have survived an attack—I am finally both happy and healthy again.

I truly believe that despite the horror of our experiences, those of us who have been victimized can fight our way back through the pain, the fear, and the anger—to a joyous, fulfilling life beyond survival.